F. T. Dufferin

Letters from High Latitudes

Being Some Account of a Voyage, in 1856, in the Schooner Yacht

F. T. Dufferin

Letters from High Latitudes

Being Some Account of a Voyage, in 1856, in the Schooner Yacht

ISBN/EAN: 9783337157975

Printed in Europe, USA, Canada, Australia, Japan

Cover: Foto ©Andreas Hilbeck / pixelio.de

More available books at **www.hansebooks.com**

FIRST GLIMPSE OF JAN MAYEN.

LETTERS
FROM
HIGH LATITUDES;

*BEING SOME ACCOUNT OF A VOYAGE, IN 1856,
IN THE SCHOONER YACHT "FOAM,"*

TO

ICELAND, JAN MAYEN, AND SPITZBERGEN.

BY LORD DUFFERIN.
GOVERNOR GENERAL OF THE DOMINION OF CANADA.

SIXTH EDITION.

LONDON:
JOHN MURRAY, ALBEMARLE STREET.
1873.

"But since it pleased a vanished eye,
I go to plant it on his tomb,
That if it can, it there may bloom,
Or dying—there at least may die."

"He,
To whom a thousand memories call,
Not being less, but more than all
The gentleness he seemed to be,

So wore his outward best, and joined
Each office of the social hour
To noble manners, as the flower
And native growth of noble mind."

In Memoriam.

Watson and Hazell, Printers, London and Aylesbury

TO

"THAT TRUE NORTH"

I DEDICATE

THIS EDITION.

"Witness, too, the silent cry,
The prayer of many a race, and creed, and clime,
Thunderless lightnings striking under sea
From sunset to sunrise of all thy realm,
And that true North."

PREFACE TO THE CANADIAN EDITION.

A CYNIC has suggested that after a certain interval the return to life of our dearest relative might often occasion as much perplexity as pleasure.

However harshly this sentiment may grate on the ears of Constancy, I confess to a kindred feeling of embarrassment in being suddenly confronted, after so many years, with the alien self that reappears in the following pages ; but I am told that the friendly community with which I am now connected, and with whose fortunes my own are temporarily interwoven, may be disposed to take an interest in the youthful yatching experiences of their present Governor General.

But for this I should never have had the hardihood to appear as an author before the public of this Continent, whose geographical position and fiscal arrangements enable its inhabitants to skim the cream from the literature of Europe, without troubling themselves either with its sedimentary deposits, or the irritating restrictions of its copyrights. Once indeed through the "enterprise" of a transatlantic Editor, whose nationality shall be nameless, a mutilated issue of these "Letters" obtained an ephemeral publicity in a provincial serial, but in spite of my spirited impressario having prefaced his piracy by the assertion that "he had commissioned a British Lord at a handsome salary" "to discover the North Pole" and to furnish his Magazine with "an account of his adventures," confirmed as it was by such a transfiguration of the dates, tenses, and superscriptions in my narrative as might best colour this ingenious fiction—the speculation must have proved a financial failure, as no per centage on his profits has hitherto reached my hands.

Notwithstanding this discouraging experience, I am still in hopes that the Canadian reader, apart from any personal interest with which he may regard the author, will not grudge an occasional half-hour to a description of those out-land countries that share with his Dominion the Aurora's ruby affluence, and are wrapped by winter in the same silver mantle as his own; whose early mariners—500 years before Columbus—swept through the gulfs of his St. Lawrence, and struck the headlands of his Acadie; and whose modern inhabitants, in the simplicity of their lives, in the nobleness of their courtesy, in the freedom of their political institutions, and in their masculine energy exemplify and prefigure within their lesser limits the qualities, virtues, and attainments proper to a great Northern people.

And here I should be disposed to end my brief apology for this Edition, were it not that I am tempted to seize the opportunity of answering a question that has been frequently put to me—"What has become of Wilson?"

This kind and faithful servant remained with me for many years after my return from the North, environed by something of an heroic halo in the eyes of the ladies of his acquaintance, and of the public whom he frequented. He subsequently accompanied me on an eighteen months' cruise to the Mediterranean, as well as on my visit to Syria as British Commissioner, but neither the sunshine of the South nor the glitter of the parti-coloured East, mercurialized the melancholy of his temperament. In the congenial atmosphere of the graveyards of Egypt he displayed indeed a transient sprightliness, which the occasional exhumation of a mummy, and such traffic with the dead and their appurtenances as my excavations at Thebes afforded him, stimulated into spasms of hilarity.

Of the Pyramids he was disposed to think but lightly, until informed that they had served for sepulchres; but on quitting the heights of Gizeh I observed that he had selected two skulls as the appropriate memorials of his visit. With his brows bound in the folds of a yellow turban, a striped Arab mantle enveloping his person, and seated on a donkey, these fleshless countenances grinning from under either arm,—his own, the least jovial of the three,—he presented, I confess, something of a weird and ghoul-like appearance as, wending round the ransacked tombs of the Pharaohs, we passed to our boats through the purple haze of evening.

He continued to the end to solemnize his announcements with phrases of dolorous import. One day at Thebes I was lying in my berth prostrate with a feverish attack, my nerves in that impressionable state peculiar to sickness in a tropical climate; suddenly Wilson enters the cabin and proclaims in his hollow tones, "If you please, my Lord, the *Corpse* is come aboard!" by which dignified but depressing title he was pleased to designate a mummy which my people had just brought down from a rock-temple I had recently discovered.

His bedside visits, however, were not always so innocuous. On our arrival at Beirût some months afterwards, we found a traveller at the hotel stricken with Syrian fever —a disease which seldom pardons. The patient's life hung by a thread. The doctors had enjoined the most absolute quiet, and every inmate of the house passed his door breathless and on tiptoe. One kind lady, who had constituted herself his nurse, was allowed to visit him. But on an unlucky Sunday afternoon she was absent for a brief half hour at Church.

Forthwith Wilson stole upon his victim, and gliding into a chair at the bed-head, whispered forth at intervals these sentences of dole : " Well, sir ! you do look bad ! " " Syrian fever, I understand, sir?" "Ah! they say people don't recover from Syrian fever." "I am Wilson, sir." "THE WILSON !" with which ghostlike revelation of his identity he concluded his dismal Avatar, the particulars of which the sick man happily survived to relate.

I could multiply these paragraphs by the relation of a hundred similar traits of my poor follower's saturnine humour. It would be more difficult to give an adequate idea of his kindness and affectionate serviceableness, his resolution in danger, his versatility of resource, and unassailable integrity; only those who have travelled much in wild countries can understand what an infinite enhancement of one's pleasure, comfort and security, is born of such faithful comradeship. If every now and then I have endeavoured to enliven my story with glimpses of the share my poor servant took in our daily life, the reader will feel that a loving hand has guided the pencil. To this day I never prepare for a journey without a sigh of regret for my lost travelling companion.

Some time after our return to England Wilson's health became affected by an obscure disease, which subsequently developed very distressing symptoms, and after much suffering, borne with great patience, he died in the Hospital for incurables at Wimbledon.

Ottawa, 1873.

CONTENTS.

LETTER I.

PROTESILAUS STUMBLES ON THE THRESHOLD . .   PAGE 1

LETTER II.

THE ICELANDER—A MODERN SIR PATRICK SPENS . .   2

LETTER III.

LOCH GOIL—THE SAGA OF CLAN CAMPBELL   4

LETTER IV.

THROUGH THE SOUNDS—STORNAWAY—THE SETTING UP OF THE FIGURE-HEAD—FITZ'S FORAY—"OH WEEL MAY THE BOATIE ROW, THAT WINS THE BAIRNS'S BREAD"—SIR PATRICK SPENS JOINS -- UP ANCHOR   8

LETTER V.

THE NORTH ATLANTIC—SPANISH WAVES—OUR CABIN IN A GALE—SEA-SICKNESS FROM A SCIENTIFIC POINT OF VIEW—WILSON—A PASSENGER COMMITS SUICIDE—FIRST SIGHT OF ICELAND—FLOKI OF THE RAVENS—THE NORSE MAYFLOWER—FAXA FIORD—WE LAND IN THULE   13

CONTENTS.

LETTER VI.

REYKJAVIK—LATIN CONVERSATION—I BECOME THE PROPRIETOR OF TWENTY-SIX HORSES—EIDER DUCKS—BESSESTAD—SNORRO STURLESON—THE OLD GREENLAND COLONY—FINLAND—A GENOESE SKIPPER IN THE FIFTEENTH CENTURY—AN ICELANDIC DINNER—SKOAL—AN AFTER-DINNER SPEECH IN LATIN —WINGED RABBITS—DUCROW—START OF THE BAGGAGE-TRAIN 21

LETTER VII.

KISSES—WILSON ON HORSEBACK—A LAVA PLATEAU—THING-VALLA—ALMANNAGIA—RABNAGIA—OUR TENT—THE SHIVERED PLAIN—WITCH-DROWNING—A PARLIAMENTARY DEBATE, A.D. 1000—THANGBRAND THE MISSIONARY—A GERMAN GNAT-CATCHER—THE MYSTICAL MOUNTAINS—SIR OLAF—HECKLA— SKAPTA JOKUL—THE FIRE DELUGE OF 1783—WE REACH THE GEYSIR—STROKR—FITZ'S BONNE FORTUNE—MORE KISSES— AN ERUPTION—PRINCE NAPOLEON—RETURN—TRADE—POPULATION—A MUTINY—THE "REINE HORTENSE"—THE SEVEN DUTCHMEN—A BALL—LOW DRESSES—NORTHWARD HO ! . 45

LETTER VIII.

START FROM REYKJAVIK—SNAEFELL—THE LADY OF FRODA—A BERSERK TRAGEDY—THE CHAMPION OF BREIDAVIK—ONUNDER FIORD—THE LAST NIGHT—CROSSING THE ARCTIC CIRCLE— FÊTE ON BOARD THE "REINE HORTENSE"—LE PÈRE ARCTIQUE —WE FALL IN WITH THE ICE—THE "SAXON" DISAPPEARS —MIST—A PARTING IN A LONELY SPOT—JAN MAYEN—MOUNT BEERENBERG — AN UNPLEASANT POSITION — SHIFT OF WIND AND EXTRICATION—"TO NORROWAY OVER THE FAEM"—A NASTY COAST—HAMMERFEST 101

LETTER IX.

EXTRACT FROM THE "MONITEUR" OF THE 31ST JULY . 140

LETTER X.

BUCOLICS—THE GOAT—MAID MARIAN—A LAPP LADY—LAPP LOVE-MAKING—THE SEA-HORSEMAN—THE GULF STREAM— ARCTIC CURRENTS—A DINGY EXPEDITION—A SCHOOL OF PERIPATETIC FISHES—ALTEN—THE CHÂTELAINE OF KAAFIORD— STILL NORTHWARD HO ! 149

CONTENTS.

LETTER XI.

WE SAIL FOR BEAR ISLAND, AND SPITZBERGEN—CHERIE ISLAND—BARENTZ—SIR HUGH WILLOUGHBY—PARRY'S ATTEMPT TO REACH THE NORTH POLE—AGAIN AMONGST THE ICE—ICE-BLINK—FIRST SIGHT OF SPITZBERGEN—WILSON—DECAY OF OUR HOPES—CONSTANT STRUGGLE WITH THE ICE—WE REACH THE 80° N. LAT.—A FREER SEA—WE LAND IN SPITZBERGEN—ENGLISH BAY—LADY EDITH'S GLACIER—A MIDNIGHT PHOTOGRAPH—NO REINDEER TO BE SEEN—ET EGO IN ARCTIS—WINTER IN SPITZBERGEN—PTARMIGAN—THE BEAR-SAGA—THE "FOAM" MONUMENT—SOUTHWARDS—SIGHT THE GREENLAND ICE—A GALE—WILSON ON THE MÄLSTROM—BREAKERS AHEAD—ROOST—TAKING A SIGHT—THRONDHJEM . . . 168

LETTER XII.

THRONDHJEM—HARALD HAARFAGER—KING HACON'S LAST BATTLE—OLAF TRYGGVESSON—THE "LONG SERPENT"—ST. OLAVE—THORMOD THE SCALD—THE JARL OF LADÉ—THE CATHEDRAL—HARALD HARDRADA—THE BATTLE OF STANFORD BRIDGE—A NORSE BALL—ODIN—AND HIS PALADINS 214

LETTER XIII.

COPENHAGEN—BERGEN—THE BLACK DEATH—SIGURDR—HOMEWARDS 240

LIST OF ILLUSTRATIONS.

	PAGE
FIRST GLIMPSE OF JAN MAYEN	*Frontispiece*
Wilson	44
Snorro	47
THE LAKE OF THINGVALLA	51
Plain of Thingvalla	52
ALMANNA-GJA—THINGVALLA—THE OXERAA	53
Ground Plan of Thingvalla	54
THINGVALLA	59
The Althing	60
The Great Geysir	72
Sketch of Waterworks	79
An Icelandic Lady	97
Remains of Basaltic Dykes	102
Mountains of Norway	136, 139
TAKING A SIGHT	137
THE ICELANDIC FOX	151
A Lapp Lady	153
A Lapp Lady's Bonnet	154
IN THE ICE	175
Sigurdr	179
THE MIDNIGHT SUN OFF SPITZBERGEN	183
"ET EGO IN ARCTIS"	191
"THE GIRLS AT HOME HAVE GOT HOLD OF THE TOW-ROPE"	211

—"It is a strange thing, that in sea voyages, where there is nothing to be seen, but sky and sea, men should make Diaries; but in land-travel, wherein so much is to be observed, for the most part, they omit it; as if chance were fitter to be registered than observation."—BACON.

TO THE

FIGURE-HEAD OF "THE FOAM."

I.

Calm sculptured image of as sweet a face
    As ever lighted up an English home,—
Whose mute companionship has deigned to grace
    Our wanderings o'er a thousand leagues of foam,—

II.

Our progress was your triumph duly hailed
    By ocean's inmates; herald dolphins played
Before our stem, tall ships that sunward sailed
    With stately curtseys due obeisance paid.

III.

Fair Fortune's fairer harbinger! you smoothed
    Our way before us, through the frantic fling
Of roystering waves—as once Athene soothed
    The deeps that raged around the wandering King:

IV.

The scowling tempest rose in vain to clutch
    His forkèd bolts; you smiled,—they harmless turned
To sheets of splendour at his palsied touch,
    And all their anger perished ere it burned.

V.

Now tinkling waves a peal of welcome rang
    Against the sheathing of our brazen bows,—
No gladder hymn the rosy Nereids sang,
    When, clad in sunshine, Aphrodite rose.

VI.

Anon, a mightier passion stirred the deep—
    Presumptuous billows scaled the quivering deck;
Up to your very lips would dare to leap,
    And fling their silver arms about your neck;

VII.

The uncouth winds stole kisses from your cheek,
    Then, wild with exultation, hurried on,
And boasting bade their laggard comrades seek
    The momentary bliss themselves had won,

VIII.

Who, following, filled our prosperous sails until
    We reached eternal winter's drear domain,
Where suns of June but frozen light distil,
    And, baffled, quickly abdicate their reign.

IX.

Yet even here your gracious beauty shed
    Deep calm; old Ocean slumbered 'neath its spell;
And Summer seemed to follow where you led,
    As loth to bid your kindred smile farewell.

X.

The ominous shapes of drifting ice, that pack
    The desolate channels of the polar flood,
Clustered like wolves around our Northward track,
    Till swayed by that sweet power to altered mood,

XI.

They cowered, and ranged themselves on either side,
    Like vassal ranks who watch some passing Queen
Through her white columned halls in silence glide,
    Nor mingling meet till she no more is seen.

XII.

And we with confident souls still followed you,
  Where stern those serried files of icebergs rose,—
As James of Douglas followed,—staunch and true,
  The honoured heart he flung amongst his foes ;

XIII.

Till in my sailors' child-like hearts there grew
  A vague, half-sportive reverence for that Form,
Which, like commissioned angel, onward flew,
  And with a halcyon spell conjured the storm !

XIV.

What marvel then, if—when our wearied hull
  In some lone haven found a brief repose,
Rude hands, by love made delicate, would cull
  A grateful garland for your Goddess' brows ?

XV.

What marvel if their leader, too, would lay
  His fragile wreath of evanescent rhyme
At her dear feet whose image cheered his way,
  And warmed with old home thoughts the lonely time,

XVI.

When as he watched that sculptured life-like smile
  Through many an anxious hour of Arctic gloom,
Its magic influence would half beguile
  The bleak and barren ocean tracts to bloom —

XVII.

With well remembered woods, and Highland hills
  That cluster round a castle's stately towers ;
And gleaming lawns, and glens, and murmuring rills,
  Where Edith plays amid the summer flowers !

Dramatis Personæ.

SIGURDR, *Son of* JONAS, *Icelander; Law Student.*
CHARLES E. FITZGERALD, *Surgeon; Photographer; Botanist.*
LORD DUFFERIN, *Navigator; Sagaman; Artist.*
WILLIAM WILSON, *Valet; Gardener; Cape Colonist.*
ALBERT GRANT, *Steward; Watchmaker; Bird-stuffer.*
JOHN BEVIS, *First Cook; afterwards Ducrow.*
WILLIAM WEBSTER, *Second Cook; Carpenter; late of Her Majesty's Foot Guards; afterwards Maid Marian.*
EBENEZER WYSE, *Master; Californian Gold-digger.*
WILLIAM LEVERETT, *Mate.*
WILLIAM TAYLOR, *Butcher.*
CHARLES PARNE,
THOMAS SCARLETT,
THOMAS PILCHER, } *Seamen.*
HENRY LEVERETT,
JOHN LOCK,
WILLIAM WYNHALL, *Ship-boy.*
Voice of a French Captain.
A German Gnat-catcher.
An early Village Cock.
A Goat.
An Icelandic Fox.
A White Bear.
Ladies and Cavaliers of the ICELANDIC, NORSE, LAPPISH, *and* FRENCH *tongues.*

SCENE.—*Sometimes on board the* "FOAM," *sometimes in* ICELAND, SPITZBERGEN, *and* NORWAY.

GOD SAVE THE QUEEN!

LETTERS
FROM HIGH LATITUDES.

LETTER I.

PROTESILAUS STUMBLES ON THE THRESHOLD.

Glasgow, Monday, June 2, 1856.

OUR start has not been prosperous. Yesterday evening, on passing Carlisle, a telegraphic message was put into my hand, announcing the fact of the "*Foam*" having been obliged to put into Holyhead, in consequence of the sudden illness of my Master. As the success of our expedition entirely depends on our getting off before the season is further advanced, you can understand how disagreeable it is to have received this check at its very outset. As yet, of course, I know nothing of the nature of the illness with which he has been seized. However, I have ordered the schooner to proceed at once to Oban, and I have sent back the Doctor to Holyhead to overhaul the sick man. It is rather early in the day for him to enter upon the exercise of his functions.

LETTER II.

THE ICELANDER—A MODERN SIR PATRICK SPENS.

Greenock, Tuesday, June 3, 1856.

I FOUND the Icelander awaiting my arrival here,—pacing up and down the coffee-room like a Polar bear.

At first he was a little shy, and, not having yet had much opportunity of practising his English, it was some time before I could set him perfectly at his ease. He has something so frank and honest in his face and bearing, that I am certain he will turn out a pleasant companion. There being no hatred so intense as that which you feel towards a disagreeable shipmate, this assurance has relieved me of a great anxiety, and I already feel I shall hereafter reckon Sigurdr (pronounced Segurthur), the son of Jonas, among the number of my best friends.

As most educated English people firmly believe the Icelanders to be a "Squawmuck," blubber-eating, seal-skin-clad race, I think it right to tell you that Sigurdr is apparelled in good broadcloth, and all the inconveniences of civilization, his costume culminating in the orthodox chimney-pot of the nineteenth century. He is about twenty-seven, very intelligent-looking, and—all women would think—lovely to behold. A high forehead, straight, delicate features, dark blue eyes, auburn hair and beard, and the complexion of—Lady S——d! His early life was passed in Iceland; but he is now residing at Copenhagen as a law student. Through the introduction of a mutual friend, he has been induced to come with me, and do us the honours of his native land.

"O whar will I get a skeely skipper,
To sail this gude ship o' mine?"

Such, alas! has been the burden of my song for these last

four-and-twenty hours, as I have sat in the Tontine Tower, drinking the bad port wine; for, after spending a fortune in telegraphic messages to Holyhead, it has been decided that B—— cannot come on, and I have been forced to rig up a Glasgow merchant skipper into a jury sailing-master.

Any such arrangement is, at the best, unsatisfactory; but to abandon the cruise is the only alternative. However, considering I had but a few hours to look about me, I have been more fortunate than might have been expected. I have had the luck to stumble on a young fellow, very highly recommended by the Captain of the Port. He returned just a fortnight ago from a trip to Australia, and having since married a wife, is naturally anxious not to lose this opportunity of going to sea again for a few months.

I start to-morrow for Oban, *via* Inverary, which I wish to show to my Icelander. At Oban I join the schooner, and proceed to Stornaway, in the Hebrides; whither the undomestic Mr. Ebenezer Wyse (a descendant, probably, of some Westland Covenanter) is to follow me by the steamer.

LETTER III.

LOCH GOIL—THE SAGA OF CLAN CAMPBELL.

Oban, June 5, 1856.

I HAVE seldom enjoyed anything so much as our journey yesterday. Getting clear at last of the smells, smoke, noise, and squalor of Greenock, to plunge into the very heart of the Highland hills, robed as they were in the sunshine of a beautiful summer day, was enough to make one beside oneself with delight; and the Icelander enjoyed it as much as I did. Having crossed the Clyde, alive with innumerable vessels, its waves dancing and sparkling in the sunlight, we suddenly shot into the still and solemn Loch Goil, whose waters, dark with mountain shadows, seemed almost to belong to a different element from that of the yellow, rushing, ship-laden river we had left. In fact, in the space of ten minutes we had got into another world, centuries remote from the steaming, weaving, delving Britain, south of Clyde.

After a sail of about three hours, we reached the head of the loch, and then took coach along the worst mountain road in Europe, towards the country of the world-invading Campbells. A steady pull of three hours more, up a wild bare glen, brought us to the top of the mica-slate ridge which pens up Loch Fyne, on its western side, and disclosed what I have always thought the loveliest scene in Scotland.

* Far below at our feet, and stretching away on either hand among the mountains, lay the blue waters of the lake.

On its other side, encompassed by a level belt of pasture-land and corn-fields, the white little town of Inverary glittered like a gem on the sea-shore; while to the right, amid lawns and gardens, and gleaming banks of wood, that hung down into the water, rose the dark towers of the Castle; the whole environed by an amphitheatre of tumbled porphyry hills, beyond whose fir-crowned crags rose the bare blue mountain-tops of Lorn.

It was a perfect picture of peace and seclusion, and I confess I had great pride in being able to show my companion so fair a specimen of one of our lordly island homes —the birthplace of a race of nobles whose names sparkle down the page of their country's history as conspicuously as the golden letters in an illuminated missal.

While descending towards the strand, I tried to amuse Sigurdr with a sketch of the fortunes of the great house of Argyll.

I told him how in ancient days three warriors came from Green Ierne, to dwell in the wild glens of Cowal and Lochow, —how one of them, the swart Breachdan, all for the love of blue-eyed Eila, swam the Gulf, once with a clew of thread, then with a hempen rope, last with an iron chain; but this time, alas! the returning tide sucks down the over-tasked hero into its swirling vortex;—how Diarmid O' Duin, *i.e.* son of "the Brown," slew with his own hand the mighty boar, whose head still scowls over the escutcheon of the Campbells;—how in later times, while the murdered Duncan's son, afterwards the great Malcolm Canmore, was yet an exile at the court of his Northumbrian uncle, ere Birnam wood had marched to Dunsinane, the first Campbell *i.e.* Campus-bellus, Beau-champ, a Norman knight and nephew of the Conqueror, having won the hand of the lady Eva, sole heiress of the race of Diarmid, became master of the lands and lordships of Argyll;—how six generations later— each of them notable in their day—the valiant Sir Colin created for his posterity a title prouder than any within a sovereign's power to bestow, which no forfeiture could attaint, no act of parliament recall; for though he cease to be Duke or Earl, the head of the Clan Campbell will still remain Mac Calan More,—and how at last the same Sir Colin fell at the String of Cowal, beneath the sword of that fierce lord, whose granddaughter was destined to bind the

honours of his own heirless house round the coronet of his
slain foeman's descendant;—how Sir Neill at Bannockburn
fought side by side with the Bruce whose sister he had
married; how Colin, the first Earl, wooed and won the Lady
Isabel, sprung from the race of Somerled, Lord of the Isles,
thus adding the galleys of Lorn to the blazonry of Argyll;—
how the next Earl died at Flodden, and his successor fought
not less disastrously at Pinkie;—how Archibald, fifth Earl,
whose wife was at supper with the Queen, her half-sister,
when Rizzio was murdered, fell on the field of Langside,
smitten not by the hand of the enemy, but by the finger of
God; how Colin, Earl and boy-General at fifteen, was
dragged away by force, with tears in his eyes, from the unhappy skirmish at Glenlivit, where his brave Highlanders
were being swept down by the artillery of Huntley and Errol,—
destined to regild his spurs in future years on the soil of Spain.

Then I told him of the Great Rebellion, and how, amid
the tumult of the next fifty years, the Grim Marquis—
Gillespie Grumach, as his squint caused him to be called—
Montrose's fatal foe, staked life and fortunes in the deadly
game engaged in by the fierce spirits of that generation, and
losing, paid the forfeit with his head, as calmly as became a
brave and noble gentleman, leaving an example, which his
son—already twice rescued from the scaffold, once by a
daughter of the ever-gallant house of Lindsay, again a prisoner, and a rebel, ·because four years too soon to be a
patriot—as nobly imitated;—how, at last, the clouds of mis-
fortune cleared away, and honours clustered where only
merit had been before; the martyr's aureole, almost become
hereditary, being replaced in the next generation by a ducal
coronet, itself to be regilt in its turn with a less sinister
lustre by him—

> "The State's whole thunder born to wield,
> And shake alike the senate and the field;"

who baffled Walpole in the cabinet, and conquered with
Marlborough at Ramilies, Oudenarde, and Malplaquet;—
and, last,—how at that present moment, even while we were

speaking, the heir to all these noble reminiscences, the young chief of this princely line, had already won, at the age of twenty-nine, by the manly vigour of his intellect and his hereditary independence of character, the confidence of his fellow-countrymen, and a seat at the council board of his sovereign.

Having thus duly indoctrinated Sigurdr with the Sagas of the family, as soon as we had crossed the lake I took him up to the Castle, and acted cicerone to its pictures and heirlooms,—the gleaming stands of muskets, whose fire wrought such fatal ruin at Culloden;—the portrait of the beautiful Irish girl, twice a Duchess, whom the cunning artist has painted with a sunflower that turns *from* the sun to look at her;—Gillespie Grumach himself, as grim and sinister-looking as in life;—the trumpets to carry the voice from the hall door to Dunnaquaich;—the fair beech avenues, planted by the old Marquis, now looking with their smooth grey boles, and overhanging branches, like the cloisters of an abbey;—the vale of Esechasan, to which, on the evening before his execution, the Earl wrote such touching verses;—the quaint old kitchen-garden;—the ruins of the ancient Castle, where worthy Major Dalgetty is said to have passed such uncomfortable moments;—the Celtic cross from lone Iona:—all and everything I showed off with as much pride and pleasure, I think, as if they had been my own possessions; and the more so as the Icelander himself evidently sympathised with such Scald-like gossip.

Having thoroughly overrun the woods and lawns of Inverary, we had a game of chess, and went to bed pretty well tired.

The next morning, before breakfast, I went off in a boat to Ardkinglass to see my little cousins; and then returning about twelve, we got a post-chaise, and crossing the boastful Loch Awe in a ferry-boat, reached Oban at nightfall. Here I had the satisfaction of finding the schooner already arrived, and of being joined by the Doctor, just returned from his fruitless expedition to Holyhead.

LETTER IV.

THROUGH THE SOUNDS—STORNAWAY—THE SETTING UP OF THE
FIGURE-HEAD—FITZ'S FORAY—OH WEEL MAY THE BOATIE ROW,
THAT WINS THE BAIRNS'S BREAD—SIR PATRICK SPENS JOINS—UP
ANCHOR.

Stornaway, Island of Lewis, Hebrides,
June 9, 1856.

WE reached these Islands of the West the day before yesterday, after a fine run from Oban.

I had intended taking Staffa and Iona on my way, but it came on so thick with heavy weather from the south-west, that to have landed on either island would have been out of the question. So we bore up under Mull at one in the morning, tore through the Sound at daylight, rounded Ardnamurchan under a double-reefed mainsail at two P.M., and shot into the Sound of Skye the same evening, leaving the hills of Moidart (one of whose "*seven men*" was an ancestor of your own), and the jaws of the hospitable Loch Hourn, reddening in the stormy sunset.

At Kylakin we were obliged to bring up for the night; but getting under weigh again at daylight, we took a fair wind with us along the east coast of Skye, passed Raasa and Rona, and so across the Minch to Stornaway.

Stornaway is a little fishing-town with a beautiful harbour, from out of which was sailing, as we entered, a fleet of herring-boats, their brown sails gleaming like gold against the dark angry water as they fluttered out to sea, unmindful of the leaden clouds banked up along the west, and all the symptoms of an approaching gale. The next morning it was upon us; but brought up as we were under the lea of a high rock, the tempest tore harmlessly over our heads, and left us at liberty to make the final preparations for departure.

Fitz, whose talents for discerning where the vegetables, fowls, and pretty ladies of a place were to be found, I had already had occasion to admire, went ashore to forage ; while I remained on board to superintend the fixing of our sacred figure-head—executed in bronze by Marochetti—and brought along with me by rail, still warm from the furnace.

For the performance of this solemnity I luckily possessed a functionary equal to the occasion, in the shape of the second cook. Originally a guardsman, he had beaten his sword into a chisel, and become carpenter; subsequently conceiving a passion for the sea, he turned his attention to the mysteries of the kitchen, and now sails with me in the alternate exercise of his two last professions. This individual, thus happily combining the chivalry inherent in the profession of arms with the skill of the craftsman and the refinement of the artist—to whose person, moreover, a paper cap, white vestments, and the sacrificial knife at his girdle, gave something of a sacerdotal character—I did not consider unfit to raise the ship's guardian image to its appointed place ; and after two hours' reverential handiwork, I had the satisfaction of seeing the well-known lovely face, with its golden hair, and smile that might charm all malice from the elements, beaming like a happy omen above our bows.

Shortly afterwards Fitz came alongside, after a most successful foray among the fish-wives. He was sitting in the stern-sheets, up to his knees in vegetables, with seven elderly hens beside him, and a dissipated-looking cock under his arm, with regard to whose qualifications its late proprietor had volunteered the most satisfactory assurances. I am also bound to mention, that protruding from his coat-pocket were certain sheets of music, with the name of " Alice Louisa," written therein in a remarkably pretty hand, which led me to believe that the Doctor had not entirely confined his energies to the acquisition of hens and vegetables. The rest of the day was spent in packing away our newly-purchased stores, and making the ship as tidy as circumstances would admit. I am afraid, however, many a smart yachtsman would have been scandalized at our decks, lumbered up with hen-coops, sacks of coal, and other necessaries, which, like the Queen of Spain's legs, not only ought never to be seen, but must not be supposed even to exist, on board a tip-top craft.

By the evening, the gale, which had been blowing all day, had increased to a perfect hurricane. At nine o'clock we let go a second anchor; and I confess, as we sat comfortably round the fire in the bright cheerful little cabin, and listened to the wind whistling and shrieking through the cordage, that none of us were sorry to find ourselves in port on such a night, instead of tossing on the wild Atlantic —though we little knew that even then the destroying angel was busy with the fleet of fishing-boats which had put to sea so gallantly on the evening of our arrival. By morning the neck of the gale was broken, and the sun shone brightly on the white rollers as they chased each other to the shore; but a Queen's ship was steaming into the bay, with sad news of ruin out to seaward,—towing behind her, boats, water-logged, or bottom upwards,—while a silent crowd of women on the quay were waiting to learn on what homes among them the bolt had fallen.

About twelve o'clock the Glasgow packet came in, and a few minutes afterwards I had the honour of receiving on my quarter-deck a gentleman who seemed a cross between the German student and swell commercial gent. On his head he wore a queer kind of smoking-cap, with the peak cocked over his left ear; then came a green shooting-jacket, and flashy silk tartan waistcoat, set off by a gold chain, hung about in innumerable festoons,—while light trousers and knotty Wellington boots completed his costume, and made the wearer look as little like a seaman as need be. It appeared, nevertheless, that the individual in question was Mr. Ebenezer Wyse, my new sailing-master; so I accepted Captain C.'s strong recommendation as a set-off against the silk tartan; explained to the new comer the position he was to occupy on board, and gave orders for sailing in an hour.

The multitudinous chain, moreover, so lavishly displayed, turned out to be an ornament of which Mr. Wyse might well be proud; and the following history of its acquisition reconciled me more than anything else to my Master's unnautical appearance.

Some time ago there was a great demand in Australia for small river steamers, which certain Scotch companies undertook to supply. The difficulty, however, was to get such fragile tea-kettles across the ocean; five started one after another in murderous succession, and each came to grief before it got half-way to the equator; the sixth alone remained with which to try a last experiment. Should she arrive, her price would more than compensate the pecuniary loss already sustained, though it could not bring to life the hands sacrificed in the mad speculation; by this time, however, even the proverbial recklessness of the seamen of the port was daunted, and the hearts of two crews had already failed them at the last moment of starting, when my friend of the chain volunteered to take the command. At the outset of his voyage everything went well; a fair wind (her machinery was stowed away, and she sailed under canvas) carried the little craft in an incredibly short time a thousand miles to the southward of the Cape, when one day, as she was running before the gale, the man at the wheel—startled at a sea which he thought was going to poop her—let go the helm; the vessel broached to, and tons of water tumbled in on the top of the deck. As soon as the confusion of the moment had subsided, it became evident that the shock had broken some of the iron plates, and that the ship was in a fair way of foundering. So frightened were the crew, that, after consultation with each other, they determined to take to the boats, and all hands came aft, to know whether there was anything the skipper would wish to carry off with him. Comprehending the madness of attempting to reach land in open boats at the distance of a thousand miles from any shore, Wyse pretended to go into the cabin to get his compass, chronometer, etc., but returning immediately with a revolver in each hand, swore he would shoot the first man who attempted to touch the boats. This timely exhibition of spirit saved their lives : soon after the weather moderated ; by undergirding the ship with chains, St. Paul fashion, the leaks were partially stopped, the steamer reached her destination, and was sold for 7,000*l.* a few days after her arrival. In token of their gratitude for the good service he had done them, the Company presented Mr. Wyse on his return with a gold watch, and the chain he wears so gloriously outside the silk tartan waistcoat.

And now, good-bye. I hear the click-click of the chain as they heave the anchor; I am rather tired and exhausted with all the worry of the last two months, and shall be heartily glad to get to sea, where fresh air will set me up again, I hope, in a few days. My next letter will be from Iceland ; and, please God, before I see English land again, I hope to have many a story to tell you of the islands that are washed by the chill waters of the Arctic Sea.

LETTER V.

THE NORTH ATLANTIC—SPANISH WAVES—OUR CABIN IN A GALE—
SEA-SICKNESS FROM A SCIENTIFIC POINT OF VIEW—WILSON—A
PASSENGER COMMITS SUICIDE—FIRST SIGHT OF ICELAND—FLOKI
OF THE RAVENS—THE NORSE MAYFLOWER—FAXA FIORD—WE
LAND IN THULE.

Reykjavik, Iceland, June 21, 1856.

WE have landed in Thule! When, in parting, you moaned so at the thought of not being able to hear of our safe arrival, I knew there would be an opportunity of writing to you almost immediately after reaching Iceland; but I said nothing about it at the time, lest something should delay this letter, and you be left to imagine all kinds of doleful reasons for its non-appearance. We anchored in Reykjavik harbour this afternoon (Saturday). H.M.S. "*Coquette*" sails for England on Monday; so that within a week you will get this.

For the last ten days we have been leading the life of the "Flying Dutchman." Never do I remember to have had such a dusting: foul winds, gales, and calms—or rather breathing spaces, which the gale took occasionally to muster up fresh energies for a blow—with a heavy head sea, that prevented our sailing even when we got aslant. On the afternoon of the day we quitted Stornaway, I got a notion how it was going to be; the sun went angrily down behind a bank of solid grey cloud, and by the time we were up with the Butt of Lewis, the whole sky was in tatters, and the mercury nowhere, with a heavy swell from the north-west.

As, two years before, I had spent a week in trying to beat through the Roost of Sumburgh under double-reefed try-sails, I was at home in the weather; and guessing we were in for it, sent down the topmasts, stowed the boats on board, handed the foresail, rove the ridge-ropes, and reefed all down. By midnight it blew a gale, which continued without intermission until the day we sighted Iceland; sometimes increasing to a hurricane, but broken now and then by sudden lulls, which used to leave us for a couple of hours at a time tumbling about on the top of the great Atlantic rollers—or Spanish waves, as they are called—until I thought the ship would roll the masts out of her. Why they should be called Spanish waves, no one seems to know; but I had always heard the seas were heavier here than in any other part of the world, and certainly they did not belie their character. The little ship behaved beautifully, and many a vessel twice her size would have been less comfortable. Indeed, few people can have any notion of the cosiness of a yacht's cabin under such circumstances. After having remained for several hours on deck, in the presence of the tempest,— peering through the darkness at those black liquid walls of water, mounting above you in ceaseless agitation, or tumbling over in cataracts of gleaming foam,—the wind roaring through the rigging,—timbers creaking as if the ship would break its heart,—the spray and rain beating in your face,— everything around in tumult,—suddenly to descend into the quiet of a snug, well-lighted little cabin, with the firelight dancing on the white rosebud chintz, the well-furnished book-shelves, and all the innumerable nick-nacks that decorate its walls,—little Edith's portrait looking so serene,— everything about you as bright and fresh as a lady's boudoir in May Fair,—the certainty of being a good three hundred miles from any troublesome shore,—all combine to inspire a feeling of comfort and security difficult to describe.

These pleasures, indeed, for the first days of our voyage, the Icelander had pretty much to himself. I was laid up with a severe bout of illness I had long felt coming on, and Fitz was sea-sick. I must say, however, I never saw any one behave with more pluck and resolution; and when we return, the first thing you do must be to thank him for his kindness to me on that occasion. Though himself almost prostrate, he looked after me as indefatigably as if he had already found his sea legs; and, sitting down on the cabin floor, with a basin on one side of him, and a pestle and mortar on the other, used to manufacture my pills, between the paroxysms of his malady, with a decorous pertinacity that could not be too much admired.

Strangely enough, too, his state of unhappiness lasted a few days longer than the eight-and-forty hours which are generally sufficient to set people on their feet again. I tried to console him by representing what an occasion it was for observing the phenomena of sea-sickness from a scientific point of view; and I must say he set to work most conscientiously to discover some remedy. Brandy, prussic acid, opium, champagne, ginger, mutton-chops, and tumblers of salt-water, were successively exhibited; but, I regret to say, after a few minutes, each in turn *re*-exhibited itself with monotonous punctuality. Indeed, at one time we thought he would never get over it; and the following conversation, which I overheard one morning between him and my servant, did not brighten his hopes of recovery.

This person's name is Wilson, and of all men I ever met he is the most desponding. Whatever is to be done, he is sure to see a lion in the path. Life in his eyes is a perpetual filling of leaky buckets, and a rolling of stones up hill. He is amazed when the bucket holds water, or the stone perches on the summit. He professes but a limited belief in his star,—and success with him is almost a disappointment. His countenance corresponds with the prevailing character of his thoughts, always hopelessly chapfallen; his voice is as of the tomb. He brushes my clothes, lays the cloth, opens the champagne, with the air of one advancing to his execution. I have never seen him smile but once, when he came to report to me that a sea had nearly swept his colleague, the steward, overboard. The son of a gardener at Chiswick, he first took to horticulture; then emigrated as a settler to the Cape, where he acquired his present complexion, which is of a grass-green; and finally served as a steward on board an Australian steam-packet.

Thinking to draw consolation from his professional experiences, I heard Fitz's voice, now very weak, say in a tone of coaxing cheerfulness,—

"Well, Wilson, I suppose this kind of thing does not last long?"

The Voice, as of the tomb.—"I don't know, Sir."

Fitz.—"But you must have often seen passengers sick."

The Voice.—"Often, Sir; *very* sick."

Fitz.—"Well; and on an average, how soon did they recover?"

The Voice.—"Some of them didn't recover, Sir."

Fitz.—"Well, but those that did?"

The Voice.—"I know'd a clergyman and his wife as were ill all the voyage; five months, Sir."

Fitz.—(Quite silent.)

The Voice; now become sepulchral.—"They sometimes dies, Sir."

Fitz.—"Ugh!"

Before the end of the voyage, however, this Job's comforter himself fell ill, and the Doctor amply revenged himself by prescribing for him.

Shortly after this, a very melancholy occurrence took place. I had observed for some days past, as we proceeded north, and the nights became shorter, that the cock we shipped at Stornaway had become quite bewildered on the subject of that meteorological phenomenon called the Dawn of Day. In fact, I doubt whether he ever slept for more than five minutes at a stretch, without waking up in a state of nervous agitation, lest it should be cock-crow. At last, when night ceased altogether, his constitution could no longer stand the shock. He crowed once or twice sarcastically, then went melancholy mad: finally, taking a calenture, he cackled lowly (probably of green fields), and leaping overboard, drowned himself. The mysterious manner in which every day a fresh member of his harem used to disappear, may also have preyed upon his spirits.

At last, on the morning of the eighth day, we began to

look out for land. The weather had greatly improved during the night; and, for the first time since leaving the Hebrides, the sun had got the better of the clouds, and driven them in confusion before his face. The sea, losing its dead leaden colour, had become quite crisp and burnished, darkling into a deep sapphire blue against the horizon; beyond which, at about nine o'clock, there suddenly shot up towards the zenith, a pale, gold aureole, such as precedes the appearance of the good fairy at a pantomime farce; then, gradually lifting its huge back above the water, rose a silver pyramid of snow, which I knew must be the cone of an ice mountain, miles away in the interior of the island. From the moment we got hold of the land, our cruise, as you may suppose, doubled in interest. Unfortunately, however, the fair morning did not keep its promise; about one o'clock, the glittering mountain vanished in mist; the sky again became like an inverted pewter cup, and we had to return for two more days to our old practice of threshing to windward. So provoked was I at this relapse of the weather, that, perceiving a whale blowing *convenient*, I could not help suggesting to Sigurdr, son of Jonas, that it was an occasion for observing the traditions of his family; but he excused himself on the plea of their having become obsolete.

The mountain we had seen in the morning was the southeast extremity of the island, the very landfall made by one of its first discoverers.[1] This gentleman not having a compass, (he lived about A.D. 864,) nor knowing exactly where

---

[1] There is in Strabo an account of a voyage made by a citizen of the Greek colony of Marseilles, in the time of Alexander the Great, through the Pillars of Hercules, along the coasts of France and Spain, up the English Channel, and so across the North Sea, past an island he calls Thule; his further progress, he asserted, was hindered by a barrier of a peculiar nature,—neither earth, air, nor sky, but a compound of all three, forming a thick viscid substance which it was impossible to penetrate. Now, whether this same Thule was one of the Shetland Islands, and the impassable substance merely a fog,—or Iceland, and the barricade beyond, a wall of ice, it is impossible to say. Probably Pythias did not get beyond the Shetlands.

the land lay, took on board with him, at starting, three consecrated ravens—as an M.P. would take three well-trained pointers to his moor. Having sailed a certain distance, he let loose one, which flew back : by this he judged he had not got half-way. Proceeding onwards, he loosed the second, which, after circling in the air for some minutes in apparent uncertainty, also made off home, as though it still remained a nice point which were the shorter course toward terra firma. But the third, on obtaining his liberty a few days later, flew forward, and by following the direction in which he had disappeared, Rabna Floki, or Floki of the Ravens, as he came to be called, triumphantly made the land.

The real colonists did not arrive till some years later, for I do not much believe a story they tell of Christian relics, supposed to have been left by Irish fishermen, found on the Westmann islands. A Scandinavian king, named Harold Haarfager (a contemporary of our own King Alfred's), having murdered, burnt, and otherwise exterminated all his brother kings who at that time grew as thick as blackberries in Norway, first consolidated their dominions into one realm, as Edgar did the Heptarchy, and then proceeded to invade the Udal rights of the landholders. Some of them, animated with that love of liberty innate in the race of the noble Northmen, rather than submit to his oppressions, determined to look for a new home amid the desolate regions of the icy sea. Freighting a dragon-shaped galley—the "*Mayflower*" of the period—with their wives and children, and all the household monuments that were dear to them, they saw the blue peaks of their dear Norway hills sink down into the sea behind, and manfully set their faces towards the west, where—some vague report had whispered—a new land might be found. Arrived in sight of Iceland, the leader of the expedition threw the sacred pillars belonging to his former dwelling into the water, in order that the gods might determine the site of his new home : carried by the tide, no one could say in what direction, they were at last discovered, at the end of three years, in a sheltered bay on the west side of the island, and Ingolf[1] came and abode there, and the place became in the course of years Reykjavik, the capital of the country.

Sigurdr having scouted the idea of acting Iphigenia, there was nothing for it but steadily to beat over the remaining hundred and fifty miles, which still separated us from Cape Reikianess. After going for two days hard at it, and sighting the Westmann islands, we ran plump into a fog, and lay to. In a few hours, however, it cleared up into a lovely sunny day. with a warm summer breeze just rippling up the water. Before us lay the long wished-for Cape, with the Meal-sack, —a queer stump of basalt, that flops up out of the sea, fifteen miles south-west of Cape Reikianess, its flat top white with guano, like the mouth of a bag of flour,—five miles on our port bow; and seldom have I remembered a pleasanter four-and-twenty hours than those spent stealing up along the gnarled and crumpled lava flat that forms the western coast of Guldbrand Syssel. Such fishing, shooting, looking through telescopes, and talking of what was to be done on our arrival! Like Antæus, Sigurdr seemed twice the man he was before, at sight of his native land; and the Doctor grew nearly lunatic when after stalking a solent goose asleep on the water, the bird flew away at the moment the schooner hove within shot.

The panorama of the bay of Faxa Fiord is magnificent, —with a width of fifty miles from horn to horn, the one running down into a rocky ridge of pumice, the other towering to the height of five thousand feet in a pyramid of eternal snow, while round the intervening semicircle crowd the peaks of a hundred noble mountains. As you approach the shore, you are very much reminded of the west coast of Scotland, except that everything is more *intense*—the atmosphere clearer, the light more vivid, the air more bracing, the hills steeper, loftier, more tormented, as the French say, and more gaunt; while between their base and the sea stretches

---

[1] It was in consequence of a domestic feud that Ingolf himself was forced to emigrate.

a dirty greenish slope, patched with houses which themselves, both roof and walls, are of a mouldy green, as if some long-since inhabited country had been fished up out of the bottom of the sea.

The effects of light and shadow are the purest I ever saw, the contrasts of colour most astonishing,—one square front of a mountain jutting out in a blaze of gold against the flank of another, dyed of the darkest purple, while up against the azure sky beyond, rise peaks of glittering snow and ice. The snow, however, beyond serving as an ornamental fringe to the distance, plays but a very poor part at this season of the year in Iceland. While I write, the thermometer is above 70°. Last night we remained playing at chess on deck till bedtime, without thinking of calling for coats, and my people live in their shirt-sleeves, and— astonishment at the climate.

And now, good-bye. I cannot tell you how I am enjoying myself, body and soul. Already I feel much stronger, and before I return I trust to have laid in a stock of health sufficient to last the family for several generations.

Remember me to ———, and tell her she looks too lovely; her face has become of a beautiful bright green— a complexion which her golden crown sets off to the greatest advantage. I wish she could have seen, as we sped across, how passionately the waves of the Atlantic flung their liquid arms about her neck, and how proudly she broke through their embraces, leaving them far behind, moaning and lamenting.

LETTER VI.

REYKJAVIK—LATIN CONVERSATION—I BECOME THE PROPRIETOR OF TWENTY-SIX HORSES — EIDER DUCKS — BESSESTAD — SNORRO STURLESON—THE OLD GREENLAND COLONY—FINLAND—A GENOESE SKIPPER IN THE FIFTEENTH CENTURY—AN ICELANDIC DINNER—SKOAL—AN AFTER-DINNER SPEECH IN LATIN—WINGED RABBITS—DUCROW—START OF THE BAGGAGE-TRAIN.

Reykjavik, June 28, 1856.

NOTWITHSTANDING that its site, as I mentioned in my last letter, was determined by auspices not less divine than those of Rome or Athens, Reykjavik is not so fine a city as either, though its public buildings may be thought to be in better repair. In fact, the town consists of a collection of wooden sheds, one story high—rising here and there into a gable end of greater pretentions—built along the lava beach, and flanked at either end by a suburb of turf huts.

On every side of it extends a desolate plain of lava that once must have boiled up red-hot from some distant gateway of hell, and fallen hissing into the sea. No tree or bush relieves the dreariness of the landscape, and the mountains are too distant to serve as a background to the buildings; but before the door of each merchant's house facing the sea, there flies a gay little pennon; and as you walk along the silent streets, whose dust no carriage-wheel has ever desecrated, the rows of flower-pots that peep out of the windows, between curtains of white muslin, at once convince you that notwithstanding their unpretending appearance, within each dwelling reign the elegance and comfort of a woman-tended home.

Thanks to Sigurdr's popularity among his countrymen, by the second day after our arrival we found ourselves no longer in a strange land. With a frank energetic cordiality that quite took one by surprise, the gentlemen of the place at once welcomed us to their firesides, and made us feel that we could give them no greater pleasure than by claiming their hospitality. As, however, it is necessary, if we are to reach Jan Mayen and Spitzbergen this summer, that our stay in Iceland should not be prolonged above a certain date, I determined at once to make preparations for our expedition to the Geysirs and the interior of the country. Our plan at present, after visiting the hot springs, is to return to Reykjavik, and stretch right across the middle of the island to the north coast—scarcely ever visited by strangers. Thence we shall sail straight away to Jan Mayen.

In pursuance of this arrangement, the first thing to do was to buy some horses. Away, accordingly, we went in the gig to the little pier leading up to the merchant's house who had kindly promised Sigurdr to provide them. Everything in the country that is not made of wood is made of lava. The pier was constructed out of huge boulders of lava, the shingle is lava, the sea-sand is pounded lava, the mud on the roads is lava paste, the foundations of the houses are lava blocks, and in dry weather you are blinded with lava dust. Immediately upon landing I was presented to a fine, burly gentleman, who, I was informed, could let me have a steppe-ful of horses if I desired, and a few minutes afterwards I picked myself up in the middle of a Latin oration on the subject of the weather. Having suddenly lost my nominative case, I concluded abruptly with the figure syncope, and a bow, to which my interlocutor politely replied "Ita." Many of the inhabitants speak English, and one or two French, but in default of either of these, your only chance is Latin. At first I found great difficulty in brushing up anything sufficiently conversational, more especially as it was necessary to broaden out the vowels in the high Roman fashion; but a little practice soon made me more fluent, and I got at last to brandish my "Pergratum est," etc. in the face of a new acquaintance, without any misgivings. On this occasion I thought it more prudent to let Sigurdr make the necessary arrangements for our journey, and in a few minutes I had the satisfaction of learning that I had become the proprietor of twenty-six horses, as many bridles and pack-saddles, and three guides.

There being no roads in Iceland, all the traffic of the country is conducted by means of horses, along the bridle-tracks which centuries of travel have worn in the lava plains. As but little hay is to be had, the winter is a season of fasting for all cattle, and it is not until spring is well advanced, and the horses have had time to grow a little fat on the young grass, that you can go a journey. I was a good deal taken aback when the number of my stud was announced to me ; but it appears that what with the photographic apparatus, which I am anxious to take, and our tent, it would be impossible to do with fewer animals. The price of each pony is very moderate, and I am told I shall have no difficulty in disposing of all of them, at the conclusion of our expedition.

These preliminaries happily concluded, Mr. J—— invited us into his house, where his wife and daughter—a sunshiny young lady of eighteen—were waiting to receive us. As Latin here was quite useless, we had to entrust Sigurdr with all the pretty things we desired to convey to our entertainers ; but it is my firm opinion that that gentleman took a dirty advantage of us, and intercepting the choicest flowers of our eloquence, appropriated them to the advancement of his own interests. However, such expressions of respectful admiration as he suffered to reach their destination were received very graciously, and rewarded with a shower of smiles.

The next few days were spent in making short expeditions in the neighbourhood, in preparing our baggage-train, and in paying visits. It would be too long for me to enumerate all the marks of kindness and hospitality I received during this short period. Suffice it to say, that I had the satisfaction of making many very interesting acquaintances, of beholding a great number of very pretty faces, and of partaking of an innumerable quantity of luncheons. In fact, to break bread, or, more correctly speaking, to crack a bottle with the master of the house, is as essential an element of a morning call as the making a bow or shaking hands, and to refuse to take off your glass would be as great an incivility as to decline taking off your hat. From earliest times, as the grand old ballad of the King of Thule tells us, a beaker was considered the fittest token a lady could present to her true-love—

Dem sterbend seine Buhle
Einen goldnen Becher gab.

And in one of the most ancient Eddaic songs it is written, " Drink, Runes, must thou know, if thou wilt maintain thy power over the maiden thou lovest. Thou shalt score them on the drinking-horn, on the back of thy hand, and the word NAUD " (*need*—necessity) " on thy nail." Moreover, when it is remembered that the ladies of the house themselves minister on these occasions, it will be easily understood that all flinching is out of the question. What is a man to do, when a wicked little golden-haired maiden insists on pouring him out a bumper, and dumb show is his only means of remonstrance? Why, of course, if death were in the cup, he must make her a leg, and drain it to the bottom, as I did. In conclusion, I am bound to add that, notwithstanding the bacchanalian character prevailing in these visits, I derived from them much interesting and useful information; and I have invariably found the gentlemen to whom I have been presented persons of education and refinement, combined with a happy, healthy, jovial temperament, that invests their conversation with a peculiar charm.

At this moment people are in a great state of excitement at the expected arrival of H.I.H. Prince Napoleon, and two days ago a large full-rigged ship came in laden with coal for his use. The day after we left Stornaway, we had seen her scudding away before the gale on a due west course, and guessed she was bound for Iceland, and running down the longitude; but as we arrived here four days before her, our course seems to have been a better one. The only other ship here is the French frigate "*Artemise*," Commodore

Dumas, by whom I have been treated with the greatest kindness and civility.

On Saturday we went to Vedey, a beautiful little green island where the eider ducks breed, and build nests with the soft under-down plucked from their own bosoms. After the little ones are hatched, and their birthplaces deserted, the nests are gathered, cleaned, and stuffed into pillow-cases, for pretty ladies in Europe to lay their soft, warm cheeks upon, and sleep the sleep of the innocent; while long-legged, broad-shouldered Englishmen protrude from between them at German inns, like the ham from a sandwich, and cannot sleep, however innocent.

The next day, being Sunday, I read prayers on board, and then went for a short time to the cathedral church,— the only stone building in Reykjavik. It is a moderate-sized, unpretending place, capable of holding three or four hundred persons, erected in very ancient times, but lately restored. The Icelanders are of the Lutheran religion; and a Lutheran clergyman, in a black gown, etc., with a ruff round his neck, such as our bishops are painted in about the time of James the First, was preaching a sermon. It was the first time I had heard Icelandic spoken continuously, and it struck me as a singularly sweet caressing language, although I disliked the particular cadence, amounting almost to a chant, with which each sentence ended.

As in every church where prayers have been offered up since the world began, the majority of the congregation were women, some few dressed in bonnets, and the rest in the national black silk skull-cap, set jauntily on one side of the head, with a long black tassel hanging down to the shoulder, or else in a quaint mitre of white linen, of which a drawing alone could give you an idea; the remainder of an Icelandic lady's costume, when not superseded by Paris fashions, consists of a black bodice fastened in front with silver clasps, over which is drawn a cloth jacket, ornamented with a multitude of silver buttons; round the neck goes a stiff ruff of velvet, figured with silver lace, and a silver belt, often beautifully chased, binds the long dark wadmal petticoat round the waist. Sometimes the ornaments are of gold instead of silver, and very costly.

Before dismissing his people, the preacher descended from the pulpit, and putting on a splendid cope of crimson velvet (in which some bishop had in ages past been murdered), turned his back to the congregation, and chanted some Latin sentences in good round Roman style. Though still retaining in their ceremonies a few vestiges of the old religion, though altars, candles, pictures, and crucifixes yet remain in many of their churches, the Icelanders are staunch Protestants, and, by all accounts, the most devout, innocent pure-hearted people in the world. Crime, theft, debauchery, cruelty, are unknown amongst them; they have neither prison, gallows, soldiers, nor police ; and in the manner of the lives they lead among their secluded valleys, there is something of a patriarchal simplicity, that reminds one of the Old World princes, of whom it has been said, that they were "upright and perfect, eschewing evil, and in their hearts no guile."

The law with regard to marriage, however, is sufficiently peculiar. When, from some unhappy incompatibility or temper, a married couple live so miserably together as to render life insupportable, it is competent for them to apply to the Danish Governor of the island for a divorce. If, after the lapse of three years from the date of the application, both are still of the same mind, and equally eager to be free, the divorce is granted, and each is at liberty to marry again.

The next day it had been arranged that we were to take an experimental trip on our new ponies, under the guidance of the learned and jovial Rector of the College. Unfortunately the weather was dull and rainy, but we were determined to enjoy ourselves in spite of everything, and a pleasanter ride I have seldom had. The steed Sigurdr had purchased for me was a long-tailed, hog-maned, shaggy, cow-houghed creature, thirteen hands high, of a bright yellow colour, with admirable action, and sure-footed enough to walk downstairs backwards. The Doctor was not less well mounted; in fact, the Icelandic pony is quite a peculiar race, much stronger, faster, and better bred than the Highland shelty, and descended probably from pure-blooded sires that scoured the steppes of Asia, long before Odin and his paladins had peopled the valleys of Scandinavia.

The first few miles of our ride lay across an undulating plain of dolorite, to a farm situated at the head of an inlet of the sea. At a distance, the farm-steading looked like a little oasis of green, amid the grey stony slopes that surrounded it, and on a nearer approach not unlike the vestiges of a Celtic earthwork, with the tumulus of a hero or two in the centre; but the mounds turned out to be nothing more than the grass roofs of the house and offices, and the banks and dykes but circumvallations round the plot of most carefully cleaned meadow, called the "tùn," which always surrounds every Icelandic farm. This word "tùn" is evidently identical with our own Irish "*townland*," the Cornish "*town*," and the Scotch "*toon*,"—terms which, in their local signification, do not mean a congregation of streets and buildings, but the yard, and spaces of grass immediately adjoining a single house; just as in German we have "*tzaun*," and in the Dutch "*tuyn*," a garden.

Turning to the right, round the head of a little bay, we passed within forty yards of an enormous eagle, seated on a crag; but we had no rifle, and all he did was to rise heavily into the air, flap his wings like a barn-door fowl, and plump lazily down twenty yards farther off. Soon after, the district we traversed became more igneous, wrinkled, cracked, and ropy than anything we had yet seen, and another two hours' scamper over such a track as till then I would not have believed horses could have traversed, even at a foot's pace, brought us to the solitary farm-house of Bessestad. Fresh from the neat homesteads of England that we had left sparkling in the bright spring weather, and sheltered by immemorial elms,—the scene before us looked inexpressibly desolate. In front rose a cluster of weather-beaten wooden buildings, and huts like ice-houses, surrounded by a scanty plot of grass, reclaimed from the craggy plain of broken lava that stretched—the home of ravens and foxes—on either side to the horizon. Beyond, lay a low black breadth of moorland, intersected by patches of what was neither land nor water, and last, the sullen sea ; while above our heads a wind, saturated with the damps of the Atlantic, went moaning over the landscape. Yet this was Bessestad, the ancient home of Snorro Sturleson !

On dismounting from our horses and entering the house things began to look more cheery; a dear old lady, to whom we were successively presented by the Rector, received us, with the air of a princess, ushered us into her best room, made us sit down on the sofa—the place of honour—and assisted by her niece, a pale lily-like maiden, named after Jarl Hakon's Thora, proceeded to serve us with hot coffee, rusks, and sweetmeats. At first it used to give me a very disagreeable feeling to be waited upon by the woman-kind of the household, and I was always starting up, and attempting to take the dishes out of their hands, to their infinite surprise ; but now I have succeeded in learning to accept their ministrations with the same unembarrassed dignity as my neighbours. In the end, indeed, I have rather got to like it, especially when they are as pretty as Miss Thora. To add, moreover, to our content, it appeared that that young lady spoke a little French ; so that we had no longer any need to pay our court by proxy, which many persons besides ourselves have found to be unsatisfactory. Our hostess lives quite alone. Her son, whom I have the pleasure of knowing, is far away, pursuing a career of honour and usefulness at Copenhagen, and it seems quite enough for his mother to know that he is holding his head high among the princes of literature, and the statesmen of Europe, provided only news of his success and advancing reputation shall occasionally reach her across the ocean.

Of the rooms and the interior arrangement of the house,
I do not know that I have anything particular to tell you ;
they seemed to me like those of a good old-fashioned farm-
house, the walls wainscoted with deal, and the doors and
staircase of the same material. A few prints, a photograph,
some book-shelves, one or two little pictures, decorated the
parlour, and a neat iron stove, and massive chests of drawers,
served to furnish it very completely. But you must not, I
fear, take the drawing-room of Bessestad as an average specimen of the comfort of an Icelandic *intérieur*. The greater
proportion of the inhabitants of the island live much more
rudely. The walls of only the more substantial farmsteads
are wainscoted with deal, or even partially screened with
drift-wood. In most houses the bare blocks of lava, pointed
with moss, are left in all their natural ruggedness. Instead
of wood, the rafters are made of the ribs of whales. The
same room but too often serves as the dining, sitting, and
sleeping place for the whole family ; a hole in the roof is
the only chimney, and a horse's skull the most luxurious
fauteuil into which it is possible for them to induct a stranger.
The *parquet* is that originally laid down by Nature,—the
beds are merely boxes filled with feathers or sea-weed,—
and by all accounts the nightly packing is pretty close, and
very indiscriminate.

After drinking several cups of coffee, and consuming at
least a barrel of rusks, we rose to go, in spite of Miss
Thora's intimation that a fresh jorum of coffee was being
brewed. The horses were resaddled ; and with an eloquent
exchange of bows, curtseys, and kindly smiles, we took
leave of our courteous entertainers, and sallied forth into
the wind and rain. It was a regular race home, single file,
the Rector leading ; but as we sped along in silence, amid
the unchangeable features of this strange land, I could not
help thinking of him whose shrewd observing eye must
have rested, six hundred and fifty years ago, on the selfsame
crags, and tarns, and distant mountain-tops ; perhaps on the
very day he rode out in the pride of his wealth, talent, and

political influence, to meet his murderers at Reikholt. And mingling with his memory would rise the pale face of Thora, —not the little lady of the coffee and buscuits we had just left, but that other Thora, so tender and true, who turned back King Olaf's hell-hounds from the hiding-place of the great Jarl of Ladé.

In order that you may understand why the forlorn barrack we had just left, and its solitary inmates, should have set me thinking of the men and women " of a thousand summers back," it is necessary I should tell you a little about this same Snorro Sturleson, whose memory so haunted me.

Colonized as Iceland had been,—not, as is generally the case, when a new land is brought into occupation, by the poverty-stricken dregs of a redundant population, nor by a gang of outcasts and ruffians, expelled from the bosom of a society which they contaminated,—but by men who in their own land had been both rich and noble,—with possessions to be taxed, and a spirit too haughty to endure taxation,—already acquainted with whatever of refinement and learning the age they lived in was capable of supplying,—it is not surprising that we should find its inhabitants, even from the first infancy of the republic, endowed with an amount of intellectual energy hardly to be expected in so secluded a community.

Perhaps it was this very seclusion which stimulated into almost miraculous exuberance the mental powers already innate in the people. Undistracted during several successive centuries by the bloody wars, and still more bloody political convulsions, which for too long a period rendered the sword of the warrior so much more important to European society than the pen of the scholar, the Icelandic settlers, devoting the long leisure of their winter nights to intellectual occupations, became the first of any European nation to create for themselves a native literature. Indeed, so much more accustomed did they get to use their heads than their hands, than if an Icelander were injured he often avenged himself, not by cutting the throat of his antagonist, but by ridiculing him in some pasquinade,—sometimes, indeed, he did both; and when the King of Denmark maltreats the crew of an Icelandic vessel shipwrecked on his coast, their indignant countrymen send the barbarous monarch word, that by way of reprisal, they intend making as many lampoons on him as there are promontories in his dominions. Almost all the ancient Scandinavian manuscripts are Icelandic; the negotiations between the Courts of the North were conducted by Icelandic diplomatists; the earliest topographical survey with which we are acquainted was Icelandic; the cosmogony of the Odin religion was formulated, and its doctrinal traditions and ritual reduced to a system, by Icelandic archæologists; and the first historical composition ever written by any European in the vernacular, was the product of Icelandic genius. The title of this important work is *"The Heimskringla,"* or *world-circle*,[1] and its author was— Snorro Sturleson ! It consists of an account of the reigns of the Norwegian kings from mythic times down to about A.D. 1150, that is to say, a few years before the death of our own Henry II.; but detailed by the old Sagaman with so much art and cleverness as almost to combine the dramatic power of Macaulay with Clarendon's delicate delineation of character, and the charming loquacity of Mr. Pepys. His stirring sea-fights, his tender love-stories, and delightful bits of domestic gossip, are really inimitable;—you actually live with the people he brings upon the stage, as intimately as you do with Falstaff, Percy, or Prince Hal; and there is something in the bearing of those old heroic figures who form his *dramatis personæ*, so grand and noble, that it is impossible to read the story of their earnest stirring lives without a feeling of almost passionate interest—an effect which no tale frozen up in the monkish Latin of the Saxon annalists has ever produced upon me.

As for Snorro's own life, it was eventful and tragic enough.

[1] So called because Heimskringla (world-circle) is the first word in the opening sentence of the manuscript which catches the eye.

Unscrupulous, turbulent, greedy of money, he married two heiresses—the one, however, becoming the *colleague*, not the successor of the other. This arrangement naturally led to embarrassment. His wealth created envy, his excessive haughtiness disgusted his sturdy fellow-countrymen. He was suspected of desiring to make the republic an appanage of the Norwegian crown, in the hope of himself becoming viceroy; and at last, on a dark September night, of the year 1241, he was murdered in his house at Reikholt by his three sons-in-law.

The same century which produced the Herodotean work of Sturleson also gave birth to a whole body of miscellaneous Icelandic literature,—though in Britain and elsewhere bookmaking was entirely confined to the monks, and merely consisted in the compilation of a series of bald annals locked up in bad Latin. It is true, Thomas of Ercildoune was a contemporary of Snorro's; but he is known to us more as a magician than as a man of letters; whereas histories, memoirs, romances, biographies, poetry, statistics, novels, calendars, specimens of almost every kind of composition, are to be found even among the meagre relics which have survived the literary decadence that supervened on the extinction of the republic.

It is to these same spirited chroniclers that we are indebted for the preservation of two of the most remarkable facts in the history of the world: the colonization of Greenland by Europeans in the 10th century, and the discovery of America by the Icelanders at the commencement of the 11th.

The story is rather curious.

Shortly after the arrival of the first settlers in Iceland, a mariner of the name of Eric the Red discovers a country away to the west, which, in consequence of its fruitful appearance, he calls Greenland. In the course of a few years the new land has become so thickly inhabited that it is necessary to erect the district into an episcopal see; and at last, in 1448, we have a brief of Pope Nicolas "granting to his beloved children of Greenland, in consideration of their having erected many sacred buildings and a splendid cathedral,"—a new bishop and a fresh supply of priests. At the commencement, however, of the next century, this colony of Greenland, with its bishops, priests and people, its one hundred and ninety townships, its cathedral, its churches, its monasteries, suddenly fades into oblivion, like the fabric of a dream. The memory of its existence perishes, and the allusions made to it in the old Scandinavian Sagas gradually come to be considered poetical inventions or pious frauds. At last, after a lapse of four hundred years, some Danish missionaries set out to convert the Esquimaux; and there, far within Davis' Straits, are discovered vestiges of the ancient settlement,—remains of houses, paths, walls, churches, tombstones, and inscriptions.[1]

What could have been the calamity which suddenly annihilated this Christian people, it is impossible to say; whether they were massacred by some warlike tribe of natives, or swept off to the last man by the terrible pestilence of 1349, called "The Black Death," or,—most horrible conjecture of all,—beleaguered by vast masses of ice setting down from the Polar Sea along the eastern coast of Greenland, and thus miserably frozen,—we are never likely to know—so utterly did they perish, so mysterious has been their doom.

On the other hand, certain traditions, with regard to the

[1] On one tombstone there was written in Runic, "Vigdis M. D. Hvilir Her; Glwde Gude Sal Hennar." "Vigdessa rests here; God gladden her soul." But the most interesting of these inscriptions is one discovered, in 1824, in an island in Baffin's Bay, in latitude 72° 55', as it shows how boldly these Northmen must have penetrated into regions supposed to have been unvisited by man before the voyages of our modern navigators:—" Erling Sighvatson and Biomo Thordarson, and Eindrid Oddson, on Saturday before Ascension-week, raised these marks and cleared ground, 1135." This date of Ascension-week implies that these three men wintered here, which must lead us to imagine that at that time, seven hundred years ago, the climate was less inclement than it is now.

discovery of a vast continent by their forefathers away in the south-west, seems never entirely to have died out of the memory of the Icelanders; and in the month of February, 1477, there arrives at Reykjavik, in a barque belonging to the port of Bristol, a certain long-visaged, grey-eyed Genoese mariner, who was observed to take an amazing interest in hunting up whatever was known on the subject. Whether Columbus—for it was no less a personage than he —really learned anything to confirm him in his noble resolutions, is uncertain; but we have still extant an historical manuscript, written at all events before the year 1395, that is to say, one hundred years prior to Columbus' voyage, which contains a minute account of how a certain person named Lief, while sailing over to Greenland, was driven out of his course by contrary winds, until he found himself off an extensive and unknown coast, which increased in beauty and fertility as he descended south, and how, in consequence of the representation Lief made on his return, successive expeditions were undertaken in the same direction. On two occasions their wives seem to have accompanied the adventurers; of one ship's company the skipper was a lady: while two parties even wintered in the new land, built houses, and prepared to colonize. For some reason, however, the intention was abandoned; and in process of time these early voyages came to be considered as aprocryphal as the Phœnician circumnavigation of Africa in the time of Pharaoh Necho.

It is quite uncertain how low a latitude in America the Northmen ever reached; but from the description given of the scenery, products, and inhabitants,—from the mildness of the weather,—and from the length of the day on the 21st of December,—it is conjectured they could not have descended much farther than Newfoundland, Nova Scotia, or, at most, the coast of Massachusetts.[1]

[1] There is a certain piece of rock on the Taunton river, in Massachusetts, called the Deighton Stone, on which are to be seen rude configurations, for a long time supposed to be a Runic inscription executed

But to return to more material matters.

Yesterday—no—the day before—in fact I forget the date of the day—I don't believe it had one—all I know is, I have not been in bed since,—we dined at the Governor's;— though dinner is too modest a term to apply to the entertainment.

The invitation was for four o'clock, and at half-past three we pulled ashore in the gig; I, innocent that I was, in a well-fitting white waistcoat.

The Government House, like all the others, is built of wood, on the top of a hillock; the only accession of dignity it can boast being a little bit of mangy kitchen-garden that hangs down in front to the road, like a soiled apron. There was no lock, handle, bell, or knocker to the door, but immediately on our approach, a servant presented himself, and ushered us into the room where Count Trampe was waiting to welcome us. After having been presented to his wife, we proceeded to shake hands with the other guests, most of whom I already knew; and I was glad to find that, at all events in Iceland, people do not consider it necessary to pass the ten minutes which precede the announcement of dinner, as if they had assembled to assist at the opening of their entertainer's will, instead of his oysters. The company consisted of the chief dignitaries of the island, including the Bishop, the Chief Justice, etc. etc., some of them in uniform, and all with holiday faces. As soon as the door was opened, Count Trampe tucked me under his arm—two other gentlemen did the same to my two companions—and we streamed into the dining-room. The table was very prettily arranged with flowers, plate, and a forest of glasses. Fitzgerald and I were placed on either side of our host, the other guests, in due order, beyond. On my left sat the Rector, and opposite, next to Fitz, the chief physician of the island. Then began a series of transactions of which I have no distinct recollection; in fact, the events of the next five hours

by these Scandinavian voyagers; but there can be now no longer any doubt of this inscription, such as it is, being of Indian execution.

recur to me in as great disarray as reappear the vestiges of a country that has been disfigured by some deluge. If I give you anything like a connected account of what passed, you must thank Sigurdr's more solid temperament; for the Doctor looked quite foolish when I asked him—tried to feel my pulse—could not find it—and then wrote the following prescription, which I believe to be nothing more than an invoice of the number of bottles he himself disposed of.[1]

I gather, then, from evidence—internal and otherwise— that the dinner was excellent, and that we were helped in Benjamite proportions; but as before the soup was finished I was already hard at work hob-nobbing with my two neighbours, it is not to be expected I should remember the bill of fare.

With the peculiar manners used in Scandinavian skoaldrinking I was already well acquainted. In the nice conduct of a wine-glass I knew that I excelled, and having an hereditary horror of heel-taps, I prepared with a firm heart to respond to the friendly provocations of my host. I only wish you could have seen how his kind face beamed with approval when I chinked my first bumper against his, and having emptied it at a draught, turned it towards him bottom upwards, with the orthodox twist. Soon, however, things began to look more serious even than I had expected. I knew well that to refuse a toast, or to half empty your glass, was considered churlish. I had come determined to accept my host's hospitality as cordially as it was offered. I was willing, at a pinch, to *payer de ma personne;* should he not be content with seeing me *at* his table, I was ready, if need were, to remain *under* it! but at the rate we were then going

---

[1] Copy of Dr. F.'s prescription :—

℞		
	vin : claret :	iii btls.
	vin : champ :	iv btls.
	vin : sherr :	½ btl.
	vin : Rheni :	ii btls.
	aqua vitæ	viii gls.
	trigint : poc: ægrot : cap : quotid :	

C. E. F.

Reik : die Martis, Junii 27.

it seemed probable this consummation would take place before the second course : so, after having exchanged a dozen rounds of sherry and champagne with my two neighbours, I pretended not to observe that my glass had been refilled ; and, like the sea-captain, who, slipping from between his two opponents, left them to blaze away at each other the long night through,—withdrew from the combat. But it would not do ; with untasted bumpers, and dejected faces, they politely waited until I should give the signal for a renewal of *host*ilities, as they well deserved to be called. Then there came over me a horrid, wicked feeling. What if I should endeavour to floor the Governor, and so literally turn the tables on him ! It is true I had lived for five-and-twenty years without touching wine,—but was not I my great-grandfather's great-grandson, and an Irish peer to boot? Were there not traditions, too, on the other side of the house, of casks of claret brought up into the dining-room, the door locked, and the key thrown out of the window ? With such antecedents to sustain me, I ought to be able to hold my own against the staunchest toper in Iceland ! So, with a devil glittering in my left eye, I winked defiance right and left, and away we went at it again for another five-and-forty minutes. At last their fire slackened : I had partially quelled both the Governor and the Rector, and still survived. It is true I did not feel comfortable ; but it was in the neighbourhood of my waistcoat, not my head, I suffered. " I am not well, but I will not out," I soliloquized, with Lepidus[1]— " $\delta \acute{u} \varsigma \; \mu o \iota \; \tau \grave{o} \; \pi \tau \epsilon \rho \acute{o} \nu$," I would have added, had I dared. Still the neck of the banquet was broken—Fitzgerald's chair was not yet empty,—could we hold out perhaps a quarter of an hour longer, our reputation was established ; guess then my horror, when the Icelandic Doctor, shouting his favourite dogma, by way of battle cry, "Si trigintis guttis, morbum curare velis, erras," gave the signal for an unexpected onslaught, and the twenty guests poured down on me in succession. I really thought I should have run away

[1] Antony and Cleopatra.

from the house; but the true family blood, I suppose, began to show itself, and with a calmness almost frightful, I received them one by one.

After this began the public toasts.

Although up to this time I had kept a certain portion of my wits about me, the subsequent hours of the entertainment became henceforth developed in a dreamy mystery. I can perfectly recall the look of the sheaf of glasses that stood before me, six in number; I could draw the pattern of each: I remember feeling a lazy wonder they should always be full, though I did nothing but empty them,—and at last solved the phenomenon by concluding I had become a kind of Danaid, whose punishment, not whose sentence, had been reversed: then suddenly I felt as if I were disembodied,—a distant spectator of my own performances, and of the feast at which my person remained seated. The voices of my host, of the Rector, of the Chief Justice, became thin and low, as though they reached me through a whispering tube; and when I rose to speak, it was as to an audience in another sphere, and in a language of another state of being: yet, however unintelligible to myself, I must have been in some sort understood, for at the end of each sentence, cheers, faint as the roar of waters on a far-off strand, floated towards me; and if I am to believe a report of the proceedings subsequently shown us, I must have become polyglot in my cups. According to that report it seems the Governor threw off (I wonder he did not do something else), with the Queen's health in French: to which I responded in the same language. Then the Rector, in English, proposed my health,—under the circumstances a cruel mockery,—but to which, ill as I was, I responded very gallantly by drinking to the *beaux yeux* of the Countess. Then somebody else drank success to Great Britain, and I see it was followed by really a very learned discourse by Lord D., in honour of the ancient Icelanders; during which he alluded to their discovery of America, and Columbus' visit. Then came a couple of speeches in Icelandic, after which the Bishop, in a magnificent Latin oration of some twenty minutes, a second time proposes my health ; to which, utterly at my wits' end, I had the audacity to reply in the same language. As it is fit so great an effort of oratory should not perish, I send you some of its choicest specimens :—

"Viri illustres," I began, "insolitus ut sum ad publicum loquendum, ego propero respondere ad complimentum quod recte reverendus prelaticus mihi fecit, in proponendo meam salutem : et supplico vos credere quod multum gratificatus et flattificatus sum honore tam distincto.

"Bibere, viri illustres, res est, quæ in omnibus terris, 'domum venit ad hominum negotia et pectora :'[1] (1) requirit 'haustum longum, haustum fortem, et haustum omnes simul:' (2) ut canit Poeta, 'unum tactum Naturæ totum orben facit consanguineum,' (3) et hominis Natura est—bibere (4).

"Viri illustres, alterum est sentimentum equaliter universale : terra communis super quam septentrionales et meridionales, eâdem enthusiasmâ convenire possunt : est necesse quod id nominarem ? Ad pulchrum sexum devotio !

"Amor regit palatium, castra, lucum : (5) Dubito sub quo capite vestram jucundam civitatem numerare debeam. Palatium ? non Regem ! Castra ? non milites ! lucum ? non ullam arborem habetis ! Tamen Cupido vos dominat haud aliter quam alios,—et virginum Islandarum pulchritudo, per omnes regiones cognita est.

"Bibamus salutem earum, et confusionem ad omnes bacularios : speramus quod eæ caræ et benedictæ creaturæ

---

[1] As the happiness of these quotations seemed to produce a very pleasing effect on my auditors, I subjoin a translation of them for the benefit of the unlearned :—

1. "Comes home to men's business and bosoms."—*Paterfamilias, Times.*

2. "A long pull, a strong pull, and a pull all together."—*Nelson at the Nile.*

3. "One touch of nature makes the whole world kin."—*Jeremy Bentham.*

4. Apothegm by the late Lord Mountcoffeehouse.

5. "Love rules the court, the camp, the grove."—*Venerable Bede.*

invenient tot maritos quot velint,—quòd geminos quottanis habeant, et quod earum filiæ, maternum exemplum sequentes, gentem Islandicam perpetuent in sæcula sæculorum."

The last words mechanically rolled out, in the same " ore rotundo" with which the poor old Dean of Christchurch used to finish his Gloria, etc. in the Cathedral.

Then followed more speeches,—a great chinking of glasses, —a Babel of conversation,—a kind of dance round the table, where we successively gave each alternate hand, as in the last figure of the Lancers,—a hearty embrace from the Governor,—and finally,—silence, daylight, and fresh air, as we stumbled forth into the street.

Now what was to be done? To go to bed was impossible. It was eleven o'clock by our watches, and as bright as noon. Fitz said it was twenty-two o'clock; but by this time he had reached that point of enlargement of the mind, and development of the visual organs, which is expressed by the term " seeing double,"—though he now pretends he was only reckoning time in the Venetian manner. We were in the position of three fast young men about Reykjavik, determined to make a night of it, but without the wherewithal. There were neither knockers to steal, nor watchmen to bonnet. At last we remembered that the apothecary's wife had a conversazione, to which she had kindly invited us; and accordingly, off we went to her house. Here we found a number of French officers, a piano, and a young lady; in consequence of which the drum soon became a ball. Finally, it was proposed we should dance a reel; the second lieutenant of the "*Artemise*" had once seen one when his ship was riding out a gale in the Clyde;—the little lady had frequently studied a picture of the Highland fling on the outside of a copy of Scotch music;—I could dance a jig—the set was complete, all we wanted was the music. Luckily the lady of the house knew the song of " Annie Laurie,"—played fast it made an excellent reel tune. As you may suppose, all succeeded admirably; we nearly died of laughing, and I only wish Lord Breadalbane had been by to see.

At one in the morning, our *danseuse* retiring to rest, the ball necessarily terminated; but the Governor's dinner still forbidding bed, we determined on a sail in the cutter to some islands about three-quarters of a mile out to sea; and I do not think I shall ever forget the delicious sensation of lying down lazily in the stern-sheets, and listening to the rippling of the water against the bows of the boat, as she glided away towards them. The dreamy, misty landscape, —each headland silently sleeping in the unearthly light,— Snœfell, from whose far-off peaks the midnight sun, though lost to us, had never faded,—the Plutonic crags that stood around, so gaunt and weird,—the quaint fresh life I had been lately leading,—all combined to promise such an existence of novelty and excitement in that strange Arctic region on the threshold of which we were now pausing, that I could not sufficiently congratulate myself on our good fortune. Soon, however, the grating of our keel upon the strand disturbed my reflections, and by the time I had unaccountably stepped up to my knees in the water, I was thoroughly awake, and in a condition to explore the island. It seemed to be about three-quarters of a mile long, not very broad, and a complete rabbit-warren; in fact, I could not walk a dozen yards without tripping up in the numerous burrows by which the ground was honeycombed: at last, on turning a corner, we suddenly came on a dozen rabbits, gravely sitting at the mouths of their holes. They were quite white, without ears, and with scarlet noses. I made several desperate attempts to catch some of these singular animals, but though one or two allowed me to come pretty near, just as I thought my prize was secure, in some unaccountable manner—it made unto itself wings, and literally flew away! Moreover, if my eyesight did not share the peculiar development which affected that of the Doctor's, I should say that these rabbits flew in *pairs*. Red-nosed, winged rabbits! I had never heard or read of the species; and I naturally grew enthusiastic in the chase, hoping to bring home a choice specimen to astonish our English naturalists. With some difficulty we managed to catch one or two, which had run into their holes instead of flying away. They bit and scratched like tiger-cats, and screamed like parrots; indeed, on a nearer inspection, I am obliged to confess that they assumed the appearance of birds,[1] which may perhaps account for their powers of flight. A slight confusion still remains in my mind as to the real nature of the creatures.

At about nine o'clock we returned to breakfast; and the rest of the day was spent in taking leave of our friends, and organizing the baggage-train, which was to start at midnight, under the command of the cook. The cavalcade consisted of eighteen horses, but of these only one-half were laden, two animals being told off to each burthen, which is shifted from the back of the one to that of the other every four hours. The pack-saddles were rude, but serviceable articles, with hooks on either side, on which a pair of oblong little chests were slung; strips of turf being stuffed beneath to prevent the creature's back being galled. Such of our goods as could not be conveniently stowed away in the chests were fitted on to the top, in whatever manner their size and weight admitted, each pony carrying about 140 lbs. The photographic apparatus caused us the greatest trouble, and had to be distributed between two beasts. As was to be expected, the guides who assisted us packed the nitrate of silver bath upside down; an outrage the nature of which you cannot appreciate. At last everything was pretty well arranged,—guns, powder, shot, tea-kettles, rice, tents, beds, portable soups, etc. all stowed away,—when the desponding Wilson came to me, his chin sweeping the ground, to say—that he very much feared the cook would die of the ride,—that he had never been on horseback in his life,—that as an experiment he had hired a pony that very morning at his own charges,—had been run away with,—but having been caught and brought home by an honest Icelander, was now lying down—that position being the one he found most convenient.

---

[1] The Puffin (*Alca arctica*). In Icelandic, *Sæ-papagoie*; In Scotland, *Pries'*; and in Cornwall, *Pope*.

As the first day's journey was two-and-thirty miles, and would probably necessitate his being twelve or thirteen hours in the saddle, I began to be really alarmed for my poor *chef;* but finding on inquiry that these gloomy prognostics were entirely voluntary on the part of Mr. Wilson, that the officer in question was full of zeal, and only too anxious to add horsemanship to his other accomplishments, I did not interfere. As for Wilson himself, it is not a marvel if he should see things a little *askew;* for some unaccountable reason, he chose to sleep last night in the open air, on the top of a hencoop, and naturally awoke this morning with a crick in his neck, and his face so immovably fixed over his left shoulder, that the efforts of all the ship's company have not been able to twist it back: with the help of a tackle, however, I think we shall eventually brace it square again.

At two we went to lunch with the Rector. The entertainment bore a strong family likeness to our last night's dinner; but as I wanted afterwards to exhibit my magic lantern to his little daughter Raghnilder, and a select party of her young friends, we contrived to elude doing full justice to it. During the remainder of the evening, like Job's children, we went about feasting from house to house, taking leave of friends who could not have been kinder had they known us all our lives, and interchanging little gifts and souvenirs. With the Governor I have left a print from the Princess Royal's drawing of the dead soldier in the Crimea. From the Rector of the cathedral church I have received some very curious books—almost the first printed in the island; I have been very anxious to obtain some specimens of ancient Icelandic manuscripts, but the island has long since been ransacked of its literary treasures; and to the kindness of the French consul I am indebted for a charming little white fox, the drollest and prettiest little beast I ever saw.

Having dined on board the "*Artemise*," we adjourned at eleven o'clock to the beach to witness the departure of the baggage. The ponies were all drawn up in one long file, the head of each being tied to the tail of the one immediately before him. Additional articles were stowed away here and there among the boxes. The last instructions were given by Sigurdr to the guides, and everything was declared ready for a start. With the air of an equestrian star, descending into the arena of Astley's Amphitheatre, the cook then stepped forward, made me a superb bow, and was assisted into the saddle. My little cabin-boy accompanied him as aide-de-camp.

The jovial Wilson rides with us to-morrow. Unless we get his head round during the night, he will have to sit facing his horse's tail, in order to see before him.

We do not seem to run any danger of falling short of provisions, as by all accounts there are birds enough in the interior of the country to feed an Israelitish emigration.

WILSON.

LETTER VII.

KISSES—WILSON ON HORSEBACK—A LAVA PLATEAU—THINGVALLA—
ALMANNAGIA—RABNAGIA—OUR TENT—THE SHIVERED PLAIN—
WITCH-DROWNING — A PARLIAMENTARY DEBATE, A. D. 1000—
THANGBRAND THE MISSIONARY—A GERMAN GNAT-CATCHER—THE
MYSTICAL MOUNTAINS—SIR OLAF—HECKLA—SKAPTA JOKUL—THE
FIRE DELUGE OF 1783—WE REACH THE GEYSIR—STROKR—FITZ'S
BONNE FORTUNE—MORE KISSES—AN ERUPTION—PRINCE NAPO-
LEON—RETURN—TRADE—POPULATION—A MUTINY—THE REINE
HORTENSE — THE SEVEN DUTCHMEN—A BALL—LOW DRESSES—
NORTHWARD HO !

Reykjavik, July 7, 1856.

At last I have seen the famous Geysirs, of which every one has heard so much; but I have also seen Thingvalla, of which no one has heard anything. The Geysirs are certainly wonderful marvels of nature, but more wonderful, more marvellous is Thingvalla; and if the one repay you for crossing the Spanish Sea, it would be worth while to go round the world to reach the other.

Of the boiling fountains I think I can give you a good idea, but whether I can contrive to draw for you anything like a comprehensible picture of the shape and nature of the Almannagja, the Hrafnagja, and the lava vale, called Thingvalla, that lies between them, I am doubtful. Before coming to Iceland I had read every account that had been written of Thingvalla by any former traveller, and when I saw it, it appeared to me a place of which I had never heard; so I suppose I shall come to grief in as melancholy a manner as my predecessors, whose ineffectual pages whiten the entrance to the valley they have failed to describe.

Having superintended—as I think I mentioned to you in my last letter—the midnight departure of the cook, guides, and luggage, we returned on board for a good night's rest, which we all needed. The start was settled for the next morning at eleven o'clock, and you may suppose we were not sorry to find, on waking, the bright joyous sunshine pouring down through the cabin skylight, and illuminating the white-robed, well-furnished breakfast-table with more than usual splendour. At the appointed hour we rowed ashore to where our eight ponies—two being assigned to each of us, to be ridden alternately—were standing ready bridled and saddled, at the house of one of our kindest friends. Of course, though but just risen from breakfast, the inevitable invitation to eat and drink awaited us; and another half-hour was spent in sipping cups of coffee poured out for us with much laughter by our hostess and her pretty daughter. At last, the necessary libations accomplished, we rose to go. Turning round to Fitz, I whispered, how I had always understood it was the proper thing in Iceland for travellers departing on a journey to kiss the ladies who had been good enough to entertain them,—little imagining he would take me at my word. Guess then my horror, when I suddenly saw him; with an intrepidity I envied but dared not imitate, first embrace the mamma, by way of prelude, and then proceed, in the most natural manner possible, to make the same tender advances to the daughter. I confess I remained dumb with consternation; the room swam round before me; I expected the next minute we should be packed neck and crop into the street, and that the young lady would have gone off into hysterics. It turned out, however, that such was the very last thing she was thinking of doing. With a simple frankness that became her more than all the boarding-school graces in the world, her eyes dancing with mischief and good humour, she met him half way, and pouting out two rosy lips, gave him as hearty a kiss as it might ever be the good fortune of one of us he-creatures to receive. From that moment I determined to conform for the future to the customs of the inhabitants.

Fresh from favours such as these, it was not surprising we should start in the highest spirits. With a courtesy peculiar to Iceland, Dr. Hjaltelin, the most jovial of doctors,—and another gentleman, insisted on conveying us the first dozen miles of our journey; and as we clattered away through the wooden streets, I think a merrier party never set out from Reykjavik. In front scampered the three spare ponies, without bridles, saddles, or any sense of moral responsibility, flinging up their heels, biting and neighing like mad things;

then came Sigurdr, now become our chief, surrounded by the rest of the cavalcade; and finally, at a little distance, plunged in profound melancholy, rode Wilson. Never shall I forget his appearance. During the night his head had come partially straight, but by way of precaution, I suppose, he had conceived the idea of burying it down to the chin in a huge seal-skin helmet I had given him against the inclemencies of the Polar Sea. As on this occasion the thermometer was at 81°, and a *coup-de-soleil* was the chief thing to be feared, a ton of fur round his skull was scarcely necessary. Seamen's trousers, a bright scarlet jersey, and jack-boots fringed with cat-skin, completed his costume ; and as he proceeded along in his usual state of chronic consternation, with my rifle slung at his back and a couple of telescopes over his shoulder, he looked the image of Robinson Crusoe, fresh from having seen the foot-print.

A couple of hours' ride across the lava plain we had previously traversed brought us to a river, where our Reykjavik friends, after showing us a salmon weir, finally took their leave, with many kind wishes for our prosperity. On looking through the clear water that hissed and bubbled through the wooden sluice, the Doctor had caught sight of an apparently dead salmon, jammed up against its wooden bars ; but on pulling him out, he proved to be still breathing, though his tail was immovably twisted into his mouth. A consultation taking place, the Doctors both agreed that it was a case of pleurosthotonos, brought on by mechanical injury to the spine (we had just been talking of Palmer's trial), and that he was perfectly fit for food. In accordance with this verdict, he was knocked on the head, and slung at Wilson's saddle-bow. Left to ourselves, we now pushed on as rapidly as we could, though the track across the lava was so uneven, that every moment I expected Snorro (for thus have I christened my pony) would be on his nose. In another hour we were among the hills. The scenery of this part of the journey was not very beautiful, the mountains not being remarkable either for their size or shape ; but here and there we came upon pretty bits, not unlike some of the barren parts of Scotland, with quiet blue lakes sleeping in the solitude.

After wandering along for some time in a broad open valley, that gradually narrowed to a glen, we reached a grassy patch. As it was past three o'clock, Sigurdr proposed a halt.

SADNESS AND JOLLITY.

Unbridling and unsaddling our steeds, we turned them loose upon the pasture, and sat ourselves down on a sunny knoll to lunch. For the first time since landing in Iceland I felt hungry; as, for the first time, four successive hours had elapsed without our having been compelled to take a snack. The appetites of the ponies seemed equally good, though probably with them hunger was no such novelty. Wilson alone looked sad. He confided to me privately that he feared his trousers would not last such jolting many days; but his dolefulness, like a bit of minor in a sparkling melody, only made our jollity more radiant. In about half an hour Sigurdr gave the signal for a start; and having caught, saddled, and bridled three unridden ponies, we drove Snorro and his companions to the front, and proceeded on our way rejoicing. After an hour's gradual ascent through a picturesque ravine, we emerged upon an immense desolate plateau of lava, that stretched away for miles and miles like a great stony sea. A more barren desert you cannot conceive. Innumerable boulders, relics of the glacial period, encumbered the track. We could only go at a foot-pace. Not a blade of grass, not a strip of green, enlivened the prospect, and the only sound we heard was the croak of the curlew and the wail of the plover. Hour after hour we plodded on, but the grey waste seemed interminable, boundless; and the only consolation Sigurdr would vouchsafe was, that our journey's end lay on this side of some purple mountains that peeped like the tents of a demon leaguer above the stony horizon.

As it was already eight o'clock, and we had been told the entire distance from Reykjavik to Thingvalla was only five-and-thirty miles, I could not comprehend how so great a space should still separate us from our destination. Concluding more time had been lost in shooting, lunching, etc., by the way than we had supposed, I put my pony into a canter, and determined to make short work of the dozen miles which seemed still to lie between us and the hills, on this side of which I understood from Sigurdr our encampment for the night was to be pitched.

Judge then of my astonishment when, a few minutes afterwards, I was arrested in full career by a tremendous precipice, or rather chasm, which suddenly gaped beneath my feet, and completely separated the barren plateau we had been so painfully traversing from a lovely, gay, sunlit flat, ten miles broad, that lay—sunk at a level lower by a hundred feet—between us and the opposite mountains. I was never so completely taken by surprise; Sigurdr's purposely vague description of our halting-place was accounted for.

We had reached the famous Almanna Gja. Like a black rampart in the distance, the corresponding chasm of the Hrafna Gja cut across the lower slope of the distant hills, and between them now slept in beauty and sunshine the broad verdant[1] plain of Thingvalla.

Ages ago,—who shall say how long?—some vast commotion shook the foundations of the island, and bubbling up from sources far away amid the inland hills, a fiery deluge must have rushed down between their ridges, until, escaping from the narrower gorges, it found space to spread itself into one broad sheet of molten stone over an entire district of country, reducing its varied surface to one vast blackened level.

One of two things then occurred : either the vitrified mass contracting as it cooled,—the centre area of fifty square miles burst asunder at either side from the adjoining plateau, and sinking down to its present level, left the two parallel Gjas, or chasms, which form its lateral boundaries, to mark the limits of the disruption ; or else, while the pith or marrow of the lava was still in a fluid state, its upper surface became solid, and formed a roof beneath which the molten stream flowed on to lower levels, leaving a vast cavern into which the upper crust subsequently plumped down.[2]

---

[1] The plain of Thingvalla is in a great measure clothed with birch brushwood.

[2] I feel it is very presumptuous in me to hazard a conjecture on a subject with which my want of geological knowledge renders me quite incompetent to deal; but however incorrect either of the above suppositions may be justly considered by the philosophers, they will

THE LAKE OF THINGVALLA

The enclosed section will perhaps help you a little to comprehend what I am afraid my description will have failed to bring before you.

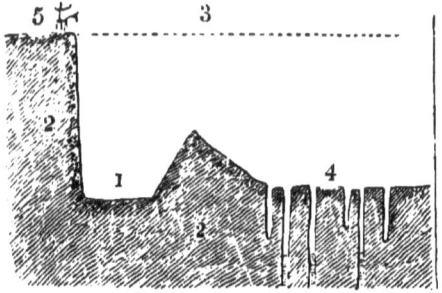 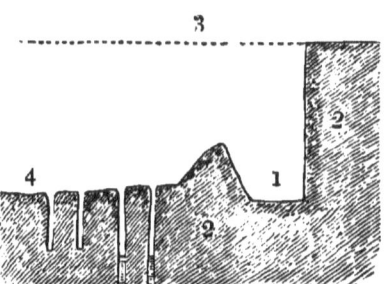

1 Gjas.   2 Lava deluge.   3 Original surface.
4 Thingvalla sunk to a lower level.   5 Astonished traveller.

1. Are the two chasms called respectively Almanna Gja,[1] or Main Gja, and Hrafna Gja, or Raven's Gja. In the act of disruption the sinking mass fell in, as it were, upon itself, so that one side of the Gja slopes a good deal back as it ascends; the other side is perfectly perpendicular, and at the spot I saw it upwards of one hundred feet high. In the lapse of years the bottom of the Almanna Gja has become gradually filled up to an even surface, covered with the most beautiful turf, except where a river, leaping from the higher plateau over the precipice, has chosen it for a bed. You must not suppose, however, that the disruption and land-slip of Thingvalla took place quite in the spick and span manner the section might lead you to imagine; in some places the rock has split asunder very unevenly, and the Hrafna Gja is altogether a very untidy rent, the sides having fallen in in many places, and almost filled up the ravine with ruins. On

perhaps serve to convey to the unlearned reader, for whose amusement (not instruction) these letters are intended, the impression conveyed to my mind by what I saw, and so help out the picture I am trying to fill in for him.

[1] Almanna may be translated *main;* it means literally *all men's;* when applied to a road, it would mean the road along which all the world travel.

ALMANNA-GJA—THINGVALLA—THE ONERA

the other hand, in the Almanna Gja, you can easily distinguish on the one face marks and formations exactly corresponding, though at a different level, with those on the face opposite, so cleanly were they separated.

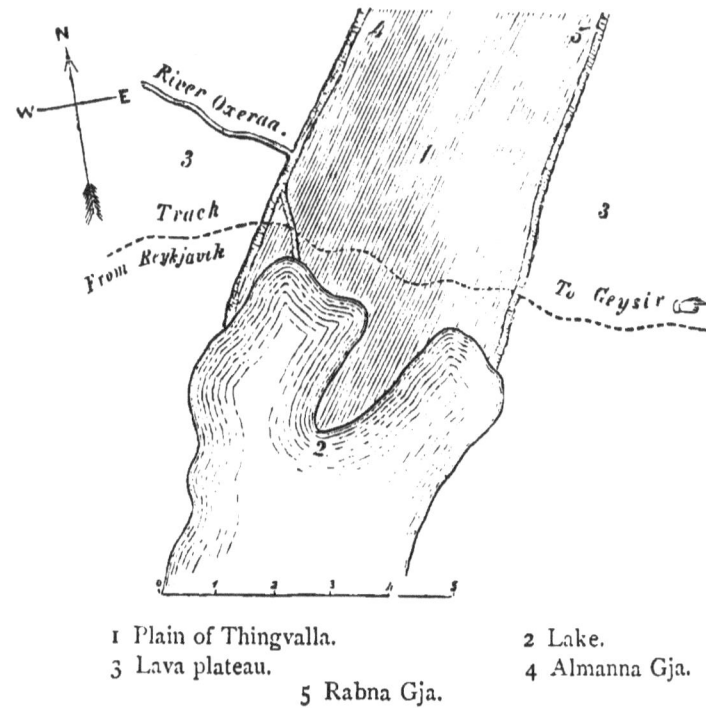

1 Plain of Thingvalla.
3 Lava plateau.
5 Rabna Gja.
2 Lake.
4 Almanna Gja.

2. Is the sea of lava now lying on the top of the original surface. Its depth I had no means of ascertaining.

3. Is the level of the surface first formed when the lava was still hot.

4. Is the plain of Thingvalla, eight miles broad, its surface shattered into a network of innumerable crevices and fissures fifty or sixty feet deep, and each wide enough to have swallowed the entire company of Korah. At the foot of the plain lies a vast lake, into which, indeed, it may be said to slope, with a gradual inclination from the north, the imprisoned waters having burst up through the lava strata, as it subsided beneath them. Gazing down through their emerald depths,

you can still follow the pattern traced on the surface of the bottom, by cracks and chasms similar to those into which the dry portion of Thingvalla has been shivered.

The accompanying ground plan will, I trust, complete what is wanting to fill up the picture I so long to conjure up before the mind's eye. It is the last card I have to play, and, if unsuccessful, I must give up the task in despair.

But to return to where I left myself, on the edge of the cliff, gazing down with astonished eyes over the panorama of land and water embedded at my feet. I could scarcely speak for pleasure and surprise; Fitz was equally taken aback, and as for Wilson, he looked as if he thought we had arrived at the end of the world. After having allowed us sufficient time to admire the prospect Sigurdr turned to the left, along the edge of the precipice, until we reached a narrow pathway accidentally formed down a longitudinal niche in the splintered face of the cliff, which led across the bottom, and up the opposite side of the Gja, into the plain of Thingvalla. By rights our tents ought to have arrived before us, but when we reached the little glebe where we expected to find them pitched, no signs of servants, guides, or horses were to be seen.

As we had not overtaken them ourselves, their non-appearance was inexplicable. Wilson suggested that, the cook having died on the road, the rest of the party must have turned aside to bury him; and that we had passed unperceived during the interesting ceremony. Be the cause what it might, the result was not agreeable. We were very tired, very hungry, and it had just begun to rain.

It is true there was a clergyman's house and a church, both built of stones covered with turf sods, close by; at the one, perhaps, we could get milk, and in the other we could sleep, as our betters—including Madame Pfeiffer—had done before us; but its inside looked so dark, and damp, and cold, and charnel-like, that one really doubted whether lying in the churchyard would not be snugger. You may guess, then, how great was my relief when our belated baggage-train was descried against the sky-line, as it slowly wended its way along the purple edge of the precipice towards the staircase by which we had already descended.

Half an hour afterwards the little plot of grass selected for the site of our encampment was covered over with poles, boxes, cauldrons, tea-kettles, and all the paraphernalia of a gipsy settlement. Wilson's Kaffir experience came at once into play, and under his solemn but effective superintendence, in less than twenty minutes the horn-headed tent rose, dry and taut, upon the sward. Having carpeted the floor with oil-skin rugs, and arranged our three beds with their clean crisp sheets, blankets, and coverlets complete, at the back, he proceeded to lay out the dinner-table at the tent door with as much decorum as if we were expecting the Archbishop of Canterbury. All this time the cook, who looked a little pale, and moved, I observed with difficulty, was mysteriously closeted with a spirit-lamp inside a diminutive tent of his own, through the door of which the most delicious whiffs occasionally permeated. Olaf and his comrades had driven off the horses to their pastures; and Sigurdr and I were deep in a game of chess. Luckily, the shower, which threatened us a moment, had blown over. Though now almost nine o'clock P.M., it was as bright as mid-day; the sky burned like a dome of gold, and silence and deep peace brooded over the fair grass-robed plain, that once had been so fearfully convulsed.

You may be quite sure our dinner went off merrily; the tetanus-afflicted salmon proved excellent, the plover and ptarmigan were done to a turn, the mulligatawny beyond all praise; but, alas! I regret to add, that he—the artist, by whose skill these triumphs had been achieved—his task accomplished,—no longer sustained by the factitious energy resulting from his professional enthusiasm,—at last succumbed, and, retiring to the recesses of his tent, like Psyche in the "Princess," lay down, "and neither spoke nor stirred."

After another game or two of chess, a pleasant chat, a gentle stroll, we also turned in ; and for the next eight hours perfect silence reigned throughout our little encampment, except when Wilson's sob-like snores shook to their foundation the canvas walls that sheltered him.

When I awoke—I do not know at what hour, for from this time we kept no account of day or night—the white sunlight was streaming into the tent, and the whole landscape was gleaming and glowing in the beauty of one of the hottest summer-days I ever remember. We breakfasted in our shirt-sleeves, and I was forced to wrap my head in a white handkerchief for fear of the sun. As we were all a little stiff after our ride, I could not resist the temptation of spending the day where we were, and examining more leisurely the wonderful features of the neighbourhood. Independently of its natural curiosities, Thingvalla was most interesting to me on account of the historical associations connected with it. Here, long ago, at a period when feudal despotism was the only government known throughout Europe, free parliaments used to sit in peace, and regulate the affairs of the young Republic; and to this hour the precincts of its Commons House of Parliament are as distinct and unchanged as on the day when the high-hearted fathers of the emigration first consecrated them to the service of a free nation. By a freak of nature, as the subsiding plain cracked and shivered into twenty thousand fissures, an irregular oval area, of about two hundred feet by fifty, was left almost entirely surrounded by a crevice so deep and broad as to be utterly impassable;— at one extremity alone a scanty causeway connected it with the adjoining level, and allowed of access to its interior. It is true, just at one point the encircling chasm grows so narrow as to be within the possibility of a jump; and an ancient worthy, named Flosi, pursued by his enemies, did actually take it at a fly; but as leaping an inch short would have entailed certain drowning in the bright green waters that sleep forty feet below, you can conceive there was never much danger of this entrance becoming a thoroughfare. I confess that for one moment, while contemplating the scene of Flosi's exploit, I felt,—like a true Briton,—an idiotic desire to be able to say that I had done the same;—that I survive to write this letter is a proof of my having come subsequently to my senses.

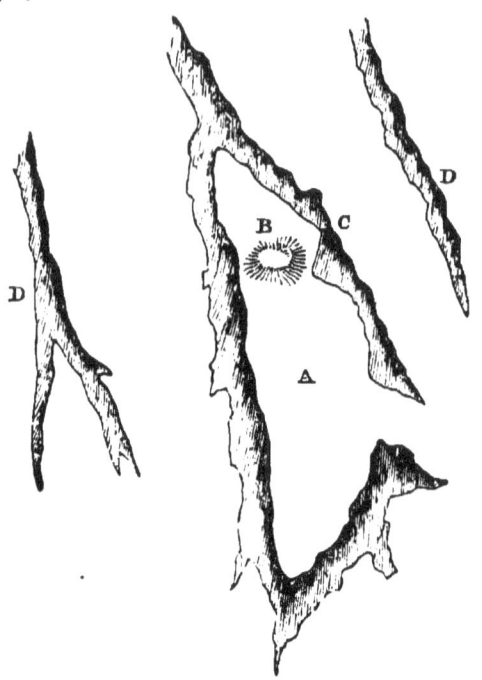

A. The Althing.
C. The place where Flosi jumped.
B. The Hill of Laws.
D. Adjacent Chasms.

This spot then, erected by nature almost into a fortress, the founders of the Icelandic constitution chose for the meetings of their Thing,[1] or Parliament, armed guards defended the entrance, while the grave bonders deliberated in security within: to this day, at the upper end of the place of meeting, may be seen the three hammocks, where sat in state the chiefs and judges of the land.

But those grand old times have long since passed away. Along the banks of the Oxeraa no longer glisten the tents and booths of the assembled lieges; no longer stalwart berserks guard the narrow entrance to the Althing; ravens alone sit on the sacred Logberg; and the floor of the old Icelandic

[1] From *thing*, to speak. We have a vestige of the same word in Dingwall, a town of Ross-shire.

THINGVALLA. Almanna gjá. The Althing

House of Commons is ignominiously cropped by the sheep of the parson. For three hundred years did the gallant little Republic maintain its independence—three hundred years of unequalled literary and political vigour. At last its day of doom drew near. Like the Scotch nobles in the time of Elizabeth, their own chieftains intrigued against the liberties of the Icelandic people; and in 1261 the island became an appanage of the Norwegian crown. Yet even then the deed embodying the concession of their independence was drawn up in such haughty terms as to resemble rather the offer of an equal alliance than the renunciation of imperial rights. Soon, however, the apathy which invariably benumbs the faculties of a people too entirely relieved from the discipline and obligation of self-government, lapped in complete inactivity, moral, political, and intellectual,—these once stirring islanders. On the amalgamation of the three Scandinavian monarchies, at the union of Calmar, the allegiance of the people of Iceland was passively transferred to the Danish crown. Ever since that time, Danish proconsuls have administered their government, and Danish restrictions have regulated their trade. The traditions of their ancient autonomy have become as unsubstantial and obsolete as those which record the vanished fame of their poets and historians, and the exploits of their mariners. It is true, the adoption of the Lutheran religion galvanized for a moment into the semblance of activity the old literary spirit. A printing-press was introduced as early as 1530, and ever since the sixteenth century many works of merit have been produced from time to time by Icelandic genius. Shakespeare, Milton, and Pope have been translated into the native tongue; one of the best printed newspapers I have ever seen is now published at Reykjavik; and the Colleges of Copenhagen are adorned by many an illustrious Icelandic scholar; but the glory of the old days is departed, and it is across a wide desolate flat of ignoble annals, as dull and arid as their own lava plains, that the student has to look back upon the glorious drama of Iceland's early history. As I gazed around on the silent, deserted plain, and paced to and fro along the untrodden grass that now clothed the Althing, I could scarcely believe it had ever been the battle-field where such keen and energetic wits encountered,—that the fire-scathed rocks I saw before me were the very same that had once inspired one of the most successful rhetorical appeals ever hazarded in a public assembly.

As an account of the debate to which I allude has been carefully preserved, I may as well give you an abstract of it. A more characteristic leaf out of the Parliamentary Annals of Iceland you could scarcely have.

In the summer of the year 1000, when Ethelred the Unready ruled in England, and fourteen years after Hugh Capet had succeeded the last Carlovingian on the throne of France,—the Icelandic legislature was convened for the consideration of a very important subject—no less important, indeed, than an inquiry into the merits of a new religion lately brought into the country by certain emissaries of Olaf Tryggveson,—the first Christian king of Norway,—and the same who pulled down London bridge.

The assembly met. The Norse missionaries were called upon to enunciate to the House the tenets of the faith they were commissioned to disclose; and the debate began. Great and fierce was the difference of opinion. The good old Tory party, supported by all the authority of the Odin establishment, were violent in opposition. The Whigs advocated the new arrangement, and, as the king supported their own views, insisted strongly on the Divine right. Several liberal members permitted themselves to speak sarcastically of the Valhalla tap, and the ankles of Freya. The discussion was at its height, when suddenly a fearful peal of subterranean thunder roared around the Althing. "Listen!" cried an orator of the Pagan party; "how angry is Odin that we should even consider the subject of a new religion. His fires will consume us." To which a ready debater on the other side replied, by "begging leave to ask the honourable gentleman,—with whom were the gods angry when these rocks were melted?"—pointing to the devastated plain around him. Taking advantage of so good a hit, the Treasury "whips" immediately called for a division; and the Christian religion was adopted by a large majority.

The first Christian missionaries who came to Iceland seem to have had a rather peculiar manner of enforcing the truths of the Gospel. Their leader was a person of the name of Thangbrand. Like the Protestant clergymen Queen Elizabeth despatched to convert Ireland, he was bundled over to Iceland principally because he was too disreputable to be allowed to live in Norway. The old Chronicler gives a very quaint description of him. "Thangbrand," he says, "was a passionate, ungovernable person, and a great man-slayer; but a good scholar, and clever. Thorvald, and Veterlid the Scald, composed a lampoon against him; but he killed them both outright. Thangbrand was two years in Iceland, and was the death of three men before he left it."

From the Althing we strolled over to the Almanna Gja, visiting the Pool of Execution on our way. As I have already mentioned, a river from the plateau above leaps over the precipice into the bottom of the Gja, and flows for a certain distance between its walls. At the foot of the fall the waters linger for a moment in a dark, deep, brimming pool, hemmed in by a circle of ruined rocks; to this pool, in ancient times, all women convicted of capital crimes were immediately taken, and drowned. Witchcraft seems to have been the principal weakness of ladies in those days, throughout the Scandinavian countries. For a long period no disgrace was attached to its profession. Odin himself, we are expressly told, was a great adept, and always found himself very much exhausted at the end of his performance; which leads me to think that perhaps he dabbled in electro-biology. At last the advent of Christianity threw discredit on the practice; severe punishments were denounced against all who indulged in it; and, in the end, its mysteries became the monopoly of the Laplanders.

All criminals, men and women, were tried by juries; and that the accused had the power of challenging the jurymen empannelled to try them, appears from the following extract from the Book of Laws:—" The judges shall go out on Washday, *i.e.*, Saturday, and continue out for challenges, until the sun comes on Thingvalla on the Lord's-day." And again, " The power of challenging shall cease as soon as the sun can no longer be seen above the western brink of the chasm, from the Logberg."

Turning aside from what, I dare say, was the scene of many an unrecorded tragedy, we descended the gorge of the Almanna Gja, towards the lake; and I took advantage of the opportunity again to examine its marvellous construction. The perpendicular walls of rock rose on either hand from the flat greensward that carpeted its bottom, pretty much as the waters of the Red Sea must have risen on each side of the fugitive Israelites. A blaze of light smote the face of one cliff, while the other lay in the deepest shadow; and on the rugged surface of each might still be traced corresponding articulations, that once had dovetailed into each other, ere the igneous mass was rent asunder. So unchanged, so recent seemed the vestiges of this convulsion, that I felt as if I had been admitted to witness one of nature's grandest and most violent operations, almost in the very act of its execution. A walk of about twenty minutes brought us to the borders of the lake—a glorious expanse of water, fifteen miles long, by eight miles broad, occupying a basin formed by the same hills, which must also, I imagine, have arrested the further progress of the lava torrent. A lovelier scene I have seldom witnessed. In the foreground lay huge masses of rock and lava, tossed about like the ruins of a world, and washed by waters as bright and green as polished malachite. Beyond, a bevy of distant mountains, robed by the transparent atmosphere in tints unknown to Europe, peeped over each other's shoulders into the silver mirror at their feet, while here and there from among their purple ridges columns of white vapour rose like altar smoke toward the tranquil heaven.

On returning home we found dinner waiting for us. I had invited the clergyman, and a German gentleman who was lodging with him, to give us the pleasure of their company; and in ten minutes we had all become the best of friends. It is true the conversation was carried on in rather a wild jargon, made up of six different languages—Icelandic, English, German, Latin, Danish, French—but in spite of the difficulty with which he expressed himself, it was impossible not to be struck with the simple earnest character of my German convive. He was about five-and-twenty, a "*doctor philosophiæ*," and had come to Iceland to catch gnats. After having caught gnats in Iceland, he intended, he said, to spend some years in catching gnats in Spain—the privacy ot Spanish gnats, as it appears, not having been hitherto invaded. The truth is, my guest was an entomologist, and in the pursuit of the objects of his study was evidently prepared to approach hardships and danger with a serenity that would not have been unworthy of the apostle of a new religion. It was almost touching to hear him describe the intensity of his joy when perhaps days and nights of fruitless labours were at last rewarded by the discovery of some hitherto unknown little fly; and it was with my whole heart that, at parting, I wished him success in his career, and the fame that so much conscientious labour merited. From my allusion to this last reward, however, he seemed almost to shrink, and, with a sincerity it was impossible to doubt, disclaimed as ignoble so poor a motive as a thirst for fame. His was one of those calm laborious minds, seldom found but among the Teutonic race, that—pursuing day by day with single-minded energy some special object—live in a noble obscurity, and die at last content with the consciousness of having added one other stone to that tower of knowledge men are building up toward heaven, even though the world should never learn what strong and patient hands have placed it there.

The next morning we started for the Geysirs : this time dividing the baggage-train, and sending on the cook in light marching order, with the materials for dinner. The weather still remained unclouded, and each mile we advanced disclosed some new wonder in the unearthly landscape. A three hours' ride brought us to the Rabna Gja, the eastern boundary of Thingvalla, and, winding up its rugged face, we took our last look over the lovely plain beneath us, and then manfully set forward across the same kind of arid lava plateau. as that which we had already traversed before arriving at the Almanna Gja. But instead of the boundless immensity which had then so much disheartened us, the present prospect was terminated by a range of quaint particoloured hills, which rose before us in such fantastic shapes that I could not take my eyes off them. I do not know whether it was the strong coffee or the invigorating air that stimulated my imagination; but I certainly felt convinced I was coming to some mystical spot—out of space, out of time—where I should suddenly light upon a green-scaled griffin, or golden-haired princess, or other *bonne fortune* of the olden days. Certainly a more appropriate scene for such an encounter could not be conceived, than that which displayed itself, when we wheeled at last round the flank of the scorched ridge we had been approaching. A perfectly smooth grassy plain, about a league square, and shaped like a horse-shoe, opened before us, encompassed by bare cinderlike hills, that rose round—red, black, and yellow—in a hundred uncouth peaks of ash and slag. Not a vestige of vegetation relieved the aridity of their vitrified sides, while the verdant carpet at their feet only made the fire-moulded circle seem more weird and impassable. Had I had a trumpet and a lance, I should have blown a blast of defiance on the one, and having shaken the other toward the four corners of the world, would have calmly waited to see what next might betide. Three arrows shot bravely forward would have probably resulted in the discovery of a trap-door with an iron ring; but having neither trumpet, lance, nor arrow, we simply alighted and lunched: yet even then I could not help thinking how lucky it was that, not eating dates, we could not inadvertently fling their stones into the eye of any inquisitive genie who might be in the neighbourhood.

After the usual hour's rest and change of horses, we galloped away to the other side of the plain, and, doubling the further horn of the semicircle, suddenly found ourselves in a district as unlike the cinder mountains we had quitted as they had differed from the volcanic scenery of the day before. On the left lay a long rampart of green hills, opening up every now and then into Scottish glens and gorges, while from their roots to the horizon stretched a vast breadth of meadowland, watered by two or three rivers, that wound, and twisted, and coiled about, like blue serpents. Here and there, white volumes of vapour, that rose in endless wreaths from the ground, told of mighty cauldrons at work beneath that moist cool verdant carpet; while large silvery lakes, and flat-topped isolated hills, relieved the monotony of the level land, and carried on the eye to where the three snowy peaks of Mount Hecla shone cold and clear against the sky.

Of course it was rather tantalizing to pass so near this famous burning mountain without having an opportunity of ascending it; but the expedition would have taken up too much time. In appearance Hecla differs very little from the innumerable other volcanic hills with which the island is studded. Its cone consists of a pyramid of stone and scoriæ, rising to the height of about five thousand feet, and welded together by bands of molten matter which have issued from its sides. From A.D. 1004 to 1766 there have been twenty-three eruptions, occurring at intervals which have varied in duration from six to seventy-six years. The one of 1766 was remarkably violent. It commenced on the 5th of April by the appearance of a huge pillar of black sand mounting slowly into the heavens, accompanied by subterranean thunders, and all the other symptoms which precede volcanic disturbances. Then a coronet of flame encircled the crater; masses of red rock, pumice, and magnetic stones were flung out with tremendous violence to an incredible distance, and in such continuous multitudes as to resemble a swarm of bees clustering over the mountain. One boulder of pumice six feet in circumference was pitched twenty miles away; another of magnetic iron fell at a distance of fifteen. The surface of the earth was covered, for a circuit of one hundred and fifty miles, with a layer of sand four inches deep; the air was so darkened by it, that at a place one hundred and forty miles off, white paper held up at a little distance could not be distinguished from black. The fishermen could not put to sea on account of the darkness, and the inhabitants of the Orkney islands were frightened out of their senses by showers of what they thought must be black snow. On the 9th of April, the lava began to overflow, and ran for five miles in a south-westerly direction, whilst, some days later,— in order that no element might be wanting to mingle in this devil's charivari,—a vast column of water, like Robin Hood's second arrow, split up through the cinder pillar to the height of several hundred feet; the horror of the spectacle being further enhanced by an accompaniment of subterranean cannonading and dire reports, heard at a distance of fifty miles.

Striking as all this must have been, it sinks into comparative tameness and insignificance, beside the infinitely more terrible phenomena which attended the eruption of another volcano, called Skapta Jokul.

Of all countries in Europe, Iceland is the one which has been the most minutely mapped, not even excepting the ordnance survey of Ireland. The Danish Government seem to have had a hobby about it, and the result has been a chart so beautifully executed, that every little crevice, each mountain torrent, each flood of lava, is laid down with an accuracy perfectly astonishing. One huge blank, however, in the south-west corner of this map of Iceland, mars the integrity of its almost microscopic delineations. To every other part of the island the engineer has succeeded in penetrating; one vast space alone of about four hundred square miles has defied his investigation. Over the area occupied by the Skapta Jokul, amid its mountain-cradled fields of snow and icy ridges, no human foot has ever wandered. Yet it is from the bosom of this desert district that has descended the most frightful visitation ever known to have desolated the island.

This event occurred in the year 1783. The preceding winter and spring had been unusually mild. Toward the end of May, a light bluish fog began to float along the confines of the untrodden tracts of Skapta, accompanied in the beginning of June by a great trembling of the earth. On the 8th of that month, immense pillars of smoke collected over the hill country towards the north, and coming down against the wind in a southerly direction, enveloped the whole district of Sida in darkness. A whirlwind of ashes then swept over the face of the country, and on the 10th, innumerable fire spouts were seen leaping and flaring amid the icy hollows of the mountain, while the river Skapta, one of the largest in the island, having first rolled down to the plain a vast volume of fetid waters mixed with sand, suddenly disappeared.

Two days afterwards a stream of lava, issuing from sources to which no one has ever been able to penetrate, came sliding down the bed of the dried-up river, and in a little time, —though the channel was six hundred feet deep and two hundred broad,—the glowing deluge overflowed its banks, crossed the low country of Medalland, ripping the turf up before it like a table-cloth, and poured into a great lake whose affrighted waters flew hissing and screaming into the air at the approach of the fiery intruder. Within a few more days the basin of the lake itself was completely filled, and having separated into two streams, the unexhausted torrent again recommenced its march ; in one direction overflowing some ancient lava fields,—in the other, re-entering the channel of the Skapta, and leaping down the lofty cataract of Stapafoss. But this was not all ; while one lava flood had chosen the Skapta for its bed, another, descending in a different direction, was working like ruin within and on either side the banks of the Hverfisfliot, rushing into the plain, by all accounts, with even greater fury and velocity. Whether the two issued from the same crater it is impossible to say, as the sources of both were far away within the heart of the unapproachable desert, and even the extent of the lava flow can only be measured from the spot where it entered the inhabited districts. The stream which flowed down Skapta is calculated to be about fifty miles in length by twelve or fifteen at its greatest breadth; that which rolled down the Hverfisfliot, at forty miles in length by seven in breadth. Where it was imprisoned, between the high banks of Skapta, the lava is five or six hundred feet thick; but as soon as it spread out into the plain its depth never exceeded one hundred feet. The eruption of sand, ashes, pumice, and lava, continued till the end of August, when the Plutonic drama concluded with a violent earthquake.

For a whole year a canopy of cinder-laden cloud hung over the island. Sand and ashes irretrievably overwhelmed thousands of acres of fertile pasturage. The Faroe islands, the Shetlands, and the Orkneys were deluged with volcanic dust, which perceptibly contaminated even the pure skies of England and Holland. Mephitic vapours tainted the atmosphere of the entire island;—even the grass, which no cinder rain had stifled, completely withered up;—the fish perished in the poisoned sea. A murrain broke out among the cattle, and a disease resembling scurvy attacked the inhabitants themselves. Stephenson has calculated that 9,000 men, 28,000 horses, 11,000 cattle, 190,000 sheep, died from the effects of this one eruption. The most moderate calculation puts the number of human deaths at upwards of 1,300; and of cattle, etc. at about 156,000.

The whole of this century had proved most fatal to the unfortunate people of Iceland. At its commencement smallpox destroyed more than 16,000 persons; nearly 10,000 more perished by a famine consequent on a succession of inclement seasons; while from time to time the southern coasts were considerably depopulated by the incursions of English and even Algerine pirates.

The rest of our day's journey lay through a country less interesting than the district we had traversed before luncheon.

For the most part we kept on along the foot of the hills, stopping now and then for a drink of milk at the occasional farms perched upon their slopes. Sometimes turning up a green and even bushy glen, (there are no trees in Iceland, the nearest approach to anything of the kind being a low dwarf birch, hardly worthy of being called a shrub,) we would cut across the shoulder of some projecting spur, and obtain a wider prospect of the level land upon our right; or else keeping more down in the flat, we had to flounder for half an hour up to the horses' shoulders in an Irish bog. After about five hours of this work we reached the banks of a broad and rather singular river, called the Brúará. Halfway across it was perfectly fordable; but exactly in the middle was a deep cleft, into which the waters from either side spilt themselves, and then in a collected volume roared over a precipice a little lower down. Across this cleft some wooden planks were thrown, giving the traveller an opportunity of boasting that he had crossed a river on a bridge which itself was under water. By this time we had all begun to be very tired, and very hungry;—it was 11 o'clock P.M. We had been twelve or thirteen hours on horseback, not to mention occasional half-hours of pretty severe walking after the ptarmigan and plover. Many were the questions we addressed to Sigurdr on the distance yet remaining, and many the conjectures we hazarded as to whether the cook would have arrived in time to get dinner ready for us. At last, after another two hours' weary jogging, we descried, straight in front, a low steep brown rugged hill, standing entirely detached from the range at the foot of which we had been riding; and in a few minutes more, wheeling round its outer end, we found ourselves in the presence of the steaming Geysirs.

I do not know that I can give you a better notion of the appearance of the place than by saying that it looked as if —for about a quarter of a mile—the ground had been honey-combed by disease into numerous sores and orifices; not a blade of grass grew on its hot, inflamed surface, which consisted of unwholesome-looking red livid clay, or crumpled shreds and shards of slough-like incrustations. Naturally enough, our first impulse on dismounting was to scamper off at once to the Great Geysir. As it lay at the furthest end of the congeries of hot springs, in order to reach it we had to run the gauntlet of all the pools of boiling water and scalding quagmires of soft clay that intervened, and consequently arrived on the spot with our ankles nicely poulticed. But the occasion justified our eagerness. A smooth silicious basin, seventy-two feet in diameter and four feet deep, with a hole at the bottom as in a washing-basin on board a steamer, stood before us brimful of water just upon the simmer; while up into the air above our heads rose a great column of vapour, looking as if it was going to turn into the Fisherman's Genie. The ground about the brim was composed of layers of incrusted silica, like the outside of an oyster, sloping gently down on all sides from the edge of the basin.

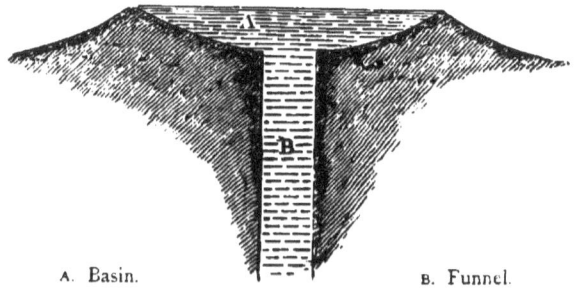

A. Basin.   B. Funnel.

Having satisfied our curiosity with this cursory inspection of what we had come so far to see, hunger compelled us to look about with great anxiety for the cook; and you may fancy our delight at seeing that functionary in the very act of dishing up dinner on a neighbouring hillock. Sent forward at an early hour, under the chaperonage of a guide, he had arrived about two hours before us, and seizing with a general's eye the key of the position, at once turned an idle babbling little Geysir into a camp-kettle, dug a bake-house in the hot soft clay, and improvising a kitchen-range at a neighbouring vent, had made himself completely master of the situation. It was about one o'clock in the morning when we sat down to dinner, and as light as day.

As the baggage-train with our tents and beds had not yet arrived, we fully appreciated our luck in being treated to so dry a night; and having eaten everything we could lay hands on, were sat quietly down to chess, and coffee brewed in Geysir water; when suddenly it seemed as if beneath our very feet a quantity of subterraneous cannon were going off; the whole earth shook, and Sigurdr, starting to his feet, upset the chess-board (I was just beginning to get the best of the game), and flung off full speed towards the great basin. By the time we reached its brim, however, the noise had ceased, and all we could see was a slight movement in the centre, as if an angel had passed by and troubled the water. Irritated at this false alarm, we determined to revenge ourselves by going and tormenting the Strokr. Strokr—or *the churn*—you must know, is an unfortunate Geysir, with so little command over his temper and his stomach, that you can get a *rise* out of him whenever you like. All that is necessary is to collect a quantity of sods, and throw them down his funnel. As he has no basin to protect him from these liberties, you can approach to the very edge of the pipe, about five feet in diameter, and look down at the boiling water which is perpetually seething at the bottom. In a few minutes the dose of turf you have just administered begins to disagree with him; he works himself up into an awful passion—tormented by the qualms of incipient sickness, he groans and hisses, and boils up, and spits at you with malicious vehemence, until at last, with a roar of mingled pain and rage, he throws up into the air a column of water forty feet high, which carries with it all the sods that have been chucked in, and scatters them scalded and half-digested at your feet. So irritated has the poor thing's stomach become by the discipline it has undergone, that even long after all the foreign matter has been thrown off, it goes on retching and sputtering, until at last nature is exhausted, when, sobbing and sighing to itself, it sinks back into the bottom of its den.

Put into the highest spirits by the success of this performance, we turned away to examine the remaining springs. I do not know, however, that any of the rest are worthy of particular mention. They all resemble in character the two I have described, the only difference being that they are infinitely smaller, and of much less power and importance. One other remarkable formation in the neighbourhood must not be passed unnoticed. Imagine a large irregular opening in the surface of the soft white clay, filled to the very brim with scalding water, perfectly still, and of as bright a blue as that of the Grotto Azzuro at Capri, through whose transparent depths you can see down into the mouth of a vast subaqueous cavern, which runs, Heaven knows how far, in a horizontal direction beneath your feet. Its walls and varied cavities really looked as if they were built of the purest lupis lazuli—and so thin seemed the crust that roofed it in, we almost fancied it might break through, and tumble us all into the fearful beautiful bath.

Having by this time taken a pretty good look at the principal features of our new domain, I wrapped myself up in a cloak and went to sleep; leaving orders that I should not be called until after the tent had arrived, and our beds were ready. Sigurdr followed my example, but the Doctor went out shooting.

As our principal object in coming so far was to see an eruption of the Great Geysir, it was of course necessary we should wait his pleasure; in fact, our movements entirely depended upon his. For the next two or three days, therefore, like pilgrims round some ancient shrine, we patiently kept watch; but he scarcely deigned to vouchsafe us the slightest manifestation of his latent energies. Two or three times the cannonading we had heard immediately after our arrival recommenced,—and once an eruption to the height of about ten feet occurred; but so brief was its duration, that by the time we were on the spot, although the tent was not eighty yards distant, all was over. As after every effort of the fountain the water in the basin mysteriously ebbs back into the funnel, this performance, though unsatisfactory in itself, gave us an opportunity of approaching the mouth of the pipe, and looking down into its scalded gullet. In an hour afterwards, the basin was brimful as ever.

Tethered down by our curiosity to a particular spot for an indefinite period, we had to while away the hours as best we could. We played chess, collected specimens, photographed the encampment, the guides, the ponies, and one or two astonished natives. Every now and then we went out shooting over the neighbouring flats, and once I ventured on a longer expedition among the mountains to our left. The views I got were beautiful,—ridge rising beyond ridge in eternal silence, like gigantic ocean waves, whose tumult has been suddenly frozen into stone;—but the dread of the Geysir going off during my absence made me almost too fidgety to enjoy them. The weather luckily remained beautiful, with the exception of one little spell of rain, which came to make us all the more grateful for the sunshine,— and we fed like princes. Independently of the game, duck, plover, ptarmigan, and bittern, with which our own guns supplied us, a young lamb was always in the larder,—not to mention reindeer tongues, skier,—a kind of sour curds, excellent when well made,—milk, cheese whose taste and nature baffles description, biscuit and bread, sent us as a free gift by the lady of a neighbouring farm. In fact, so noble is Icelandic hospitality, that I really believe there was nothing within fifty miles round we might not have obtained for the asking, had we desired it. As for Fitz, he became quite the *enfant gâté* of a neighbouring family.

Having unluckily caught cold, instead of sleeping in the tent, he determined to seek shelter under a solid roof-tree, and, conducted by our guide Olaf, set off on his pony at bed-time in search of a habitation. The next morning he reappeared so unusually radiant that I could not help inquiring what good fortune had in the meantime befallen him: upon which he gave me such an account of his last night's reception at the farm, that I was almost tempted to bundle tent and beds down the throat of our irritable friend Strokr, and throw myself for the future upon the hospitality of the inhabitants. It is true, I had read in Van Troil of something of the kind, but until now I never fully believed it. The Doctor shall tell his own history.

"No sooner," said he, "had I presented myself at the door, and made known my errand, than I was immediately welcomed by the whole family, and triumphantly inducted into the guest quarters: everything the house could produce was set before me, and the whole society stood by to see that I enjoyed myself. As I had but just dined an additional repast was no longer essential to my happiness; but all explanation was useless, and I did my best to give them satisfaction. Immediately on rising from the table, the young lady of the house—(old Van Troil says it is either the mother or the daughter of the house, if she be grown up, who performs this office)—proposed by signs to conduct me to my apartment; taking in one hand a large plate of skier, and in the other a bottle of brandy, she led the way through a passage built of turf and stones to the place where I was to sleep. Having watched her deposit—not without misgivings, for I knew it was expected both should be disposed of before morning—the skier by my bedside, and the brandy-bottle under the pillow, I was preparing to make her a polite bow, and to wish her a very good night, when she advanced towards me, and with a winning grace difficult to resist, insisted upon helping me off with my coat, and then,—proceeding to extremities,—with my shoes and stockings. At this most critical part of the proceedings, I naturally imagined her share of the performance would conclude, and that I should at last be restored to that privacy which at such seasons is generally considered appropriate. Not a bit of it. Before I knew where I was, I found myself sitting in a chair, in my shirt, trouserless, while my fair tire-woman was engaged in neatly folding up the ravished garments on a neighbouring chair. She then in the most simple manner in the world, helped me into bed, tucked me up, and having said a quantity of pretty things in Icelandic, gave me a hearty kiss and departed. If," he added, "you see anything remarkable in my appearance, it is probably because—

> 'This very morn I've felt the sweet surprise
> Of unexpected lips on sealed eyes;'"

by which he poetically intimated the pleasing ceremony which had awaked him to the duties of the day. I think it needless to subjoin that the Doctor's cold did not get better as long as we remained in the neighbourhood, and that, had it not been for the daily increasing fire of his looks, I should have begun to be alarmed at so protracted an indisposition.

We had now been keeping watch for three days over the Geysir, in languid expectation of the eruption which was to set us free. All the morning of the fourth day I had been playing chess with Sigurdr; Fitzgerald was photographing, Wilson was in the act of announcing luncheon, when a cry from the guides made us start to our feet, and with one common impulse rush towards the basin. The usual subterranean thunders had already commenced. A violent agitation was disturbing the centre of the pool. Suddenly a dome of water lifted itself up to the height of eight or ten feet,—then burst, and fell ; immediately after which a shining liquid column, or rather a sheaf of columns wreathed in robes of vapour, sprung into the air, and in a succession of jerking leaps, each higher than the last, flung their silver crests against the sky. For a few minutes the fountain held its own, then all at once appeared to lose its ascending energy. The unstable waters faltered, drooped, fell, "like a broken purpose," back upon themselves, and were immediately sucked down into the recesses of their pipe.

The spectacle was certainly magnificent; but no description can give any idea of its most striking features. The enormous wealth of water, its vitality, its hidden power,— the illimitable breadth of sunlit vapour, rolling out in exhaustless profusion,—all combined to make one feel the stupendous energy of nature's slightest movements.

And yet I do not believe the exhibition was so fine as some that have been seen : from the first burst upwards to the moment the last jet retreated into the pipe, was no more than a space of seven or eight minutes, and at no moment did the crown of the column reach higher than sixty or seventy feet above the surface of the basin. Now, early travellers talk of three hundred feet, which must, of course, be fabulous ; but many trustworthy persons have judged the eruptions at two hundred feet, while well-authenticated accounts—when the elevation of the jet has been actually measured—make it to have attained a height of upwards of one hundred feet.

With regard to the internal machinery by which these waterworks are set in motion, I will only say that the most received theory seems to be that which supposes the existence of a chamber in the heated earth, almost, but not quite, filled with water, and communicating with the upper air by means of a pipe, whose lower orifice, instead of being in the roof, is at the side of the cavern, and *below* the surface of the subterranean pond. The water kept by the surrounding furnaces at boiling point, generates of course a continuous supply of steam, for which some vent must be obtained ; as it cannot escape by the funnel,—the lower mouth of which is under water,—it squeezes itself up within the arching roof, until at last, compressed beyond all endurance, it strains against the rock, and pushing down the intervening waters with its broad, strong back, forces them below the level of the funnel, and dispersing part, and driving part before it, rushes forth in triumph to the upper air. The fountains, therefore, that we see mounting to the sky during an eruption, are nothing but the superincumbent mass of waters in the pipe driven up in confusion before the steam at the moment it obtains its liberation.[1]

The accompanying sketch may perhaps help you to understand my meaning.

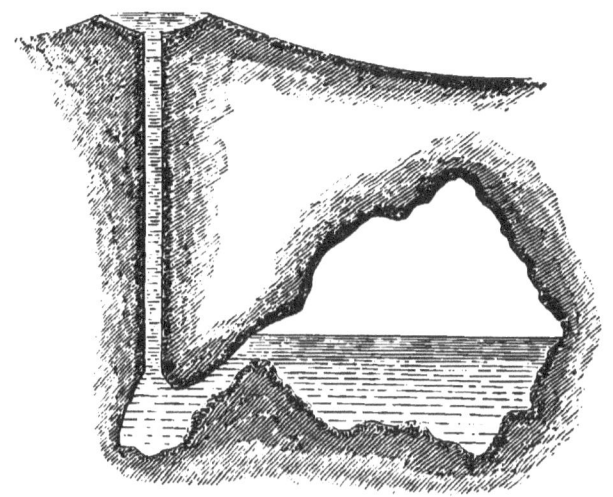

The last gulp of water had disappeared down the funnel. We were standing at the bottom of the now empty basin, gazing into each other's faces with joyous astonishment, when suddenly we perceived a horseman come frantically galloping round the base of the neighbouring hill towards us. The state of the case was only too evident. He had seen

[1] Professor Bunsen has lately announced a chemical theory, which I believe has been received with favour by the scientific world. He points to the fact that water, after being long subjected to heat, loses much of the air contained in it, has the cohesion of its molecules much increased, and requires a higher temperature to bring it to boil ; at which moment the production of vapour becomes so great, and so instantaneous, as to cause explosion. The bursting of furnace boilers is often attributable to this cause. Now, the water at the bottom of the well of the Great Geysir is found to be of constantly increasing temperature up to the moment of an eruption, when on one occasion it was as high as 261° Fahrenheit. Professor Bunsen's idea is, that on reaching some unknown point above that temperature, ebullition takes place, vapour is suddenly generated in enormous quantity, and an eruption of the superior column of water is the consequence.

the masses of vapour rising round the fountain, and guessing "what was *up*," had strained every nerve to arrive in time. As there was no mutual friend present to introduce us to each other,—of course under ordinary circumstances I should have wrapped myself in that reserve which is the birthright of every Briton, and pretended never even to have noticed his arrival ; but the sight we had just seen had quite upset my nerves,—and I confess, with shame, that I so far compromised myself, as to inaugurate a conversation with the stranger. In extenuation of my conduct, I must be allowed to add, that the new-comer was not a fellow-countryman, but of the French tongue, and of the naval profession.

Occupying then the door of my tent—by way of vantage ground, as soon as the stranger was come within earshot, I lifted up my voice, and cried in a style of Arabian familiarity, "O thou that ridest so furiously,—weary and disappointed one,—turn in, I pray thee, into the tent of thy servant, and eat bread, and drink wine, that thy soul may be comforted." To which he answered and said, "Man,— dweller in sulphureous places,—I will not eat bread, nor drink wine, neither will I enter into thy tent, until I have measured out a resting-place for my Lord the Prince."

At this interesting moment our acquaintance was interrupted by the appearance of two other horsemen—the one a painter, the other a geologist—attached to the expedition of Prince Napoleon. They informed us that His Imperial Highness had reached Reykjavik two days after we had left, that he had encamped last night at Thingvalla, and might be expected here in about four hours : they themselves having come on in advance to prepare for his arrival. My first care was to order coffee for the tired Frenchmen ; and then —feeling that long residence having given us a kind of proprietorship in the Geysirs, we were bound to do the honours of the place to the approaching band of travellers,—I summoned the cook, and enlarging in a long speech on the gravity of the occasion, gave orders that he should make a holocaust of all the remaining game, and get under way a plum-pudding, whose dimensions should do himself and England credit. A long table having been erected within the tent, Sigurdr started on a plundering expedition to the neighbouring farm, Fitzgerald undertook the ordering of the feast, while I rode on my pony across the morass, in hopes of being able to shoot a few additional plover. In a couple of hours afterwards, just as I was stalking a duck that lay innocently basking on the bosom of the river, a cloud of horsemen swept round the base of the distant mountain, and returning home, I found the encampment I had left so deserted—alive and populous with as merry a group of Frenchmen as it might ever be one's fortune to fall in with. Of course they were dressed in every variety of costumes, long boots, picturesque brigand-looking hats, with here and there a sprinkling of Scotch caps from Aberdeen; but— whatever might be the head-dress, underneath you might be sure to find a kindly, cheery face. My old friend Count Trampe, who had accompanied the expedition, at once presented me to the Prince, who was engaged in sounding the depth of the pipe of the Great Geysir,—and encouraged by the gracious reception which His Imperial Highness accorded me, I ventured to inform him that "there was a poor banquet toward," of which I trusted he—and as many of his officers as the table could hold—would condescend to partake. After a little hesitation,—caused, I presume, by fear of our being put to inconvenience,—he was kind enough to signify his acceptance of my proposal, and in a few minutes afterwards with a cordial frankness I fully appreciated, allowed me to have the satisfaction of receiving him as a guest within my tent.

Although I never had the pleasure of seeing Prince Napoleon before, I should have known him among a thousand, from his remarkable likeness to his uncle, the first Emperor. A stronger resemblance, I conceive, could scarcely exist between two persons. The same delicate, sharply cut features, thin refined mouth, and firm determined jaw. The Prince's frame, however, is built altogether on a larger scale, and his eyes, instead of being of a cold piercing blue—are soft and brown, with quite a different expression.

Though of course a little Barmicidal, the dinner went off very well, as every dinner must do where such merry companions are the convives. We had some difficulty about stowing away the legs of a tall philosopher, and to each knife three individuals were told off; but the birds were not badly cooked, and the plum-pudding arrived in time to convert a questionable success into an undoubted triumph.

On rising from table, each one strolled away in whatever direction his particular taste suggested. The painter to sketch; the geologist to break stones; the philosopher to moralize, I presume,—at least, he lighted a cigar,—and the rest to superintend the erection of the tents which had just arrived.

In an hour afterwards, sleep—though not altogether silence—for loud and strong rose the choral service intoned to Morpheus from every side—reigned supreme over the encampment, whose canvas habitations, huddled together on the desolated plateau, looked almost Crimean. This last notion, I suppose, must have mingled with my dreams, for not long afterwards I found myself in full swing towards a Russian battery, that banged and bellowed, and cannonaded about my ears in a fashion frightful to hear. Apparently I was serving in the French attack, for clear and shrill above the tempest rose the cry, "Alerte! alerte! aux armes, Monseigneur! aux armes!" The ground shook, volumes of smoke rose before my eyes, and completely hid the defences of Sebastopol; which fact, on reflection, I perceived to be the less extraordinary, as I was standing in my shirt at the door of a tent in Iceland. The premonitory symptoms of an eruption, which I had taken for a Russian cannonading, had awakened the French sleepers,—a universal cry was pervading the encampment,—and the entire settlement had turned out—chiefly in bare legs—to witness the event which the reverberating earth and steaming water seemed to prognosticate. Old Geysir, however, proved less courteous than we had begun to hope, for after labouring uneasily in his basin for a few minutes, he roused himself on his hind-legs—fell—made one more effort,—and then giving it up as a bad job, sank back into his accustomed inaction, and left the disappointed assembly to disperse to their respective dormitories.

The next morning, the whole encampment was stirring at an early hour with preparations for departure; for unsatisfactory as it had been, the French considered themselves absolved by the partial performance they had witnessed from any longer "making antechamber," as they said, to so capricious a functionary. Being very anxious to have one more trial at photographing Strokr, I ventured to suggest that the necessary bolus of sods should be administered to him. In a few minutes two or three cart-loads of turf were seething and wallowing within him. In the meantime, Fitz seized the opportunity of the Prince being at breakfast to do a picture of him seated on a chair, with his staff standing around him, and looking the image of Napoleon before the battle of Austerlitz. A good twenty minutes had now elapsed since the emetic had been given,—no symptoms of any result had as yet appeared,—and the French began to get impatient; inuendoes were hazarded to the disadvantage of Strokr's reputation for consistency,—inuendoes which I confess touched me nearly, and made me feel like a showman whose dog has misbehaved. At last the whole party rode off; but the rear horseman had not disappeared round the neighbouring hill before—splash! bang!—fifty feet up into the air drove the dilatory fountain, with a fury which amply avenged the affront put upon it, and more than vindicated my good opinion. All our endeavours, however, to photograph the eruption proved abortive. We had already attempted both Strokr and the Great Geysir, but in the case of the latter the exhibition was always concluded before the plate could be got ready; and although, as far as Strokr is concerned, you can tell within a certain period when the performance will take place, yet the interval occurring between the dose and the explosion varies so capriciously, that unless you are content to spend many days upon the spot, it would be almost impossible to hit it off exactly. On this last occasion,—although we did not prepare the plate until a good twenty minutes after the turf was thrown in,—the spring remained inactive so much longer than is usual that the collodion became quite insensitive, and the eruption left no impression whatever upon it.

Of our return journey to Reykjavik I think I have no very interesting particulars to give you. During the early part of the morning there had been a slight threatening of rain; but by twelve o'clock it had settled down into one of those still dark days, which wrap even the most familiar landscape in a mantle of mystery. A heavy, low-hung, steel-coloured pall was stretched almost entirely across the heavens, except where along the flat horizon a broad stripe of opal atmosphere let the eye wander into space, in search of the pearly gateways of Paradise. On the other side rose the contorted lava mountains, their bleak heads knocking against the solid sky and stained of an inky blackness, which changed into a still more lurid tint where the local reds struggled up through the shadow that lay brooding over the desolate scene. If within the domain of nature such another region is to be found, it can only be in the heart of those awful solitudes which science has unveiled to us amid the untrodden fastnesses of the lunar mountains. An hour before reaching our old camping-ground at Thingvalla, as if summoned by enchantment, a dull grey mist closed around us, and suddenly confounded in undistinguishable ruin the glory and the terror of the panorama we had traversed: sky, mountains, horizon, all had disappeared; and as we strained our eyes from the edge of the Rabna Gja across the monotonous grey level at our feet, it was almost difficult to believe that there lay the same magical plain, the first sight of which had become almost an epoch in our lives.

I had sent on cook, baggage, and guides, some hours before we ourselves started, so that on our arrival we found a dry, cosy tent, and a warm dinner awaiting us. The rapid transformation of the aspect of the country, which I had just witnessed, made me quite understand how completely the success of an expedition in Iceland must depend on the weather, and fully accounted for the difference I had observed in the amount of enjoyment different travellers seemed to have derived from it. It is one thing to ride forty miles a day through the most singular scenery in the world, when a radiant sun brings out every feature of the country into startling distinctness, transmuting the dull tormented earth into towers, domes, and pinnacles of gleaming metal,—and weaves for every distant summit a robe of variegated light, such as the "Delectable Mountains" must have worn for the rapt gaze of weary "Christian;"—and another to plod over the same forty miles, drenched to the skin, seeing nothing but the dim, grey roots of hills, that rise you know not how, and you care not where,—with no better employment than to look at your watch, and wonder when you shall reach your journey's end. If, in addition to this, you have to wait, as very often must be the case, for many hours after your own arrival, wet, tired, hungry, until the baggage-train, with the tents and food, shall have come up, with no alternative in the meantime but to lie shivering inside a grass-roofed church, or to share the quarters of some farmer's family, whose domestic arrangements resemble in every particular those which Macaulay describes as prevailing among the Scottish Highlanders a hundred years ago; and, if finally—after vainly waiting for some days to see an eruption which never takes place —you journey back to Reykjavik under the same melancholy conditions,—it will not be unnatural that, on returning to your native land, you should proclaim Iceland, with her Geysirs, to be a sham, a delusion, and a snare!

Fortune, however, seemed determined that of these bitternesses we should not taste; for the next morning, bright and joyous overhead bent the blue unclouded heaven; while the plain lay gleaming at our feet in all the brilliancy of enamel. I was sorely tempted to linger another day in the neighbourhood; but we have already spent more time upon the Geysirs than I had counted upon, and it will not do to remain in Iceland longer than the 15th, or Winter will have begun to barricade the passes into his Arctic dominions. My plan, on returning to Reykjavik, is to send the schooner round to wait for us in a harbour on the north coast of the island, while we ourselves strike straight across the interior on horseback.

The scenery, I am told, is magnificent. On the way we shall pass many a little nook, shut up among the hills, that has been consecrated by some touching old-world story; and the manner of life among the northern inhabitants is, I believe, more unchanged and characteristic than that of any other of the islanders. Moreover, scarcely any stranger has ever penetrated to any distance in this direction; and we shall have an opportunity of traversing a slice of that tremendous desert—piled up for thirty thousand square miles in disordered pyramids of ice and lava over the centre of the country, and periodically devastated by deluges of molten stone and boiling mud, or overwhelmed with whirlwinds of intermingled snow and cinders,—an unfinished corner of the universe, where the elements of chaos are still allowed to rage with unbridled fury.

Our last stage from Thingvalla back to Reykjavik was got over very quickly, and seemed an infinitely shorter distance than when we first performed it. We met a number of farmers returning to their homes from a kind of fair that is annually held in the little metropolis; and as I watched the long caravan-like line of pack-horses and horsemen, wearily plodding over the stony waste in single file, I found it less difficult to believe that these remote islanders should be descended from Oriental forefathers. In fact, one is constantly reminded of the East in Iceland. From the earliest ages the Icelanders have been a people dwelling in tents. In the time of the ancient Parliament, the legislators, during the entire session, lay encamped in movable booths around the place of meeting. Their domestic polity is naturally patriarchal, and the flight of their ancestors from Norway was a protest against the antagonistic principle of feudalism. No Arab could be prouder of his courser than they are of their little ponies, or reverence more deeply the sacred rights of hospitality; while the solemn salutation exchanged between two companies of travellers, passing each other in the *desert*—as they invariably call the uninhabited part of the country—would not have misbecome the stately courtesy of the most ancient worshippers of the sun.

Anything more multifarious than the landing of these caravans we met returning to the inland districts—cannot well be conceived : deal boards, rope, kegs of brandy, sacks of rye or wheaten flour, salt, soap, sugar, snuff, tobacco, coffee; everything, in fact, which was necessary to their domestic consumption during the ensuing winter. In exchange for these commodities, which of course they are obliged to get from Europe, the Icelanders export raw wool, knitted stockings, mittens, cured cod, and fish oil, whale blubber, fox skins, eider-down, feathers, and Icelandic moss. During the last few years the exports of the island have amounted to about 1,200,000 lbs. of wool and 500,000 pairs of stockings and mittens. Although Iceland is one-fifth larger than Ireland, its population consists of only about 60,000 persons, scattered along the habitable ring which runs round between the central desert and the sea ; of the whole area of 38,000 square miles it is calculated that not more than one-eighth part is occupied, the remaining 33,000 square miles consisting of naked mountains of ice, or valleys desolated by lava or volcanic ashes. Even Reykjavik itself cannot boast of more than 700 or 800 inhabitants.

During winter time the men are chiefly employed in tending cattle, picking wool, manufacturing ropes, bridles, saddles, and building boats. The fishing season commences in spring; in 1853 there were as many as 3,500 boats engaged upon the water. As summer advances—turf-cutting and hay-making begins ; while the autumn months are principally devoted to the repairing of their houses, manuring the grass lands, and killing and curing of sheep for exportation, as well as for their own use during the winter. The woman-kind of a family occupy themselves throughout the year in washing, carding, and spinning wool, in knitting gloves and stockings, and in weaving frieze and flannel for their own wear.

The ordinary food of a well-to-do Icelandic family consists of dried fish, butter, sour whey kept till fermentation takes place, curds, and skier—a very peculiar cheese unlike any I ever tasted,—a little mutton, and rye bread. As might be expected, this meagre fare is not very conducive to health; scurvy, leprosy, elephantiasis, and all cutaneous disorders, are very common, while the practice of mothers to leave off nursing their children at the end of three days, feeding them with cows' milk instead, results in a frightful mortality among the babies.

Land is held either in fee-simple, or let by the Crown to tenants on what may almost be considered perpetual leases. The rent is calculated partly on the number of acres occupied, partly on the head of cattle the farm is fit to support, and is paid in kind, either in fish or farm produce. Tenants in easy circumstances generally employ two or three labourers, who—in addition to their board and lodging—receive from ten to twelve dollars a year of wages. No property can be entailed, and if any one dies intestate, what he leaves is distributed among his children—in equal shares to the sons, in half shares to the daughters.

The public revenue arising from Crown lands, commercial charges, and a small tax on the transference of property, amounts to about 3,000*l*.; the expenditure for education, officers' salaries (the Governor has about 400*l*. a year), ecclesiastical establishments, etc., exceeds 6,000*l*. a year; so that the island is certainly not a self-supporting institution.

The clergy are paid by tithes; their stipends are exceedingly small, generally not averaging more than six or seven pounds sterling per annum; their chief dependence being upon their farms. Like St. Dunstan, they are invariably excellent blacksmiths.

As we approached Reykjavik, for the first time during the whole journey we began to have some little trouble with the relay of ponies in front. Whether it was that they were tired, or that they had arrived in a district where they had been accustomed to roam at large, I cannot tell; but every ten minutes, during the last six or seven miles, one or other of them kept starting aside into the rocky plain, across which the narrow bridle-road was carried, and cost us many a weary chase before we could drive them into the track again. At last, though not till I had been violently hugged, kissed, and nearly pulled off my horse by an enthusiastic and rather tipsy farmer, who mistook me for the Prince, we galloped, about five o'clock, triumphantly into the town, without an accident having occurred to man or horse during the whole course of the expedition—always excepting one tremendous fall sustained by Wilson. It was on the evening of the day we left the Geysirs. We were all galloping in single file down the lava pathway, when suddenly I heard a cry behind me, and then the noise as of a descending avalanche. On turning round, behold! both Wilson and his pony lay stretched upon the ground, the first some yards in advance of the other. The poor fellow evidently thought he was killed; for he neither spoke nor stirred, but lay looking up at me, with blank, beady eyes as I approached to his assistance. On further investigation, neither of the sufferers proved to be a bit the worse.

The cook, and the rest of the party, did not arrive till about midnight; but I make no doubt that when that able and spirited individual did at length reascend the side of the schooner, his cheek must have burned with pride at the reflection, that during the short period of his absence on shore he had added to his other accomplishments that of becoming a most finished cavalier. I do not mean by that to imply that he was at all *done.* Although we had enjoyed our trip so much, I was not sorry to find myself on board. The descent again, after our gipsy life, into the coquettish little cabin, with its books and dear home faces, quite penetrated me with that feeling of snug content of which I believe Englishmen alone are susceptible.

I have now to relate to you a most painful occurrence which has taken place during my absence at the Geysirs;— no less a catastrophe, in fact, than a mutiny among my hitherto most exemplary ship's company. I suppose they, too, had occasion to bear witness to the proverbial hospitality of Iceland; salt junk, and the innocuous cates which generally compose ship-board rations, could never have produced such an emergency. Suffice it to say, that "Dyspepsia and her fatal train" having taken hold of them, in a desperate hour they determined on a desperate deed,—and rushing aft in a body, demanded of my faithful steward, not only access to the penetralia of the absent Doctor's cupboard, but that he himself should administer to them whatever medicaments he could come by. In vain Mr. Grant threw himself across the cabin-door. Remonstrance was useless; my horny-handed lambs were inexorable—unless he acceded to their demands, they threatened to report him when I returned! The Doctor's sanctuary was thrown open, and all its sweets—if such they may be called—were rifled. A huge box of pills, the first that came to hand—they happened to be calomel—was served out, share and share alike, with concomitant vials of wrath, of rhubarb and senna; and it was not until the last drop of castor oil had been carefully licked up that the marauders suffered their unwilling accomplice to retire to the fastnesses of his pantry.

An avenging Nemesis, however, hovered over the violated shrine of Esculapius. By the time I returned the exigencies of justice had been more than satisfied, and the outrage already atoned for. The rebellious *hands* were become most penitent *stomachs;* and fresh from the Oriental associations suggested by our last day's ride, I involuntarily dismissed the disconsolate culprits, with the Asiatic form of condonation: "Mashallah, you have made your faces white! Go in peace!"

During our expedition to the interior, the harbour of Reykjavik had become populous with new arrivals. First of all, there was my old friend, the "*Reine Hortense*," the Emperor's yacht, a magnificent screw corvette of 1,100 tons. I had last parted with her three years ago in the Baltic, after she had towed me for eighty miles on our way from Bomarsund to Stockholm. Then there were two English screw steamers, of about 700 tons each, taken up by the French Government as tenders to the yacht; not to mention a Spanish brig, and one or two other foreigners, which, together with the frigate, the barque, and the vessels we had found here on our first arrival, made the usually deserted bay look quite lively. Until this year no steamers had ever cockneyfied its secluded waters.

This morning, directly after breakfast, I went on board the "*Reine Hortense*" to pay my respects to Prince Napoleon; and H.I.H. has just done me the honour of coming to inspect the "*Foam*." When I was first presented to him at the Geysirs, he asked me what my plans might be; and on my mentioning my resolution of sailing to the North, he most kindly proposed that I should come with him West to Greenland instead. My anxiety, however, to reach, if it were possible, Jan Mayen and Spitzbergen, prevented my accepting this most tempting offer; but in the meantime, H.I.H. has, it seems, himself determined to come to Jan Mayen, and he is kind enough to say that if I can get ready for a start by six o'clock to-morrow morning, the "*Reine Hortense*" shall take me in tow. To profit by this proposal would of course entail the giving up my plan of riding across the interior of Iceland, which I should be very loth to do; at the same time, the season is so far advanced, the mischances of our first start from England have thrown us so far behind in our programme, that it would seem almost a pity to neglect such an opportunity of overrunning the time that has been lost; and after all, these Polar islands, which so few have visited, are what I am chiefly bent on seeing. Before I close this letter the thing will have been settled one way or another; for I am to have the honour of dining with the Prince this evening, and between this and then I shall have made up my mind. After dinner there is to be a ball on board the frigate, to which all the rank, fashion, and beauty of Reykjavik have been invited.

3 A.M.

I give up seeing the rest of Iceland, and go North at once. It has cost me a struggle to come to this conclusion, but on the whole I think it will be better. Ten or fifteen days of summer-time become very precious in these latitudes, and are worth a sacrifice. At this moment we have just brought up astern of the "*Reine Hortense*," and are getting our hawsers bent, ready for a start in half an hour's time. My next letter, please God, will be dated from Hammerfest. I suppose I shall be about fifteen or twenty days getting there, but this will depend on the state of the ice about Jan Mayen. If the anchorage is clear, I shall spend a few days in examining the island, which by all accounts would appear to be most curious.

I happened first to hear of its existence from a very intelligent whaling Captain I fell in with among the Shetlands four years ago. He was sailing home to Hull, after fishing the Spitzbergen waters, and had sighted the huge mountain which forms the northern extremity of Jan Mayen, on his way south. Luckily, the weather was fine while he was passing, and the sketch he made of it at the time so filled me with amazement, that I then determined, if ever I got the chance, to go and see with my own eyes so great a marvel. Imagine a spike of igneous rock (the whole island is volcanic), shooting straight up out of the sea to the height of 6,870 feet, not broad-based like a pyramid, nor round-topped like a sugar-loaf, but needle-shaped, pointed like the spire of a church. If only my Hull skipper were as good a draughtsman as he seemed to be a seaman, we should now be on our way to one of the wonders of the world. Most people here hold out rather a doleful prospect, and say that, in the first place, it is probable the whole island will be imprisoned within the eternal fields of ice, that lie out for upwards of a hundred and fifty miles along the eastern coast of Greenland; and next, that if even the sea should be clear in its vicinity, the fogs up there are so dense and constant that the chances are very much against our hitting the land. But the fact of the last French man-of-war which sailed in that direction never having returned, has made those seas needlessly unpopular at Reykjavik.

It was during one of these fogs that Captain Fotherby, the original discoverer of Jan Mayen, stumbled upon it in 1614. While sailing southwards in a mist too thick to see a ship's length off, he suddenly heard the noise of waters breaking on a great shore; and when the gigantic bases of Mount Beerenberg gradually disclosed themselves, he thought he had discovered some new continent. Since then it has been often sighted by homeward-bound whalers, but rarely landed upon. About the year 1633 the Dutch Government, wishing to establish a settlement in the actual neighbourhood of the fishing-grounds, where the blubber might be boiled down, and the spoils of each season transported home in the smallest bulk,—actually induced seven seamen to volunteer remaining the whole winter on the island.[1] Huts were built for them, and having been furnished with an ample supply of salt provisions, they were left to resolve the problem, as to whether or no human beings could support the severities of the climate. Standing on the shore, these seven men saw their comrades' parting sails sink down beneath the sun,—then watched the sun sink, as had sunk the

---

[1] The names of the seven Dutch seamen who attempted to winter in Jan Mayen's Island were:

        Outgert Jacobson, of Grootenbrook, their commander.
        Adrian Martin Carman, of Schiedam, clerk.
        Thauniss Thaunissen, of Schermehem, cook.
        Dick Peterson, of Veenhuyse.
        Peter Peterson, of Harlem.
        Sebastian Gyse, of Defts-Haven.
        Gerard Beautin, of Bruges.

sails ;— but extracts from their own simple narrative are the most touching record I can give you of their fate :—

"The 26th of August, our fleet set sail for Holland with a strong north-east wind, and a hollow sea, which continued all that night. The 28th, the wind the same; it began to snow very hard; we then shared half a pound of tobacco betwixt us, which was to be our allowance for a week. Towards evening we went about together, to see whether we could discover anything worth our observation; but met with nothing." And so on for many a weary day of sleet and storm.

On the 8th of September they "were frightened by a noise of something falling to the ground,"—probably some volcanic disturbance. A month later, it becomes so cold that their linen, after a moment's exposure to the air, becomes frozen like a board.[2] Huge fleets of ice beleaguered the island, the sun disappears, and they spend most of their time in "rehearsing to one another the adventures that had befallen them both by sea and land." On the 12th of December they kill a bear, having already begun to feel the effects of a salt diet. At last comes New Year's Day, 1636. "After having wished each other a happy new year, and success in our enterprise, we went to prayers, to disburthen our hearts before God." On the 25th of February (the very day on which Wallenstein was murdered) the sun reappeared. By the 22nd of March scurvy had already declared itself: "For want of refreshments we began to be very heartless, and so afflicted that our legs are scarce able to bear us." On the 3rd of April, "there being no more than two of us in

[2] The climate, however, does not appear to have been then so inclement in these latitudes as it has since become. A similar deterioration in the temperature, both of Spitzbergen and Greenland, has also been observed. In Iceland we have undoubted evidence of corn having been formerly grown, as well as of the existence of timber of considerable size, though now it can scarcely produce a cabbage, or a stunted shrub of birch. M. Babinet, of the French Institute, goes a little too far when he says, in the *Journal des Débats* of the 30th December, 1856, that for many years Jan Mayen has been inaccessible.

health, we killed for them the only two pullets we had left; and they fed pretty heartily upon them, in hopes it might prove a means to recover part of their strength. We were sorry we had not a dozen more for their sake." On Easter Day, Adrian Carman, of Schiedam, their clerk, dies. "The Lord have mercy upon his soul, and upon us all, we being very sick." During the next few days they seem all to have got rapidly worse; one only is strong enough to move about. He has learnt writing from his comrades since coming to the island; and it is he who concludes the melancholy story. "The 23rd (April), the wind blew from the same corner, with small rain. We were by this time reduced to a very deplorable state, there being none of them all, except myself, that were able to help themselves, much less one another, so that the whole burden lay upon my shoulders,—and I perform my duty as well as I am able, as long as God pleases to give me strength. I am just now a-going to help our commander out of his cabin, at his request, because he imagined by this change to ease his pain, he then struggling with death." For seven days this gallant fellow goes on "striving to do his duty;" that is to say, making entries in the journal as to the state of the weather, that being the principal object their employers had in view when they left them on the island; but on the 30th of April his strength too gave way, and his failing hand could do no more than trace an incompleted sentence on the page.

Meanwhile succour and reward are on their way toward the forlorn garrison. On the 4th of June, up again above the horizon rise the sails of the Zealand fleet; but no glad faces come forth to greet the boats as they pull towards the shore; and when their comrades search for those they had hoped to find alive and well,—lo! each lies dead in his own hut,—one with an open Prayer-book by his side; another with his hand stretched out towards the ointment he had used for his stiffened joints; and the last survivor, with the unfinished journal still lying by his side.

The most recent recorded landing on the island was

effected twenty-two years ago, by the brave and pious Captain, now Dr. Scoresby,[1] on his return from a whaling cruise. He had seen the mountain of Beerenberg one hundred miles off, and, on approaching, found the coast quite clear of ice. According to his survey and observations, Jan Mayen is about sixteen miles long, by four wide ; but I hope soon, on my own authority, to be able to tell you more about it.

Certainly, this our last evening spent in Iceland will not have been the least joyous of our stay. The dinner on board the "*Reine Hortense*" was very pleasant. I renewed acquaintance with some of my old Baltic friends, and was presented to two or three of the Prince's staff who did not accompany the expedition to the Geysirs ; among others, to the Duc d'Abrantes, Marshal Junot's son. On sitting down to table, I found myself between H.I.H. and Monsieur de Saulcy, member of the French Institute, who made that famous expedition to the Dead Sea, and is one of the gayest, pleasantest persons I have ever met. Of course there was a great deal of laughing and talking, as well as much speculation with regard to the costume of the Icelandic ladies we were to see at the ball. It appears that the dove-cots of Reykjavik have been a good deal fluttered by an announcement emanating from the gallant Captain of the "*Artemise*" that his fair guests would be expected to come in low dresses; for it would seem that the practice of showing their ivory shoulders is, as yet, an idea as shocking to the pretty ladies of this country as waltzes were to our grandmothers. Nay, there was not even to be found a native milliner equal to the task of marking out that mysterious line which divides the prudish from the improper ; so that the Collet-monté faction have been in despair. As it turned out, their anxiety on this head was unnecessary ; for we found, on entering the ball-room, that, with the natural refinement which characterises this noble people, our bright-eyed partners, as if by inspiration, had hit off the exact

[1] I regret to be obliged to subjoin that Dr. Scoresby has died since the above was written.

sweep from shoulder to shoulder, at which—after those many oscillations, up and down, which the female corsage has undergone since the time of the first Director—good taste has finally arrested it.

I happened to be particularly interested in the above important question; for up to that moment I had always been haunted by a horrid paragraph I had met with some-

AN ICELANDIC LADY.

where in an Icelandic book of travels, to the effect that it was the practice of Icelandic women, from early childhood, to flatten down their bosoms as much as possible. This fact, for the honour of the island, I am now in a position to deny; and I here declare that, as far as I had the indiscretion to observe, those maligned ladies appeared to me as buxom in form as any rosy English girl I have ever seen.

It was nearly nine o'clock before we adjourned from the "*Reine Hortense*," to the ball. Already, for some time past, boats full of gay dresses had been passing under the corvette's stern on their way to the "*Artemise*," looking like flower-beds that had put to sea,—though they certainly could no longer be called a *parterre;*—and by the time we ourselves mounted her lofty sides, a mingled stream of music, light, and silver laughter, was pouring out of every port-hole. The ball-room was very prettily arranged. The upper deck had been closed in with a lofty roof of canvas, from which hung suspended glittering lustres, formed by bayonets with their points collected into an inverted pyramid, and the butt-ends serving as sockets for the tapers. Every wall was gay with flags,—the frigate's frowning armament all hid or turned to ladies' uses : 82 pounders became sofas—boarding-pikes, balustrades—pistols, candlesticks—the brass carronades set on end, pillarwise, their brawling mouths stopped with nosegays; while portraits of the Emperor and the Empress, busts, colours draped with Parisian cunning, gave to the scene an appearance of festivity that looked quite fairy-like in so sombre a region. As for our gallant host, I never saw such spirits ; he is a fine old grey-headed blow-hard of fifty odd, talking English like a native, and combining the frank openhearted cordiality of a sailor with that graceful winning gaiety peculiar to Frenchmen. I never saw anything more perfect than the kind, almost fatherly, courtesy with which he welcomed each blooming bevy of maidens that trooped up his ship's side. About two o'clock we had supper on the main-deck. I had the honour of taking down Miss Thora, of Bessestad ; and somehow—this time, I no longer found myself wandering back in search of the pale face of the old-world Thora, being, I suppose, sufficiently occupied by the soft, gentle eyes of the one beside me. With the other young ladies I did not make much acquaintance, as I experienced a difficulty in finding befitting remarks on the occasion of being presented to them. Once or twice, indeed, I hazarded, through their fathers, some little complimentary observations in Latin; but I cannot say that I found that language lend itself readily to the gallantries of the ball-room. After supper dancing recommenced, and the hilarity of the evening reached its highest pitch when half a dozen sailors, dressed in turbans made of flags (one of them a lady with the face of the tragic muse), came forward and danced the cancan, with a gravity and decorum that would have greatly edified what Gavarni calls "*la pudeur municipale.*"

At 3 o'clock A.M. I returned on board the schooner, and we are all now very busy in making final preparations for departure. Fitz is rearranging his apothecary's shop. Sigurdr is writing letters. The last strains of music have ceased on board the "*Artemise;*" the sun is already high in the heavens; the flower-beds are returning on shore,—a little draggled perhaps, as if just pelted by a thunder-storm; the "*Reine Hortense*" has got her steam up, and the real, serious part of our voyage is about to begin.

I feel that my description has not half done justice to the wonders of this interesting island; but I can refer you to your friend Sir Henry Holland for further details.; he paid a visit to Iceland in 1810, with Sir G. Mackenzie, and made himself thoroughly acquainted with its historical and scientific associations.

CONCLUDING ACT.

SCENE. *R. Y. S. "Foam": astern of the "Reine Hortense."*

DRAMATIS PERSONÆ.

VOICE OF FRENCH CAPTAIN, COMMANDING "R. H."
LORD D.
DOCTOR.
WILSON.

Voice of French Captain.—" Nous partons."
Lord D——.—" All ready, Sir!"
Wilson to Doctor (*sotto voce*).—" Sir!"

Doctor.—" Eh ? "

Wilson.—" Do you know, Sir ? "

Doctor.—" What ? "

Wilson.—" Oh, nothing, Sir ;—only we're going to the hicy regions, Sir, ain't we ? Well, I've just seen that ere brig as is come from there, Sir, and they say there's a precious lot of ice this year! (*Pause.*) Do you know, Sir, the skipper showed me the bows of his vessel, Sir? She's got seven feet of solid timber in her for'ard : *we've* only two inches, Sir ! " (*Dives below.*)

Voice of French Captain (*with a slight accent*).—" Are you ready ? "

Lord D———.—" Ay, ay, Sir ! Up anchor ! "

LETTER VIII.

START FROM REYKJAVIK — SNAEFELL—THE LADY OF FRODA — A BERSERK TRAGEDY—THE CHAMPION OF BREIDAVIK — ONUNDER FIORD—THE LAST NIGHT—CROSSING THE ARCTIC CIRCLE—FÊTE ON BOARD THE "REINE HORTENSE"—LE PÈRE ARCTIQUE—WE FALL IN WITH THE ICE—THE "SAXON" DISAPPEARS—MIST—A PARTING IN A LONELY SPOT—JAN MAYEN—MOUNT BEERENBERG—AN UNPLEASANT POSITION—SHIFT OF WIND AND EXTRICATION—"TO NORROWAY OVER THE FAEM"—A NASTY COAST—HAMMERFEST.

Hammerfest, July.

BACK in Europe again,—within reach of posts! The glad sun shining, the soft winds blowing, and roses on the cabin table,—as if the region of fog and ice we have just fled forth from were indeed the dream-land these summer sights would make it seem. I cannot tell you how gay and joyous it all appears to us, fresh from a climate that would not have been unworthy of Dante's Inferno. And yet—had it been twice as bad, what we have seen would have more than repaid us, though it has been no child's play to get to see it.

But I must begin where I left off in my last letter,—just, I think, as we were getting under way, to be towed by the "*Reine Hortense*" out of Reykjavik Harbour. Having been up all night,—as soon as we were well clear of the land, and that it was evident the towing business was doing well—I turned in for a few hours. When I came on deck again we had crossed the Faxe Fiord on our way north, and were sweeping round the base of Snaefell—an extinct volcano which rises from the sea in an icy cone to the height of 5,000 feet, and grimly looks across to Greenland. The day was beautiful; the mountain's summit beamed down upon us in unclouded splendour, and everything seemed to promise an uninterrupted view of the west coast of Iceland, along whose rugged cliffs few mariners have ever sailed. Indeed, until within these last few years, the passage, I believe, was altogether impracticable, in consequence of the continuous fields of ice which used to drift down the narrow channel between the frozen continent and the northern extremity of the island. Lately, some great change seems to have taken place in the lie of the Greenland ice; and during the summer-time you can pass through, though late in the year a solid belt binds the two shores together.

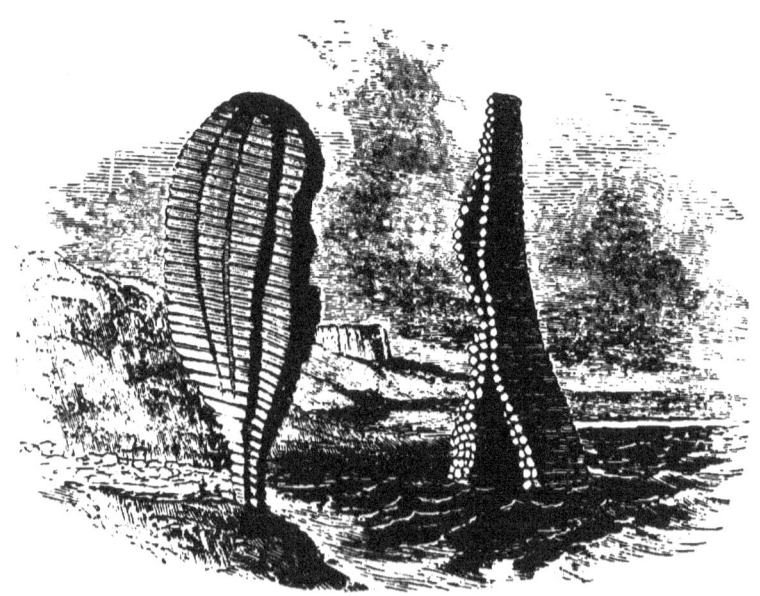

REMAINS OF BASALTIC DYKES.

But in a historical and scientific point of view, the whole country lying about the basanite roots of Snaefell is most interesting. At the feet of its southern slopes are to be seen wonderful ranges of columnar basalt, prismatic caverns, ancient craters, and specimens of almost every formation that can result from the agency of subterranean fires; while each glen, and bay, and headland, in the neighbourhood, teems with traditionary lore. On the north-western side of the mountain stretches the famous Eyrbiggja district, the most classic ground in Iceland, with the towns, or rather farmsteads, of Froda, Helgafell, and Biarnarhaf.

This last place was the scene of one of the most curious and characteristic Sagas to be found in the whole catalogue of Icelandic chronicles.

In the days when the same Jarl Hakon I have already mentioned lorded it over Norway, an Icelander of the name of Vermund, who had come to pay his court to the lord of Lade, took a violent wish to engage in his own service a couple of gigantic Berserks,[1] named Halli and Leikner, whom the Jarl had retained about his person,—fancying that two champions of such great strength and prowess would much add to his consequence on returning home. In vain the Jarl warned him that personages of that description were wont to give trouble and become unruly,—nothing would serve but he must needs carry them away with him; nay, if they would but come, they might ask as wages any boon which might be in his power to grant. The bargain accordingly was made; but, on arriving in Iceland, the first thing Halli took it into his head to require was a wife, who should be rich, nobly born, and beautiful. As such a request was difficult to comply with, Vermund, who was noted for being a man of gentle disposition, determined to turn his troublesome retainers over to his brother, Arngrim Styr, *i.e.*, the Stirring or Tumultuous One,—as being a likelier man than himself to know how to keep them in order.

Arngrim happened to have a beautiful daughter, named Asdisa, with whom the inflammable Berserk of course fell in love. Not daring openly to refuse him, Arngrim told his would-be son-in-law, that before complying with his suit, he must consult his friends, and posted off to Helgafell, where

[1] Berserk, *i.e.*, bare sark. The berserks seem to have been a description of athletes, who were in the habit of stimulating their nervous energies by the use of some intoxicating drug, which rendered them capable of feats of extraordinary strength and daring. The Berserker gang must have been something very like the Malay custom of running a muck. Their moments of excitement were followed by periods of great exhaustion.

dwelt the Pagan Pontiff Snorre. The result of this conference was an agreement on the part of Styr to give his daughter to the Berserk, provided he and his brother would *cut* a road through the lava rocks of Biarnarhaf. Halli and Leikner immediately set about executing this prodigious task; while the scornful Asdisa, arrayed in her most splendid attire, came sweeping past in silence, as if to mock their toil. The poetical reproaches addressed to the young lady on this occasion by her sturdy admirer and his mate are still extant. In the meantime, the other servants of the crafty Arngrim had constructed a subterranean bath, so contrived that at a moment's notice it could be flooded with boiling water. Their task at last concluded, the two Berserks returned home to claim their reward; but Arngrim Styr, as if in the exuberance of his affection, proposed that they should first refresh themselves in the new bath. No sooner had they descended into it, than Arngrim shut down the trap-door, and having ordered a newly-stripped bullock's hide to be stretched before the entrance, gave the signal for the boiling water to be turned on. Fearful were the struggles of the scalded giants : Halli, indeed, succeeded in bursting up the door; but his foot slipped on the bloody bull's hide, and Arngrim stabbed him to the heart. His brother was then easily forced back into the seething water.

The effusion composed by the Tumultuous One on the occasion of this exploit is also extant, and does not yield in poetical merit to those which I have already mentioned as having emanated from his victims.

As soon as the Pontiff Snorre heard of the result of Arngrim Styr's stratagem, he came over and married the Lady Asdisa. Traces of the road made by the unhappy champions can yet be detected at Biarnarhaf, and tradition still identifies the grave of the Berserks.

Connected with this same Pontiff Snorre is another of those mysterious notices of a great land in the western ocean which we find in the ancient chronicles, so interwoven with narrative we know to be true, as to make it impossible not to attach a certain amount of credit to them. This particular story is the more interesting as its *dénouement*, abruptly left in the blankest mystery by one Saga, is incidentally revealed to us in the course of another, relating to events with which the first had no connection.[1]

It seems that Snorre had a beautiful sister, named Thured of Froda, with whom a certain gallant gentleman—called Bjorn, the son of Astrand—fell head and ears in love. Unfortunately, a rich rival appears in the field; and though she had given her heart to Bjorn, Snorre—who, we have already seen, was a prudent man—insisted upon her giving her hand to his rival. Disgusted by such treatment, Bjorn sails away to the coasts of the Baltic, and joins a famous company of sea-rovers, called the Jomsburg Vikings. In this worthy society he so distinguishes himself by his valour and daring that he obtains the title of the Champion of Breidavik. After many doughty deeds, done by sea and land, he at last returns, loaded with wealth and honours, to his native country.

In the summer-time of the year 999, soon after his arrival, was held a great fair at Froda, whither all the merchants, " clad in coloured garments," congregated from the adjacent country. Thither came also Bjorn's old love, the Lady of Froda; "and Bjorn went up and spoke to her, and it was thought likely their talk would last long, since they for such a length of time had not seen each other." But to this renewal of old acquaintance both the lady's husband and her brother very much objected; and "it seemed to Snorre that it would be a good plan to kill Bjorn." So, about the time of haymaking, off he rides, with some retainers, to his victim's home, having fully instructed one of them how to deal the first blow. Bjorn was in the home-field (tùn), mending his sledge, when the cavalcade appeared in sight; and, guessing what motive had inspired the visit, went straight up to Snorre, who rode in front, " in a blue cloak," and held the knife with which he

[1] From internal evidence it is certain that the chronicle which contains these Sagas must have been written about the beginning of the thirteenth century.

had been working in such a position as to be able to stab the Pontiff to the heart, should his followers attempt to lift their hands against himself. Comprehending the position of affairs, Snorre's friends kept quiet. "Bjorn then asked the news." Snorre confesses that he had intended to kill him; but adds, "Thou tookest such a lucky grip of me at our meeting, that thou must have peace this time, however it may have been determined before." The conversation is concluded by an agreement on the part of Bjorn to leave the country, as he feels it impossible to abstain from paying visits to Thured as long as he remains in the neighbourhood. Having manned a ship, Bjorn put to sea in the summer-time. " When they sailed away, a north-east wind was blowing, which wind lasted long during that summer; but of this ship was nothing heard since this long time." And so we conclude it is all over with the poor Champion of Breidavik ! Not a bit of it. He turns up, thirty years afterwards, safe and sound, in the uttermost parts of the earth.

In the year 1029, a certain Icelander, named Gudlief, undertakes a voyage to Limerick, in Ireland. On his return home, he is driven out of his course by north-east winds, Heaven knows where. After drifting for many days to the westward, he at last falls in with land. On approaching the beach, a great crowd of people came down to meet the strangers, apparently with no friendly intentions. Shortly afterwards, a tall and venerable chieftain makes his appearance, and, to Gudlief's great astonishment, addresses him in Icelandic. Having entertained the weary mariners very honourably, and supplied them with provisions, the old man bids them speed back to Iceland, as it would be unsafe for them to remain where they were. His own name he refused to tell; but having learnt that Gudlief comes from the neighbourhood of Snaefell, he puts into his hands a sword and a ring. The ring is to be given to Thured of Froda; the sword to her son Kjartan. When Gudlief asks by whom he is to say the gifts are sent, the ancient chieftain answers, "Say they come from one who was a better friend of the Lady of

Froda than of her brother Snorre of Helgafell." Wherefore it is conjectured that this man was Bjorn, the son of Astrand, Champion of Breidavik.

After this, Madam, I hope I shall never hear you depreciate the constancy of men. Thured had better have married Bjorn after all!

I forgot to mention that when Gudlief landed on the strange coast, it seemed to him that the inhabitants spoke Irish. Now, there are many antiquaries inclined to believe in the former existence of an Irish colony to the southward of the Vinland of the Northmen. Scattered through the Sagas are several notices of a distant country in the West, which is called Ireland ed Mekla—Great Ireland, or the White Man's land. When Pizarro penetrated into the heart of Mexico, a tradition already existed of the previous arrival of white men from the East. Among the Shawnasee Indians a story is still preserved of Florida having been once inhabited by white men, who used iron instruments. In 1658, Sir Erland the Priest had in his possession a chart, even then thought ancient, of "The Land of the White Men, or Hibernia Major, situated opposite Vinland the Good;" and Gaelic philologists pretend to trace a remarkable affinity between many of the American-Indian dialects and the ancient Celtic.

But to return to the "*Foam.*" After passing the cape, away we went across the spacious Brieda Fiord, at the rate of nine or ten knots an hour, reeling and bounding at the heels of the steamer, which seemed scarcely to feel how uneven was the surface across which we were speeding. Down dropped Snaefell beneath the sea, and dim before us, clad in evening haze, rose the shadowy steeps of Bardestrand. The north-west division of Iceland consists of one huge peninsula, spread out upon the sea like a human hand, the fingers just reaching over the Arctic circle; while up between them run the gloomy fiords, sometimes to the length of twenty, thirty, and even forty miles. Anything more grand and mysterious than the appearance of their solemn portals, as we passed across from bluff to bluff, it is impossible to conceive. Each might have served as a separate entrance to some poet's hell—so drear and fatal seemed the vista one's eye just caught receding between the endless ranks of precipice and pyramid.

There is something, moreover, particularly mystical in the effect of the grey, dreamy atmosphere of an arctic night, through whose uncertain medium mountain and headland loom as impalpable as the frontiers of a demon world ; and as I kept gazing at the glimmering peaks, and monstrous crags, and shattered stratifications, heaped up along the coast in cyclopean disorder, I understood how natural it was that the Scandinavian mythology, of whose mysteries the Icelanders were ever the natural guardians and interpreters, should have assumed that broad, massive simplicity which is its most beautiful characteristic. Amid the rugged features of such a country the refinements of Paganism would have been dwarfed into insignificance. How out of place would seem a Jove with his beard in ringlets—a trim Apollo—a sleek Bacchus—an ambrosial Venus—a slim Diana, and all their attendant groups of Oreads and Cupids—amid the ocean mists, and icebound torrents, the flame-scarred mountains, and four months' night—of a land which the opposing forces of heat and cold have selected for a battle-field !

The undeveloped reasoning faculty is prone to attach an undue value and meaning to the forms of things, and the infancy of a nation's mind is always more ready to worship the *manifestations* of a Power, than to look beyond them for a cause. Was it not natural then that these northerns, dwelling in daily communion with this grand Nature, should fancy they could perceive a mysterious and independent energy in her operations ; and at last come to confound the moral contest man feels within him, with the physical strife he finds around him ; to see in the returning sun—fostering into renewed existence the winter-stifled world—even more than a *type* of that spiritual consciousness which alone can make the dead heart stir ; to discover even more than an *analogy* between the reign of cold, darkness, and desolation, and the still blanker ruin of a sin-perverted soul? But in that iron clime, amid such awful associations, the conflict going on was too terrible—the contending powers too visibly in presence of each other, for the practical, conscientious Norse mind to be content with the puny godships of a Roman Olympus. Nectar, Sensuality, and Inextinguishable Laughter were elements of felicity too mean for the nobler atmosphere of their Walhalla; and to those active temperaments and healthy minds,—invigorated and solemnized by the massive mould of the scenery around them,—Strength, Courage, Endurance, and above all Self-sacrifice—naturally seemed more essential attributes of divinity than mere elegance and beauty. And we must remember that whilst the vigorous imagination of the north was delighting itself in creating a stately dreamland, where it strove to blend, in a grand world-picture—always harmonious, though not always consistent—the influences which sustain both the physical and moral system of its universe, an undercurrent of sober Gothic common sense induced it—as a kind of protest against the too material interpretation of the symbolism it had employed—to wind up its religious scheme by sweeping into the chaos of oblivion all the glorious fabric it had evoked, and proclaiming—in the place of the transient gods and perishable heaven of its Asgaard—that One undivided Deity, at whose approach the pillars of Walhalla were to fall, and Odin and his peers to perish, with all the subtle machinery of their existence; while man—himself immortal—was summoned to receive at the hands of the Eternal All-Father the sentence that waited upon his deeds. It is true this purer system belonged only to the early ages. As in the case of every false religion, the symbolism of the Scandinavian mythology lost with each succeeding generation something of its transparency, and at last degenerated into a gross superstition. But traces still remained, even down to the times of Christian ascendency, of the deep, philosophical spirit in which it had been originally conceived; and through its homely imagery there ran a vein of tender humour, such as still characterises the warm-hearted, laughter-loving northern races. Of this mixture of philosophy and fun, the following story is no bad specimen.[1]

Once on a time the two Œsir, Thor, the Thunder god, and his brother Lopt, attended by a servant, determined to go eastward to Jotunheim, the land of the giants, in search of adventures. Crossing over a great water, they came to a desolate plain, at whose further end, tossing and waving in the wind, rose the tree tops of a great forest. After journeying for many hours along its dusty labyrinths, they began to be anxious about a resting-place for the night. "At last, Lopt perceived a very spacious house, on one side of which was an entrance as wide as the house itself; and there they took up their night-quarters. At midnight they perceived a great earthquake; the ground reeled under them and the house shook.

"Then up rose Thor and called to his companions. They sought about, and found a side building to the right, into which they went. Thor placed himself at the door; the rest went and sat down further in, and were very much afraid.

"Thor kept his hammer in his hand, ready to defend them. Then they heard a terrible noise and roaring. As it began to dawn, Thor went out, and saw a man lying in the wood not far from them; he was by no means small, and he slept and snored loudly. Then Thor understood what the noise was which they heard in the night. He buckled on his belt of power, by which he increased his divine strength. At the same instant the man awoke, and rose up. It is said that Thor was so much astonished that he did not dare to slay him with his hammer, but inquired his name. He called himself Skrymer. 'Thy name,' said he, 'I need not ask, for I know that thou art Asar-Thor. But what hast thou done with my glove?'

[1] The story of Thor's journey has been translated from the Edda both by the Howitts and Mr. Thorpe.

"Skrymer stooped and took up his glove, and Thor saw that it was the house in which they had passed the night, and that the out-building was the thumb."

Here follow incidents which do not differ widely from certain passages in the history of Jack the Giant Killer. Thor makes three several attempts to knock out the easy-going giant's brains during a slumber, in which he is represented as "snoring outrageously,"—and after each blow of the Thunder god's hammer, Skrymer merely wakes up—strokes his beard—and complains of feeling some trifling inconvenience, such as a dropped acorn on his head, a fallen leaf, or a little moss shaken from the boughs. Finally, he takes leave of them,—points out the way to Utgard Loke's palace, advises them not to give themselves airs at his court,—as unbecoming "such little fellows" as they were, and disappears in the wood; "and"—as the old chronicler slyly adds—"it is not said whether the Œsir wished ever to see him again."

They then journey on till noon; till they come to a vast palace, where a multitude of men, of whom the greater number were immensely large, sat on two benches. "After this they advanced into the presence of the king, Utgard Loke, and saluted him. He scarcely deigned to give a look, and said smiling: 'It is late to inquire after true tidings from a great distance; but is it not Thor that I see? Yet you are really bigger than I imagined. What are the exploits that you can perform? For no one is tolerated amongst us who cannot distinguish himself by some art or accomplishment.'

"'Then,' said Lopt, 'I understand an art of which I am prepared to give proof; and that is, that no one here can dispose of his food as I can.' Then answered Utgard Loke: 'Truly this *is* an art, if thou canst achieve it; which we will now see.' He called from the bench a man named Loge to contend with Lopt. They set a trough in the middle of the hall, filled with meat. Lopt placed himself at one end and Loge at the other. Both ate the best they could, and they met in the middle of the trough. Lopt had picked the meat from the bones, but Loge had eaten meat, bones, and trough altogether. All agreed Lopt was beaten. Then asked Utgard Loke what art the young man (Thor's attendant) understood? Thjalfe answered, that he would run a race with any one that Utgard Loke would appoint. There was a very good race ground on a level field. Utgard Loke called a young man named Huge, and bade him run with Thjalfe. Thjalfe runs his best, at three several attempts—according to received Saga customs,—but is of course beaten in the race.

" Then asked Utgard Loke of Thor, what were the feats that he would attempt corresponding to the fame that went abroad of him? Thor answered that he thought he could beat any one at drinking. Utgard Loke said, 'Very good;' and bade his cup-bearer bring out the horn from which his courtiers were accustomed to drink. Immediately appeared the cup-bearer, and placed the horn in Thor's hand. Utgard Loke then said, 'that to empty that horn at one pull was well done; some drained it at twice; but that he was a wretched drinker who could not finish it at the third draught.' Thor looked at the horn, and thought that it was not large, though it was tolerably long. He was very thirsty, lifted it to his mouth, and was very happy at the thought of so good a draught. When he could drink no more, he took the horn from his mouth, and saw, to his astonishment, that there was little less in it than before. Utgard Loke said: 'Well hast thou drunk, yet not much. I should never have believed but that Asar-Thor could have drunk more; however, of this I am confident, thou wilt empty it at the second time.' He drank again; but when he took away the horn from his mouth, it seemed to him that it had sunk less this time than the first; yet the horn might now be carried without spilling.

"Then said Utgard Loke : ' How is this, Thor? If thou dost not reserve thyself purposely for the third draught, thine honour must be lost; how canst thou be regarded as a great man, as the Œsir look upon thee, if thou dost not distinguish thyself in other ways more than thou hast done in this?'

"Then was Thor angry, put the horn to his mouth, drank with all his might, and strained himself to the utmost; and when he looked into the horn it was now somewhat lessened. He gave up the horn, and would not drink any more. 'Now,' said Utgard Loke, 'now is it clear that thy strength is not so great as we supposed. Wilt thou try some other game, for we see that thou canst not succeed in this?' Thor answered: 'I will now try something else; but I wonder who, amongst the Œsir, would call that a little drink! What play will you propose?'

"Utgard Loke answered: 'Young men think it mere play to lift my cat from the ground; and I would never have proposed this to Œsir Thor, if I did not perceive that thou art a much less man than I had thought thee.' Thereupon sprang an uncommonly great grey cat upon the floor. Thor advanced, took the cat round the body, and lifted it up. The cat bent its back in the same degree as Thor lifted; and when Thor had lifted one of its feet from the ground, and was not able to lift it any higher, said Utgard Loke: 'The game has terminated just as I expected. The cat is very great, and Thor is low and small, compared with the great men who are here with us.'

"Then said Thor: 'Little as you call me, I challenge any one to wrestle with me, for now I am angry.' Utgard Loke answered, looking round upon the benches: 'I see no one here who would not deem it play to wrestle with thee: but let us call hither the old Ella, my nurse; with her shall Thor prove his strength, if he will. She has given many one a fall who appeared far stronger than Thor is.' On this there entered the hall an old woman; and Utgard Loke said she would wrestle with Thor. In short, the contest went so, that the more Thor exerted himself, the firmer she stood; and now began the old woman to exert herself, and Thor to give way, and severe struggles followed. It was not long before Thor was brought down on one knee. Then Utgard Loke stepped forward, bade them cease the struggle, and said that Thor should attempt nothing more at his court. It was now drawing towards night; Utgard Loke showed Thor and his companions their lodging, where they were well accommodated.

"As soon as it was light the next morning, up rose Thor and his companions, dressed themselves, and prepared to set out. Then came Utgard Loke, and ordered the table to be set, where there wanted no good provisions, either meat or drink. When they had breakfasted, they set out on their way. Utgard Loke accompanied them out of the castle; but at parting he asked Thor how the journey had gone off; whether he had found any man more mighty than himself? Thor answered, that the enterprise had brought him much dishonour, it was not to be denied, and that he must esteem himself a man of no account, which much mortified him.

"Utgard Loke replied: 'Now will I tell thee the truth, since thou art out of my castle, where, so long as I live and reign, thou shalt never re-enter; and whither, believe me, thou hadst never come if I had known before what might thou possessest, and that thou wouldst so nearly plunge us into great trouble. False appearances have I created for thee, so that the first time when thou mettest the man in the wood it was I; and when thou wouldst open the provision-sack, I had laced it together with an iron band, so that thou couldst not find the means to undo it. After that thou struckest at me three times with the hammer. The first stroke was the weakest, and it had been my death had it hit me. Thou sawest by my castle a rock, with three deep square holes, of which one was very deep: those were the marks of thy hammer. The rock I placed in the way of the blow, without thy perceiving it.

"'So also in the games, when thou contendedst with my courtiers. When Lopt made his essay, the fact was this: he was very hungry, and ate voraciously; but he who was called Loge, was *fire*, which consumed the trough as well as the meat. And Huge (mind) was my *thought* with which Thjalfe ran a race, and it was impossible for him to match it in speed. When thou drankest from the horn, and thoughtest that its contents grew no less, it was, notwithstanding, a great marvel, such as I never believed could have taken place. The one end of the horn stood in the sea, which thou didst not perceive; and when thou comest to the shore thou wilt see how much the ocean has diminished by what thou hast drunk. *Men will call it the ebb.*

"' Further,' said he, ' most remarkable did it seem to me that thou liftedst the cat, and in truth all became terrified when they saw that thou liftedst one of its feet from the ground. For it was no cat, as it seemed unto thee, but the great serpent that lies coiled round the world. Scarcely had he length that his tail and head might reach the earth, and thou liftedst him so high up that it was but a little way to heaven. That was a marvellous wrestling that thou wrestledst with Ella (old age), for never has there been any one, nor shall there ever be, let him approach what great age he will, that Ella shall not overcome.

"' Now we must part, and it is best for us on both sides that you do not often come to me; but if it should so happen, I shall defend my castle with such other arts that you shall not be able to effect anything against me.'

"When Thor heard this discourse he grasped his hammer and lifted it into the air, but as he was about to strike he saw Utgard Loke nowhere. Then he turned back to the castle to destroy it, and he saw only a beautiful and wide plain, but no castle."

So ends the story of Thor's journey to Jotunheim.

It was now just upon the stroke of midnight. Ever since leaving England, as each four-and-twenty hours we climbed up nearer to the pole, the belt of dusk dividing day from day had been growing narrower and narrower, until having nearly reached the Arctic circle, this,—the last night we were to traverse,—had dwindled to a thread of shadow.

Only another half-dozen leagues more, and we would stand on the threshold of a four months' day! For the few preceding hours clouds had completely covered the heavens, except where a clear interval of sky, that lay along the northern horizon, promised a glowing stage for the sun's last obsequies. But like the heroes of old he had veiled his face to die, and it was not until he dropped down to the sea that the whole hemisphere overflowed with glory and the gilded pageant concerted for his funeral gathered in slow procession round his grave; reminding one of those tardy honours paid to some great prince of song, who—left during life to languish in a garret—is buried by nobles in Westminster Abbey. A few minutes more the last fiery segment had disappeared beneath the purple horizon, and all was over.

"The king is dead—the king is dead—the king is dead! Long live the king!" And up from the sea that had just entombed his sire, rose the young monarch of a new day; while the courtier clouds, in their ruby robes, turned faces still aglow with the favours of their dead lord, to borrow brighter blazonry from the smile of a new master.

A fairer or a stranger spectacle than the last Arctic sunset cannot well be conceived: Evening and Morning—like kinsmen whose hearts some baseless feud has kept asunder—clasping hands across the shadow of the vanished night.

You must forgive me if sometimes I become a little magniloquent;—for really, amid the grandeur of that fresh primæval world, it was almost impossible to prevent one's imagination from absorbing a dash of the local colouring. We seemed to have suddenly waked up among the colossal scenery of Keats' Hyperion. The pulses of young Titans beat within our veins. Time itself,—no longer frittered down into paltry divisions,—had assumed a more majestic aspect. We had the appetite of giants—was it unnatural we should also adopt "the large utterance of the early gods?"

As the "*Reine Hortense*" could not carry coals sufficient

for the entire voyage we had set out upon, it had been arranged that the steamer "*Saxon*" should accompany her as a tender, and the Onunder Fiord, on the north-west coast of the island, had been appointed as the place of rendezvous. Suddenly wheeling round therefore to the right we quitted the open sea, and dived down a long grey lane of water that ran on as far as the eye could reach between two lofty ranges of porphyry and amygdaloid. The conformation of these mountains was most curious: it looked as if the whole district was the effect of some prodigious crystallization, so geometrical was the outline of each particular hill, sometimes rising cube-like, or pentagonal, but more generally built up into a perfect pyramid, with stairs mounting in equal gradations to the summit. Here and there the cone of the pyramid would be shaven off, leaving it flat-topped like a Babylonian altar or Mexican teocalli; and as the sun's level rays,—shooting across above our heads in golden rafters from ridge to ridge,—smote brighter on some loftier peak behind, you might almost fancy you beheld the blaze of sacrificial fires. The peculiar symmetrical appearance of these rocks arises from the fact of their being built up in layers of trap, alternating with Neptunian beds; the disintegrating action of snow and frost on the more exposed strata having gradually carved their sides into flights of terraces.

It is in these Neptunian beds that the famous surturbrand is found, a species of bituminous timber, black and shining like pitch coal; but whether belonging to the common carboniferous system, or formed from ancient drift-wood, is still a point of dispute among the learned. In this neighbourhood considerable quantities both of zerlite and chabasite are also found, but, generally speaking, Iceland is less rich in minerals than one would suppose; opal, calcedony, amethyst, malachite, obsidian, agate, and feldspar, being the principal. Of sulphur the supply is inexhaustible.

After steaming down for several hours between these terraced hills, we at last reached the extremity of the fiord, where we found the "*Saxon*" looking like a black sea-dragon coiled up at the bottom of his den. Up fluttered a signal to the mast-head of the corvette, and blowing off her steam, she wore round upon her heel, to watch the effects of her summons. As if roused by the challenge of an intruder, the sleepy monster seemed suddenly to bestir itself, and then pouring out volumes of sulphureous breath, set out with many an angry snort in pursuit of the rash troubler of its solitude. At least, such I am sure might have been the notion of the poor peasant inhabitants of two or three cottages I saw scattered here and there along the loch, as, startled from their sleep, they listened to the stertorous breathing of the long snake-like ships, and watched them glide past with magic motion along the glassy surface of the water. Of course the novelty and excitement of all we had been witnessing had put sleep and bedtime quite out of our thoughts : but it was already six o'clock in the morning ; it would require a considerable time to get out of the fiord, and in a few hours after we should be within the Arctic circle, so that if we were to have any sleep at all—now was the time. Acting on these considerations, we all three turned in ; and for the next half-dozen hours I lay dreaming of a great funeral among barren mountains, where white bears in peers' robes were the pall-bearers, and a sea-dragon chief-mourner. When we came on deck again, the northern extremity of Iceland lay leagues away on our starboard quarter, faintly swimming through the haze ; up overhead blazed the white sun, and below glittered the level sea, like a pale blue disc netted in silver lace. I seldom remember a brighter day; the thermometer was at 72°, and it really felt more as if we were crossing the line than entering the frigid zone.

Animated by that joyous inspiration which induces them to make a fête of everything, the French officers, it appeared, wished to organize a kind of carnival to inaugurate their arrival in Arctic waters, and by means of a piece of chalk and a huge black board displayed from the hurricane-deck of the "*Reine Hortense*," an inquiry was made as to what suggestion I might have to offer in furtherance of this laudable object. With that poverty of invention and love of spirits which characterise my nation, I am obliged to confess that, after deep reflection, I was only able to answer, "Grog." But seeing an extra flag or two was being run up at each masthead of the Frenchman, the lucky idea occurred to me to dress the "*Foam*" in all her colours. The schooner's toilette accomplished, I went on board the "*Reine Hortense*," and you cannot imagine anything more fragile, graceful, or coquettish, than her appearance from the deck of the corvette,—as she curtsied and swayed herself on the bosom of the almost imperceptible swell, or flirted up the water with her curving bows. She really looked like a living little lady.

But from all such complacent reveries I was soon awakened by the sound of a deep voice, proceeding apparently from the very bottom of the sea, which hailed the ship in the most authoritative manner, and imperiously demanded her name, where she was going, whom she carried, and whence she came: to all which questions, a young lieutenant, standing with his hat off at the gangway, politely responded. Apparently satisfied on these points, our invisible interlocutor then announced his intention of coming on board. All the officers of the ship collected on the poop to receive him.

In a few seconds more, amid the din of the most unearthly music, and surrounded by a bevy of hideous monsters, a white-bearded, spectacled personage—clad in bear-skin, with a cocked hat over his left ear—presented himself in the gangway, and handing to the officers of the watch an enormous board, on which was written

"LE PÈRE ARCTIQUE,"

by way of visiting card,—proceeded to walk aft, and take the sun's altitude with what, as far as I could make out, seemed to be a plumber's wooden triangle. This preliminary operation having been completed, there then began a regular riot all over the ship. The yards were suddenly manned with red devils, black monkeys, and every kind of grotesque monster, while the whole ship's company, officers and men promiscuously mingled, danced the cancan upon deck. In order that the warmth of the day should not make us forget that we had arrived in his dominions, the Arctic father had stationed certain of his familiars in the tops, who at stated intervals flung down showers of hard peas, as typical of *hail*, while the powdering of each other's faces with handfuls of flour could not fail to remind everybody on board that we had reached the latitude of *snow*. At the commencement of this noisy festival I found myself standing on the hurricane deck, next to one of the grave savants attached to the expedition, who seemed to contemplate the antics that were being played at his feet with that sad smile of indulgence with which Wisdom sometimes deigns to commiserate the gaiety of Folly. Suddenly he disappeared from beside me, and the next that I saw or heard of him—he was hard at work pirouetting on the deck below with a red-tailed demon, and exhibiting in his steps a "verve" and a graceful audacity which at Paris would have certainly obtained for him the honours of expulsion at the hands of the municipal authorities. The entertainment of the day concluded with a discourse delivered out of a wind-sail by the chaplain attached to the person of the Père Arctique, which was afterwards washed down by a cauldron full of grog, served out in bumpers to the several actors in this unwonted ceremonial. As the Prince had been good enough to invite us to dinner, instead of returning to the schooner I spent the intermediate hour in pacing the quarter-deck with Baron de la Roncière,—the naval commander entrusted with the charge of the expedition. Like all the smartest officers in the French navy, he speaks English beautifully, and I shall ever remember with gratitude the cordiality with which he welcomed me on board his ship, and the thoughtful consideration of his arrangements for the little schooner which he had taken in tow. At five o'clock dinner was announced, and I question if so sumptuous a banquet has ever been served up before in that outlandish part of the world, embellished as it was by selections from the best operas played by the *corps d'orchestre* which had accompanied the Prince from Paris. During the pauses of the music the conversation naturally turned on the strange lands we were about to visit, and the best mode of spifflicating the white bears who were probably already shaking in their snow shoes: but alas! while we were in the very act of exulting in our supremacy over these new domains, the stiffened finger of the Ice king was tracing in frozen characters a "Mene, mene, tekel upharsin" on the plate glass of the cabin windows. During the last half-hour the thermometer had been gradually falling, until it was nearly down to 32°; a dense penetrating fog enveloped both the vessels—(the "*Saxon*" had long since dropped out of sight), flakes of snow began floating slowly down, and a gelid breeze from the north-west told too plainly that we had reached the frontiers of the solid ice, though we were still a good hundred miles distant from the American shore. Although at any other time the terrible climate we had dived into would have been very depressing, under present circumstances I think the change rather tended to raise our spirits, perhaps because the idea of fog and ice in the month of June seemed so completely to uncockneyfy us. At all events there was no doubt now we had got into *les mers glaciales*, as our French friends called them, and, whatever else might be in store for us, there was sure henceforth to be no lack of novelty and excitement.

By this time it was already well on in the evening, so having agreed with Monsieur de la Roncière on a code of signals in case of fogs, and that a jack hoisted at the mizen of the "*Reine Hortense*," or at the fore of the schooner, should be an intimation of a desire of one or other to cast off, we got into the boat and were dropped down alongside our own ship. Ever since leaving Iceland the steamer had been heading east-north-east by compass, but during the whole of the ensuing night she shaped a south-east course; the thick mist rendering it unwise to stand on any longer in the direction of the *banquise*, as they call the outer edge of the belt that hems in Eastern Greenland. About three A.M. it cleared up a little. By breakfast time the sun re-appeared, and we could see five or six miles ahead of the vessel. It was shortly after this, that as I was standing in the main rigging peering out over the smooth blue surface of the sea, a white twinkling point of light suddenly caught my eye about a couple of miles off on the port bow, which a telescope soon resolved into a solitary isle of ice, dancing and dipping in the sunlight. As you may suppose, the news brought everybody upon deck; and when almost immediately afterwards a string of other pieces, glittering like a diamond necklace, hove in sight, the excitement was extreme.

Here at all events was honest blue salt water frozen solid, and when, as we proceeded, the scattered fragments thickened, and passed like silver argosies on either hand, until at last we found ourselves enveloped in an innumerable fleet of bergs,—it seemed as if we could never be weary of admiring a sight so strange and beautiful. It was rather in form and colour than in size that these ice islets were remarkable; anything approaching to a real iceberg we neither saw, nor are we likely to see. In fact, the lofty ice mountains that wander like vagrant islands along the coast of America, seldom or never come to the eastward or northward of Cape Farewell. They consist of land ice, and are all generated among bays and straits within Baffin's Bay, and first enter the Atlantic a good deal to the southward of Iceland; whereas the Polar ice, among which we have been knocking about, is field ice, and—except when packed one ledge above the other, by great pressure—is comparatively flat. I do not think I saw any pieces that were piled up higher than thirty or thirty-five feet above the sea-level, although at a little distance through the mist they may have loomed much loftier.

In quaintness of form, and in brilliancy of colours, these

wonderful masses surpassed everything I had imagined; and we found endless amusement in watching their fantastic procession.

At one time it was a knight on horseback, clad in sapphire mail, a white plume above his casque. Or a cathedral window with shafts of chrysophras, new powdered by a snow-storm. Or a smooth sheer cliff of lapis lazuli; or a Banyan tree, with roots descending from its branches, and a foliage as delicate as the efflorescence of molten metal; or a fairy dragon, that breasted the water in scales of emerald; or anything else that your fancy chose to conjure up. After a little time, the mist again descended on the scene, and dulled each glittering form to a shapeless mass of white; while in spite of all our endeavours to keep upon our northerly course, we were constantly compelled to turn and wind about in every direction—sometimes standing on for several hours at a stretch to the southward and eastward. These perpetual embarrassments became at length very wearying, and in order to relieve the tedium of our progress I requested the Doctor to remove one of my teeth. This he did with the greatest ability—a wrench to starboard,— another to port,—and up it flew through the cabin sky-light.

During the whole of that afternoon and the following night we made but little Northing at all, and the next day the ice seemed more pertinaciously in our way than ever; neither could we relieve the monotony of the hours by conversing with each other on the black boards, as the mist was too thick for us too distinguish from on board one ship anything that was passing on the deck of the other. Notwithstanding the great care and skill with which the steamer threaded her way among the loose floes, it was impossible sometimes to prevent fragments of ice striking us with considerable violence on the bows; and as we lay in bed at night, I confess that until we got accustomed to the noise, it was by no means a pleasant thing to hear the pieces angrily scraping along the ship's sides—within two inches of our ears. On the evening of the fourth day it came on to blow pretty hard, and at midnight it had freshened to half a gale; but by dint of standing well away to the eastward we had succeeded in reaching comparatively open water, and I had gone to bed in great hopes that at all events the breeze would brush off the fog, and enable us to see our way a little more clearly the next morning.

At five o'clock A.M. the officer of the watch jumped down into my cabin, and awoke me with the news—"That the Frenchman was a-saying summat on his black board!" Feeling by the motion that a very heavy sea must have been knocked up during the night, I began to be afraid that something must have gone wrong with the towing-gear, or that a hawser might have become entangled in the corvette's screw—which was the catastrophe of which I had always been most apprehensive; so slipping on a pair of fur boots, which I carefully kept by the bedside in case of an emergency, and throwing a cloak over—

"Le simple appareil
D'une beauté qu'on vient d'arracher au sommeil,"

I caught hold of a telescope, and tumbled up on deck. Anything more bitter and disagreeable than the icy blast, which caught me round the waist as I emerged from the companion I never remember. With both hands occupied in levelling the telescope, I could not keep the wind from blowing the loose wrap quite off my shoulders, and except for the name of the thing, I might just as well have been standing in my shirt. Indeed, I was so irresistibly struck with my own resemblance to a coloured print I remember in youthful days,—representing that celebrated character "Puss in Boots," with a purple robe of honour streaming far behind him on the wind, to express the velocity of his magical progress—that I laughed aloud while I shivered in the blast. What with the spray and mist, moreover, it was a good ten minutes before I could make out the writing, and when at last I did spell out the letters, their meaning was not very inspiriting: "*Nous retournons à Reykjavik!*"

So evidently they had given it up as a bad job, and had come to the conclusion that the island was inaccessible. Yet it seemed very hard to have to turn back, after coming so far! We had already made upwards of 300 miles since leaving Iceland: it could not be much above 120 or 130 more to Jan Mayen; and although things looked unpromising, there still seemed such a chance of success, that I could not find it in my heart to give in; so, having run up a jack at the fore—all writing on our board was out of the question, we were so deluged with spray—I jumped down to wake Fitzgerald and Sigurdr, and tell them we were going to cast off, in case they had any letters to send home. In the meantime, I scribbled a line of thanks and good wishes to M. de la Roncière, and another to you, and guyed it with our mails on board the corvette—in a milk can.

In the meantime all was bustle on board our decks, and I think every one was heartily pleased at the thoughts of getting the little schooner again under canvas. A couple of reefs were hauled down in the mainsail and staysail, and everything got ready for making sail.

"Is all clear for'ard for slipping, Mr. Wyse?"

"Ay, ay, Sir; all clear!"

"Let go the tow-ropes!"

"All gone, Sir!"

And down went the heavy hawsers into the sea, up fluttered the staysail,—then—poising for a moment on the waves with the startled hesitation of a bird suddenly set free,—the little creature spread her wings, thrice dipped her ensign in token of adieu—receiving in return a hearty cheer from the French crew—and glided like a phantom into the North, while the "*Reine Hortense*" puffed back to Iceland.[1]

[1] It subsequently appeared that the "*Saxon*," on the second day after leaving Onunder Fiord, had unfortunately knocked a hole in her bottom against the ice, and was obliged to run ashore in a sinking state. In consequence of never having been rejoined by her tender, the "*Reine*

Ten minutes more, and we were the only denizens of that misty sea. I confess I felt excessively sorry to have lost the society of such joyous companions; they had received us always with such merry good nature: the Prince had shown himself so gracious and considerate, and he was surrounded by a staff of such clever, well-informed persons, that it was with the deepest regret I watched the fog close round the magnificent corvette, and bury her—and all whom she contained—within its bosom. Our own situation, too, was not altogether without causing me a little anxiety. We had not seen the sun for two days; it was very thick, with a heavy sea, and dodging about as we had been among the ice, at the heels of the steamer, our dead reckoning was not very much to be depended upon. The best plan I thought would be to stretch away at once clear of the ice, then run up into the latitude of Jan Mayen, and—as soon as we should have reached the parallel of its northern extremity—bear down on the land. If there was any access at all to the island, it was very evident it would be on its northern or eastern side; and now that we were alone, to keep on knocking up through a hundred miles or so of ice in a thick fog, in our fragile schooner, would have been out of the question.

The ship's course, therefore, having been shaped in accordance with this view, I stole back into bed and resumed my violated slumbers. Towards mid-day the weather began to moderate, and by four o'clock we were skimming along on a smooth sea, with all sails set. This state of prosperity continued for the next twenty-four hours; we had made about eighty knots since parting company with the Frenchman, and it was now time to

---

Hortense" found herself short of coals; and as the encumbered state of the sea rendered it already very unlikely that any access would be found open to the island, M. de la Roncière very properly judged it advisable to turn back. He re-entered the Reykjavik harbour without so much as a shovelful of coals left on board.

run down West and pick up the land. Luckily the sky was pretty clear, and as we sailed on through open water I really began to think our prospects very brilliant. But about three o'clock on the second day, specks of ice began to flicker here and there on the horizon, then larger bulks came floating by in forms as picturesque as ever— (one, I particularly remember, a human hand thrust up out of the water with outstretched forefinger, as if to warn us against proceeding farther), until at last the whole sea became clouded with hummocks that seemed to gather on our path in magical multiplicity.

Up to this time we had seen nothing of the island, yet I knew we must be within a very few miles of it; and now, to make things quite pleasant, there descended upon us a thicker fog than I should have thought the atmosphere capable of sustaining; it seemed to hang in solid festoons from the masts and spars. To say that you could not see your hand, ceased almost to be any longer figurative; even the ice was hid—except those fragments immediately adjacent, whose ghastly brilliancy the mist itself could not quite extinguish, as they glimmered round the vessel like a circle of luminous phantoms. The perfect stillness of the sea and sky added very much to the solemnity of the scene; almost every breath of wind had fallen, scarcely a ripple tinkled against the copper sheathing, as the solitary little schooner glided along at the rate of half a knot or so an hour, and the only sound we heard was the distant wash of waters, but whether on a great shore, or along a belt of solid ice, it was impossible to say. In such weather,—as the original discoverers of Jan Mayen said under similar circumstances,—"it was easier to hear land than to see it." Thus, hour after hour passed by and brought no change. Fitz and Sigurdr—who had begun quite to disbelieve in the existence of the island—went to bed, while I remained pacing up and down the deck, anxiously questioning each quarter of the grey canopy that enveloped us. At last, about four in the morning, I fancied some change was going to take place; the heavy wreaths of vapour seemed to be imperceptibly separating, and in a few minutes more the solid roof of grey suddenly split asunder, and I beheld through the gap—thousands of feet overhead, as if suspended in the crystal sky—a cone of illuminated snow.

You can imagine my delight. It was really that of an anchorite catching a glimpse of the seventh heaven. There at last was the long-sought-for mountain actually tumbling down upon our heads. Columbus could not have been more pleased when, after nights of watching, he saw the first fires of a new hemisphere dance upon the water; nor, indeed, scarcely less disappointed at their sudden disappearance than I was, when, after having gone below to wake Sigurdr, and tell him we had seen bonâ fide terra-firma, I found, on returning upon deck, that the roof of mist had closed again, and shut out all trace of the transient vision. However, I had got a clutch of the island, and no slight matter should make me let go my hold. In the meantime there was nothing for it but to wait patiently until the curtain lifted; and no child ever stared more eagerly at a green drop-scene in expectation of "the realm of dazzling splendour" promised in the bill, than I did at the motionless grey folds that hung round us. At last the hour of liberation came: a purer light seemed gradually to penetrate the atmosphere, brown turned to grey, and grey to white, and white to transparent blue, until the lost horizon entirely reappeared, except where in one direction an impenetrable veil of haze still hung suspended from the zenith to the sea. Behind that veil I knew must lie Jan Mayen.

A few minutes more, and slowly, silently, in a manner you could take no count of, its dusky hem first deepened to a violet tinge, then gradually lifting, displayed a long line of coast—in reality but the roots of Beerenberg—dyed of the darkest purple; while, obedient to a common impulse, the clouds that wrapped its summit gently disengaged themselves, and left the mountain standing in all the magnificence of his

6,870 feet, girdled by a single zone of pearly vapour, from underneath whose floating folds seven enormous glaciers rolled down into the sea ! Nature seemed to have turned scene-shifter, so artfully were the phases of this glorious spectacle successively developed.

Although—by reason of our having hit upon its side instead of its narrow end—the outline of Mount Beerenberg appeared to us more like a sugar-loaf than a spire—broader at the base and rounder at the top than I had imagined,— in size, colour, and effect, it far surpassed anything I had anticipated. The glaciers were quite an unexpected element of beauty. Imagine a mighty river of as great a volume as the Thames—started down the side of a mountain,— bursting over every impediment,—whirled into a thousand eddies,—tumbling and raging on from ledge to ledge in quivering cataracts of foam,—then suddenly struck rigid by a power so instantaneous in its action, that even the froth and fleeting wreaths of spray have stiffened into the immutability of sculpture. Unless you had seen it, it would be almost impossible to conceive the strangeness of the contrast between the actual tranquillity of these silent crystal rivers and the violent descending energy impressed upon their exterior. You must remember, too, all this is upon a scale of such prodigious magnitude, that when we succeeded subsequently in approaching the spot—where with a leap like that of Niagara one of these glaciers plunges down into the sea—the eye, no longer able to take in its fluvial character, was content to rest in simple astonishment at what then appeared a lucent precipice of grey-green ice, rising to the height of several hundred feet above the masts of the vessel.

As soon as we had got a little over our first feelings of astonishment at the panorama thus suddenly revealed to us by the lifting of the fog, I began to consider what would be the best way of getting to the anchorage on the west—or Greenland side of the island. We were still seven or eight miles from the shore, and the northern extremity of the island, round which we should have to pass, lay about five

leagues off, bearing West by North, while between us and
the land stretched a continuous breadth of floating ice.
The hummocks, however, seemed to be pretty loose with
openings here and there, so that with careful sailing I thought
we might pass through, and perhaps on the farther side of
the island come into a freer sea. Alas! after having with
some difficulty wound along until we were almost abreast
of the cape, we were stopped dead short by a solid rampart
of fixed ice, which in one direction leant upon the land,
and in the other ran away as far as the eye could reach into
the dusky North. Thus hopelessly cut off from all access
to the western and better anchorage, it only remained to
put about, and—running down along the land—attempt to
reach a kind of open roadstead on the eastern side, a little
to the south of the volcano described by Dr. Scoresby:
but in this endeavour also we were doomed to be disappointed; for after sailing some considerable distance through
a field of ice, which kept getting more closely packed as
we pushed further into it, we came upon another barrier
equally impenetrable, that stretched away from the island
toward the Southward and Eastward. Under these circumstances, the only thing to be done was to get back to
where the ice was looser, and attempt a landing wherever
a favourable opening presented itself. But even to extricate
ourselves from our present position, was now no longer of
such easy performance. Within the last hour the wind had
shifted into the North-West; that is to say, it was now blowing right down the path along which we had picked our
way; in order to return, therefore, it would be necessary
to work the ship to windward through a sea as thickly
crammed with ice as a lady's boudoir is with furniture.
Moreover, it had become evident, from the obvious closing
of the open spaces, that some considerable pressure was
acting upon the outside of the field; but whether originating
in a current or the change of wind, or another field being
driven down upon it, I could not tell. Be that as it might,
out we must get,—unless we wanted to be cracked like a

walnut-shell between the drifting ice and the solid belt to
leeward; so sending a steady hand to the helm,—for these
unusual phenomena had begun to make some of my people
lose their heads a little, no one on board having ever seen a
bit of ice before,—I stationed myself in the bows, while Mr.
Wyse conned the vessel from the square yard. Then there
began one of the prettiest and most exciting pieces of nau-
tical manœuvring that can be imagined. Every single soul
on board was summoned upon deck; to all, their several
stations and duties were assigned—always excepting the
cook, who was merely directed to make himself generally
useful. As soon as everybody was ready, down went the
helm,—about came the ship,—and the critical part of the
business commenced. Of course, in order to wind and
twist the schooner in and out among the devious channels
left between the hummocks, it was necessary she should
have considerable way on her; at the same time so narrow
were some of the passages, and so sharp their turnings, that
unless she had been the most handy vessel in the world, she
would have had a very narrow squeak for it. I never saw
anything so beautiful as her behaviour. Had she been a
living creature, she could not have dodged, and wound, and
doubled, with more conscious cunning and dexterity; and
it was quite amusing to hear the endearing way in which the
people spoke to her, each time the nimble creature contrived
to elude some more than usually threatening tongue of ice.
Once or twice, in spite of all our exertions, it was impossible to save her from a collision; all that remained to be
done, as soon as it became evident she could not clear some
particular floe, or go about in time to avoid it, was to haul
the staysail sheet a-weather in order to deaden her way as
much as possible, and—putting the helm down—let her go
right at it, so that she should receive the blow on her stem,
and not on the bluff of the bow; while all hands, armed
with spars and fenders, rushed forward to ease off the shock.
And here I feel it just to pay a tribute of admiration to the
cook, who on these occasions never failed to exhibit an im-

mense amount of misdirected energy, breaking—I remember—at the same moment, both the cabin sky-light, and an oar, in single combat with a large berg that was doing no particular harm to us, but against which he seemed suddenly to have conceived a violent spite. Luckily a considerable quantity of snow overlaid the ice, which, acting as a buffer, in some measure mitigated the violence of the concussion; while the very fragility of her build diminishing the momentum, proved in the end the little schooner's greatest security. Nevertheless, I must confess that more than once, while leaning forward in expectation of the *scrunch* I knew must come, I have caught myself half murmuring to the fair face that seemed to gaze so serenely at the cold white mass we were approaching: " O Lady, is it not now fit thou shouldest befriend the good ship of which thou art the pride ? "

At last, after having received two or three pretty severe bumps,—though the loss of a little copper was the only damage they entailed,—we made our way back to the northern end of the island, where the pack was looser, and we had at all events a little more breathing room.

It had become very cold;—so cold, indeed, that Mr. Wyse—no longer able to keep a clutch of the rigging—had a severe tumble from the yard on which he was standing. The wind was freshening, and the ice was evidently still in motion ; but although very anxious to get back again into open water, we thought it would not do to go away without landing, even if it were only for an hour. So having laid the schooner right under the cliff, and putting into the gig our own discarded figure-head, a white ensign, a flag-staff, and a tin biscuit-box, containing a paper on which I had hastily written the schooner's name, the date of her arrival, and the names of all those who sailed on board,—we pulled ashore. A ribbon of beach not more than fifteen yards wide, composed of iron-sand, augite, and pyroxene, running along under the basaltic precipice—upwards of a thousand feet high—which serves as a kind of plinth to the mountain, was the only standing room this part of the coast afforded.

With considerable difficulty, and after a good hour's climb, we succeeded in dragging the figure-head we had brought ashore with us, up a sloping patch of snow, which lay in a crevice of the cliff, and thence a little higher, to a natural pedestal formed by a broken shaft of rock ; where —after having tied the tin box round her neck, and duly planted the white ensign of St. George beside her,—we left the superseded damsel, somewhat grimly smiling across the frozen ocean at her feet, until some Bacchus of a bear should come to relieve the loneliness of my wooden Ariadne.

On descending to the water's edge, we walked some little distance along the beach without observing anything very remarkable, unless it were the network of vertical and horizontal dikes of basalt which shot in every direction through the scoriæ and conglomerate of which the cliff seemed to be composed. Innumerable sea-birds sat in the crevices and ledges of the uneven surface, or flew about us with such confiding curiosity, that by reaching out my hand I could touch their wings as they poised themselves in the air alongside. There was one old sober-sides with whom I passed a good ten minutes *tête-à-tête*, trying who could stare the other out of countenance.

It was now high time to be off. As soon then as we had collected some geological specimens, and duly christened the little cove, at the bottom of which we had landed. " Clandeboye Creek,"—we walked back to the gig. But— so rapidly was the ice drifting down upon the island,—we found it had already become doubtful whether we should not have to carry the boat over the patch which—during the couple of hours we had spent on shore—had almost cut her off from access to the water. If this was the case with the gig, it was very evident the quicker we got the schooner out to sea again the better. So immediately we returned on board, having first fired a gun in token of adieu to the desolate land we should never again set foot on, the ship was put about, and our task of working out towards the open water recommenced. As this operation was likely to require some time, directly breakfast was over, (it was now about eleven o'clock A.M.,) and after a vain attempt had been made to take a photograph of the mountain, which the mist was again beginning to envelope, I turned in to take a nap, which I rather needed,—fully expecting that by the time I awoke we should be beginning to get pretty clear of the pack. On coming on deck, however, four hours later, although we had reached away a considerable distance from the land, and had even passed the spot, where, the day before, the sea was almost free,—the floes seemed closer than ever; and, what was worse, from the mast-head not a vestige of open water was to be discovered. On every side, as far as the eye could reach, there stretched over the sea one cold white canopy of ice.

The prospect of being beset, in so slightly built a craft, was—to say the least—unpleasant; it looked very much as if fresh packs were driving down upon us from the very direction in which we were trying to push out, yet it had become a matter of doubt which course it would be best to steer. To remain stationary was out of the question; the pace at which the fields drift is sometimes very rapid,[1] and the first nip would settle the poor little schooner's business for ever. At the same time, it was quite possible that any progress we succeeded in making, instead of tending towards her liberation, might perhaps be only getting her deeper

---

[1] Dr. Scoresby states that the invariable tendency of fields of ice is to drift south-westward, and that the strange effects produced by their occasional rapid motions, is one of the most striking objects the Polar Seas present, and certainly the most terrific. They frequently acquire a rotary motion, whereby their circumference attains a velocity of several miles an hour; and it is scarcely possible to conceive the consequences produced by a body, exceeding ten thousand million tons in weight, coming in contact with another under such circumstances. The strongest ship is but an insignificant impediment between two fields in motion. Numbers of whale vessels have thus been destroyed; some have been thrown upon the ice; some have had their hulls completely torn open, or divided in two, and others have been overrun by the ice, and buried beneath its heaped fragments.

into the scrape. One thing was very certain,—Northing or Southing might be an even chance, but whatever *Easting* we could make must be to the good ; so I determined to choose whichever vein seemed to have most Easterly direction in it. Two or three openings of this sort from time to time presented themselves ; but in every case, after following them a certain distance, they proved to be but *cul-de-sacs*, and we had to return discomfited. My great hope was in a change of wind. It was already blowing very fresh from the northward and eastward ; and if it would but shift a few points, in all probability the ice would loosen as rapidly as it had collected. In the meantime, the only thing to do was to keep a sharp look-out, sail the vessel carefully, and take advantage of every chance of getting to the eastward.

It now grew colder than ever,—the distant land was almost hid with fog,—tattered dingy clouds came crowding over the heavens,—while Wilson moved uneasily about the deck, with the air of Cassandra at the conflagration of Troy. It was Sunday, the 14th of July, and I had a momentary fancy that I could hear the sweet church bells in England pealing across the cold white flats which surrounded us. At last, about five o'clock P.M., the wind shifted a point or two, then flew round into the south-east. Not long after, just as I had expected, the ice evidently began to loosen,—a promising opening was reported from the mast-head a mile or so away on the port-bow, and by nine o'clock we were spanking along, at the rate of eight knots an hour, under a double-reefed mainsail and staysail—down a continually widening channel, between two wave-lashed ridges of drift ice. Before midnight, we had regained the open sea, and were standing away

> "to Norroway,
> To Norroway, over the faem."

In the forenoon I had been too busy to have our usual Sunday church ; but as soon as we were pretty clear of the ice I managed to have a short service in the cabin.

Of our run to Hammerfest I have nothing particular to say. The distance is eight hundred miles, and we did it in eight days. On the whole, the weather was pretty fair, though cold, and often foggy. One day indeed was perfectly lovely,—the one before we made the coast of Lapland, —without a cloud to be seen for the space of twenty-four hours; giving me an opportunity of watching the sun performing his complete circle overhead, and taking a meridian altitude at midnight. We were then in 70° 25′ North latitude; *i.e.*, almost as far north as the North Cape; yet the thermometer had been up to 80° during the afternoon.

Shortly afterwards the fog came on again, and next morning it was blowing very hard from the eastward. This was the more disagreeable, as it is always very difficult, under the most favourable circumstances, to find one's way into any harbour along this coast, fenced off, as it is, from the ocean by a complicated outwork of lofty islands, which, in their turn, are hemmed in by nests of sunken rock, sown as thick as peas, for miles to seaward. There are no pilots until you are within the islands, and no longer want them,—no lighthouses or beacons of any sort; and all that you have to go by is the shape of the hill-tops; but as, on the clearest day, the outlines of the mountains have about as much variety as

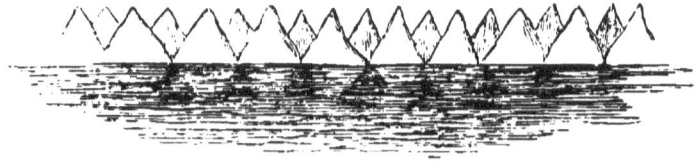

the teeth of a saw, and as on a cloudy day, which happens about seven times a week, you see nothing but the line of their dark roots,—the unfortunate mariner, who goes poking about for the narrow passage which is to lead him between the islands,—at the *back* of one of which a pilot is waiting for him,—will, in all probability, have already placed his vessel in a position to render that functionary's further attendance a work of supererogation. At least, I know it

TAKING A SIGHT

was as much surprise as pleasure that I experienced, when, after having with many misgivings ventured to slip through an opening in the monotonous barricade of mountains, we

found it was the right channel to our port. If the king of all the Goths would only stick up a lighthouse here and there along the edge of his Arctic seaboard, he would save many an honest fellow a heart-ache.

I must now finish this long letter.

Hammerfest is scarcely worthy of my wasting paper on it. When I tell you that it is the most northerly town in Europe, I think I have mentioned its only remarkable characteristic. It stands on the edge of an enormous sheet of water, completely landlocked by three islands, and consists of a congregation of wooden houses, plastered up against a steep mountain; some of which being built on piles, give the notion of the place having slipped down off the hill half-way into the sea. Its population is so and so,—its chief exports this and that; for all which, see Mr. Murray's "Handbook," where you will find all such matters much more clearly and correctly set down than I am likely to state them. At all events, it produces milk, cream—*not* butter—salad, and bad potatoes; which is what we are most interested in at present. To think that you should be all revelling this very moment in green-peas and cauliflowers! I hope you don't forget your grace before dinner.

I will write to you again before setting sail for Spitzbergen.

LETTER IX.

EXTRACT FROM THE "MONITEUR" OF THE 31ST JULY.

I HAVE received a copy of the "Moniteur" of the 31st July, containing so graphic an account of the voyage of the "*Reine Hortense*" towards Jan Mayen, and of the catastrophe to her tender the "*Saxon,*"—in consequence of which the corvette was compelled to abandon her voyage to the Northward,—that I must forward it to you.

(*Translation.*)

"*Voyage of Discovery along the Banquise, north of Iceland,* by ' LA REINE HORTENSE.'

"It fell to the lot of an officer of the French navy, M. Jules de Blosseville, to attempt to explore those distant parts, and to shed an interest over them, both by his discoveries and by his tragical and premature end.

In the spring of 1833, on the breaking up of a frost, '*La Lilloise,*' under the command of that brave officer, succeeded in passing through the *Banquise,* nearly up to latitude 69°, and in surveying about thirty leagues of coast to the south of that latitude. After having returned to her anchorage off the coast of Iceland, he sailed again in July for a second attempt. From that time nothing has been heard of '*La Lilloise.*'

* * * * *

The following year the '*Bordelaise*' was sent to look for the '*Lilloise,*' but found the whole north of Iceland blocked up by ice-fields; and returned, having been stopped in the latitude of the North Cape.

* * * * *

As a voyage to the Danish colonies on the western coast of Greenland formed part of the scheme of our arctic navigation, we were aware at our departure from Paris, that it was our business to make ourselves well acquainted with the southern part of the ice-field, from Reykjavik to Cape Farewell. But while we were touching at Peterhead, the principal port for the fitting of vessels destined for the seal fishery, the Prince, and M. de la Roncière, Commander of '*La Reine Hortense*,' gathered—from conversations with the fishermen just returned from their spring expedition— some important information on the actual state of the ice. They learnt from them that navigation was completely free this year round the whole of Iceland; that the icefield resting on Jan Mayen Island, and surrounding it to a distance of about twenty leagues, extended down the south-west along the coast of Greenland, but without blocking up the channel which separates that coast from that of Iceland. These unhoped-for circumstances opened a new field to our explorations, by allowing us to survey all that part of the *Banquise* which extends to the north of Iceland, thus forming a continuation to the observations made by the '*Recherche*,' and to those which we ourselves intended to make during our voyage to Greenland. The temptation was too great for the Prince; and Commander de la Roncière was not a man to allow an opportunity to escape for executing a project which presented itself to him with the character of daring and novelty.

But the difficulties of the enterprise were serious, and of such a nature that no one but a sailor experienced in navigation is capable of appreciating. The '*Reine Hortense*' is a charming pleasure-boat, but she offers very few of the requisites for a long voyage, and she was destitute of all the special equipment indispensable for a long sojourn in the ice. There was room but for six days' coals, and for three weeks' water. As to the sails, one may say the masts of the corvette are merely for show, and that without steam it would be impossible to reckon on her making any way regularly and uninterruptedly. Add to this, that she is built of iron,—that is to say, an iron sheet of about two centimètres thick constitutes all her planking,—and that her deck—divided into twelve great panels, is so weak that it has been thought incapable of carrying guns proportioned to her tonnage. Those who have seen the massive vessels of the fishermen of Peterhead, their enormous outside planking, their bracings and fastenings in wood and in iron, and their internal knees and stancheons, may form an idea from such precautions—imposed by long experience of the nature of the dangers that the shock—or even the pressure of the ice—may cause to a ship in the latitudes that we were going to explore.

* * * * *

The '*Cocyte*' had also been placed at the disposal of H.I.H. Prince Napoleon. This vessel which arrived at Reykjavik the same day that we did, the 30th of June—is a steam schooner, with paddles, standing the sea well, carying coals for twelve days, but with a deplorably slow rate of speed.

We found besides at Reykjavik the war transport '*La Perdrix*' and two English merchant steamers, the '*Tasmania* and the '*Saxon*,' freighted by the Admiralty to take to Iceland coals necessary for our voyage to Greenland. These five vessels, with the frigate '*Artemise*,' which performed he duties of guardship, formed the largest squadron which had ever assembled in the harbour of the capital of Iceland.

Unfortunately, these varied and numerous elements had nothing in common, and Commodore de la Roncière soon saw that extraneous help would afford us no additional security; and, in short, that the '*Reine Hortense*'— obliged to go fast—as her short supplies would not allow long voyages, had to reckon on herself alone. However, the [English] captain of the '*Saxon*' expressing a great desire to visit these northern parts, and displaying on this subject a sort of national vanity, besides promising an average speed of seven knots an hour, it was decided that—at all events, that vessel should start alone with the *Reine Hortense*,' whose

supply of coals it would be able to replenish, in the event—
a doubtful one, it is true—of our making the coast of Jan
Mayen's Island, and finding a good anchorage. The '*Reine
Hortense*' had—by the help of a supplementary load on deck
—a supply of coals for eight days; and immediately on starting, the crew as well as the passengers, were to be put on a
measured allowance of water.

A few hours before getting under way, the expedition
was completed by the junction of a new companion, quite
unexpected. We found in Reykjavik harbour a yacht belonging to Lord Dufferin. The Prince, seeing his great
desire to visit the neighbourhood of Jan Mayen, offered to
take his schooner in tow of the '*Reine Hortense.*' It was a
fortunate accident for a seeker of maritime adventures; and
an hour afterwards, the proposition having been eagerly
accepted, the Englishman was attached by two long cables
to the stern of our corvette.

On the 7th of July, 1856, at two o'clock in the morning,
after a ball given by Commander de Mas on board the
'*Artemise*,'—the '*Reine Hortense,*' with the English schooner
in tow, left Reykjavik harbour, directing her course along
the west coast of Iceland, towards Onundarfiord, where we
were to join the '*Saxon*' which had left a few hours before
us. At nine o'clock, the three vessels, steering east-north-
east, doubled the point of Cape North. At noon our observation of the latitude placed us about 67°. We had just
crossed the Arctic circle. The temperature was that of a
fine spring day, 10° centigrade (50° Farenh.).

* * * * *

The '*Reine Hortense*' diminished her speed. A rope
thrown across one of the towing-ropes enabled Lord
Dufferin to haul one of his boats to our corvette. He
himself came to dine with us, and to be present at the
ceremony of crossing the polar circle. As to the '*Saxon*,'
M. de la Roncière perceived by this time that the worthy
Englishman had presumed too much on his power. The
'*Saxon*' was evidently incapable of following us. The

captain, therefore, made her a signal that she was to take her own course, to try and reach Jan Mayen; and if she could not succeed, to direct her course on Onundarfiord, and there to wait for us. The English vessel fell rapidly astern, her hull disappeared, then her sails, and in the evening every trace of her smoke had faded from the horizon.

*   *   *   *   *

In the evening, the temperature grew gradually colder; that of the water underwent a more rapid and significant change. At twelve at night it was only three degrees centig. (about 37° Fahr.). At that moment the vessel plunged into a bank of fog, the intensity of which we were enabled to ascertain, from the continuance of daylight in these latitudes at this time of the year. There are tokens that leave no room to doubt that we are approaching the solid ice. True enough :—at two o'clock in the morning the officer on watch sees close to the ship a herd of seals, inhabitants of the field ice. A few minutes later the fog clears up suddenly; a ray of sunshine gilds the surface of the sea, lighting up millions of patches of sparkling white, extending to the farthest limit of the horizon. These are the detached hummocks which precede and announce the field ice; they increase in size and in number as we proceed. At three o'clock in the afternoon we find ourselves in front of a large pack which blocks up the sea before us. We are obliged to change our course to extricate ourselves from the ice that surrounds us.

This is an evolution requiring on the part of the commander the greatest precision of eye, and a perfect knowledge of his ship. The '*Reine Hortense*,' going half speed, with all the officers and the crew on deck, glides along between the blocks of ice, some of which she seems almost to touch, and the smallest of which would sink her instantly if a collision took place. Another danger, which it is almost impossible to guard against, threatens a vessel in those trying moments. If a piece of ice gets under the screw, it will be inevitably smashed like glass, and the consequences of such an accident might be fatal.

The little English schooner follows us bravely; bounding in our track, and avoiding only by a constant watchfulness and incessant attention to the helm the icebergs that we have cleared.

But the difficulties of this navigation are nothing in clear weather, as compared to what they are in a fog. Then, notwithstanding the slowness of the speed, it requires as much luck as skill to avoid collisions. Thus it happened that after having escaped the ice a first time, and having steered E.N.E., we found ourselvess uddenly, towards two o'clock of that same day (the 9th), not further than a quarter of a mile from the field ice which the fog had hidden from us. . Generally speaking, the *Banquise* that we coasted along for three days, and that we traced with the greatest care for nearly a hundred leagues, presented to us an irregular line of margin, running from W.S.W. to E.N.E., and thrusting forward toward the south—capes and promontories of various sizes, and serrated like the teeth of a saw. Every time that we bore up for E.N.E., we soon found ourselves in one of the gulfs of ice formed by the indentations of the *Banquise*. It was only by steering to the S.W. that we got free from the floating icebergs, to resume our former course as soon as the sea was clear.

The further we advanced to the northward, the thicker became the fog and more intense the cold (two degrees centig. below zero); and snow whirled round in squalls of wind, and fell in large flakes on the deck. The ice began to present a new aspect, and to assume those fantastic and terrible forms and colours, which painters have made familiar to us. At one time it assumed the appearance of mountain-peaks covered with snow, furrowed with valleys of green and blue; more frequently they appeared like a wide flat plateau, as high as the ship's deck, against which the sea rolled with fury, hollowing its edges into gulfs, or breaking them into perpendicular cliffs or caverns, into which the sea rushed in clouds of foam.

We often passed close by a herd of seals, which—stretched

on these floating islands, followed the ship with a stupid and puzzled look. We were forcibly struck with the contrast between the fictitious world in which we lived on board the ship, and the terrible realities of nature that surrounded us. Lounging in an elegant saloon, at the corner of a clear and sparkling fire, amidst a thousand objects of the arts and luxuries of home, we might have believed that we had not changed our residence, or our habits, or our enjoyments. One of Strauss's waltzes, or Schubert's melodies—played on the piano by the band-master—completed the illusion; and yet we had only to rub off the thin incrustation of frozen vapour that covered the panes of the windows, to look out upon the gigantic and terrible forms of the icebergs dashed against each other by a black and broken sea, and the whole panorama of Polar nature, its awful risks, and its sinister splendours.

*   *   *   *   *

Meanwhile, we progressed but very slowly. On the 10th of July we were still far from the meridian of Jan Mayen, when we suddenly found ourselves surrounded by a fog, and at the bottom of one of the bays formed by the field ice. We tacked immediately, and put the ship about, but the wind had accumulated the ice behind us. At a distance the circle that enclosed us seemed compact and without egress. We considered this as the most critical moment of our expedition. Having tried this icy barrier at several points, we found a narrow and tortuous channel, into which we ventured; and it was not till after an hour of anxieties that we got a view of the open sea, and of a passage into it. From this moment we were able to coast along the *Banquise* without interruption.

On the 11th of July at 6 A.M. we reached, at last, the meridian of Jan Mayen, at about eighteen leagues'[1] distance from the southern part of that island, but we saw the ice-field

---

[1] I think there must be some mistake here; when we parted company with the "*Reine Hortense,*" we were still upwards of 100 miles distant from the southern extremity of Jan Mayen.

stretching out before us as far as the eye could reach; hence it became evident that Jan Mayen was blocked up by the ice, at least along its south coast. To ascertain whether it might still be accessible from the north, it would have been necessary to have attempted a circuit to the eastward, the possible extent of which could not be estimated; moreover, we had consumed half our coals, and had lost all hope of being rejoined by the '*Saxon.*' Thus forced to give up any further attempts in that direction, Commodore de la Roncière, having got the ship clear of the floating ice, took a W.S.W. course, in the direction of Reykjavik.

The instant the '*Reine Hortense*' assumed this new course, a telegraphic signal—as had been previously arranged—acquainted Lord Dufferin with our determinations. Almost immediately, the young Lord sent on board us a tin box, with two letters, one for his mother, and one for our commander. In the latter he stated that—finding himself clear of the ice, and master of his own movements—he preferred continuing his voyage alone, uncertain whether he should at once push for Norway, or return to Scotland.[1] The two ropes that united the vessels were then cast off, a farewell hurrah was given, and in a moment the English schooner was lost in the fog.

Our return to Reykjavik afforded no incident worth notice; the '*Reine Hortense*,' keeping her course outside the ice, encountered no impediment, except from the intense fogs, which forced her—from the impossibility of ascertaining her position—to lie to, and anchor off the cape during part of the day and night of the 13th.

On the morning of the 14th, as we were getting out at the Dyre Fiord, where we had anchored, we met—to our great astonishment—the '*Cocyte*' proceeding northward. Her commander, Sonnart, informed us that on the evening of the 12th, the '*Saxon*'—in consequence of the injuries she had received, had been forced back to Reykjavik. She had

[1] I was purposely vague as to my plans, lest you might learn we still intended to go on.

hardly reached the ice on the 9th, when she came into collision with it; five of her timbers had been stove in, and an enormous leak had followed. Becoming water-logged, she was run ashore, the first time at Onundarfiord, and again in Reykjavik roads, whither she had been brought with the greatest difficulty."

LETTER X.

BUCOLICS—THE GOAT—MAID MARIAN—A LAPP LADY—LAPP LOVE-MAKING—THE SEA-HORSEMAN—THE GULF STREAM—ARCTIC CURRENTS—A DINGY EXPEDITION—A SCHOOL OF PERIPATETIC FISHES—ALTEN—THE CHÂTELAINE OF KAAFIORD—STILL NORTHWARD HO!

July 27th, Alten.

THIS letter ought to be an Eclogue, so pastoral a life have we been leading lately among these pleasant Nordland valleys. Perhaps it is only the unusual sight of meadows, trees and flowers, after the barren sea, and still more barren lands we have been accustomed to, that invests this neighbourhood with such a smiling character. Be that as it may, the change has been too grateful not to have made us seriously reflect on our condition; and we have at last determined that not even the envious ocean shall for the future cut us off from the pleasures of a shepherd life. Henceforth, the boatswain is no longer to be the only swain on board! We have purchased an ancient goat—a nanny-goat—so we may be able to go a-milking upon occasion. Mr. Webster, late of her Majesty's Foot-guards, carpenter, etc., takes brevet-rank as dairy-maid; and our venerable passenger is at this moment being inducted into a sumptuous barrel[1] which I have had fitted up for her reception abaft the binnacle. A spacious meadow of sweet-scented hay has been laid down in a neighbouring corner for her further accommodation; and the Doctor is tuning up his flageolet, in order to complete the bucolic character of the scene. The only personage amongst us at all disconcerted

[1] The cask in question was bought in order to be rigged up eventually into a crow's-nest, as soon as we should again find ourselves among the ice.

by these arrangements is the little white fox which has come with us from Iceland. Whether he considers the admission on board of so domestic an animal to be a reflection on his own wild Viking habits, I cannot say; but there is no impertinence—even to the nibbling of her beard when she is asleep —of which he is not guilty towards the poor old thing, who passes the greater part of her mornings in gravely butting at her irreverent tormentor.

But I must relate our last week's proceedings in a more orderly manner.

As soon as the anchor was let go in Hammerfest harbour, we went ashore; and having first ascertained that the existence of a post does not necessarily imply letters, we turned away, a little disappointed, to examine the metropolis of Finmark. A nearer inspection did not improve the impression its first appearance had made upon us; and the odour of rancid cod-liver oil, which seemed indiscriminately to proceed from every building in the town, including the church, has irretrievably confirmed us in our prejudices. Nevertheless, henceforth the place will have one redeeming association connected with it, which I am bound to mention. It was in the streets of Hammerfest that I first set eyes on a Laplander. Turning round the corner of one of the ill-built houses, we suddenly ran over a diminutive little personage in a white woollen tunic, bordered with red and yellow stripes, green trousers, fastened round the ankles, and reindeer boots, curving up at the toes like Turkish slippers. On her head— for notwithstanding the trousers, she turned out to be a lady —was perched a gay parti-coloured cap, fitting close round the face, and running up at the back into an overarching peak of red cloth. Within this peak was crammed—as I afterwards learnt—a piece of hollow wood, weighing about a quarter of a pound, into which is fitted the wearer's back hair; so that perhaps, after all, there *does* exist a more inconvenient *coiffure* than a Paris bonnet.

Hardly had we taken off our hats, and bowed a thousand apologies for our unintentional rudeness to the fair inhabitant

THE ICELANDIC FOX.

of the green trousers, before a couple of Lapp gentlemen
hove in sight. They were dressed pretty much like their
companion, except that an ordinary red night-cap replaced
the queer helmet worn by the lady; and the knife and
sporran fastened to their belts, instead of being suspended
in front as hers were, hung down against their hips. Their

A LAPP LADY.

tunics, too, may have been a trifle shorter. None of the three
were beautiful. High cheek-bones, short noses, oblique Mon-
gol eyes, no eyelashes, and enormous mouths, composed a
cast of features which their burnt-sienna complexion, and
hair like ill-got-in hay did not much enhance. The expression of their countenances was not unintelligent; and there
was a merry, half-timid, half-cunning twinkle in their eyes,

which reminded me a little of faces I had met with in the more neglected districts of Ireland. Some ethnologists, indeed, are inclined to reckon the Laplanders as a branch of the Celtic family. Others, again, maintain them to be Ugrians; while a few pretend to discover a relationship between the Lapp language and the dialects of the Australian savages, and similar outsiders of the human family; alleging that as successive stocks bubbled up from the central birthplace of

A LAPP LADY'S BONNET.

mankind in Asia, the earlier and inferior races were gradually driven outwards in concentric circles, like the rings produced by the throwing of a stone into a pond; and that consequently, those who dwell in the uttermost ends of the earth are, *ipso facto*, first cousins.

This relationship with the Polynesian Niggers, the native genealogists would probably scout with indignation, being perfectly persuaded of the extreme gentility of their descent. Their only knowledge of the patriarch Noah is as a personage who derives his principal claim to notoriety from having been the first Lapp. Their acquaintance with any sacred history—nay, with Christianity at all—is very limited. It was not until after the thirteenth century that an attempt was made to convert them; and although Charles the Fourth and Gustavus ordered portions of Scripture to be translated in Lappish, to this very day a great proportion of the race are pagans; and even the most illuminated amongst them remain slaves to the grossest superstition. When a couple is to be married, if a priest happens to be in the way, they will send for him perhaps out of complaisance; but otherwise, the young lady's papa merely strikes a flint and steel together, and the ceremony is not less irrevocably completed. When they die, a hatchet and a flint and steel are invariably buried with the defunct, in case he should find himself chilly on his long journey—an unnecessary precaution, many of the orthodox would consider, on the part of such lax religionists. When they go boar-hunting—the most important business in their lives—it is a sorcerer, with no other defence than his incantations, who marches at the head of the procession. In the internal arrangements of their tents, it is not a room to themselves, but a door to themselves, that they assign to their womankind; for woe betide the hunter if a woman has crossed the threshold over which he sallies to the chase; and for three days after the slaughter of his prey he must live apart from the female portion of his family in order to appease the evil deity whose familiar he is supposed to have destroyed. It would be endless to recount the innumerable occasions upon which the ancient rites of Jumala are still interpolated among the Christian observances they profess to have adopted.

Their manner of life I had scarcely any opportunities of observing. Our Consul kindly undertook to take us to one of their encampments; but they flit so often from place to place, it is very difficult to light upon them. Here and there, as we cruised about among the fiords, blue wreaths of smoke rising from some little green nook among the rocks would betray their temporary place of abode; but I never got a near view of a regular settlement.

In the summer-time they live in canvas tents: during winter, when the snow is on the ground, the forest Lapps build huts in the branches of trees, and so roost like birds. The principal tent is of an hexagonal form, with a fire in the centre, whose smoke rises through a hole in the roof. The gentlemen and ladies occupy different sides of the same apartment; but a long pole laid along the ground midway between them symbolizes an ideal partition, which I dare say is in the end as effectual a defence as lath and plaster prove in more civilized countries. At all events, the ladies have a doorway quite to themselves, which, doubtless, they consider a far greater privilege than the seclusion of a separate boudoir. Hunting and fishing are the principal employments of the Lapp tribes; and to slay a bear is the most honourable exploit a Lapp hero can achieve. The flesh of the slaughtered beast becomes the property—not of the man who killed him, but of him who discovered his trail, and the skin is hung up on a pole, for the wives of all who took part in the expedition to shoot at with their eyes bandaged. Fortunate is she whose arrow pierces the trophy,—not only does it become her prize, but, in the eyes of the whole settlement, her husband is looked upon thenceforth as the most fortunate of men. As long as the chase is going on, the women are not allowed to stir abroad ; but as soon as the party have safely brought home their booty, the whole female population issue from the tents, and having deliberately chewed some bark of a species of alder, they spit the red juice into their husband's faces, typifying thereby the bear's blood which has been shed in the honourable encounter.

Although the forests, the rivers, and the sea supply them in a great measure with their food, it is upon the reindeer that the Laplander is dependent for every other comfort in life. The reindeer is his estate, his horse, his cow, his companion, and friend. He has twenty-two different names for him. His coat, trousers, and shoes are made of reindeer's skin, stitched with thread manufactured from the nerves and sinews of the reindeer. Reindeer milk is the most important item in his diet. Out of reindeer horns are made almost all the utensils used in his domestic economy; and it is the reindeer that carries his baggage, and drags his sledge. But the beauty of this animal is by no means on a par with his various moral and physical endowments. His antlers, indeed, are magnificent, branching back to the length of three or four feet; but his body is poor, and his limbs thick and ungainly; neither is his pace quite so rapid as is generally supposed. The Laplanders count distances by the number of horizons they have traversed; and if a reindeer changes the horizon three times during the twenty-four hours, it is thought a good day's work. Moreover, so just an appreciation has the creature of what is due to his own great merit, that if his owner seeks to tax him beyond his strength, he not only becomes restive, but sometimes actually turns upon the inconsiderate Jehu who has over-driven him. When, therefore, a Lapp is in a great hurry, instead of taking to his sledge, he puts on a pair of skates exactly twice as long as his own body, and so flies on the wings of the wind.

Every Laplander, however poor, has his dozen or two dozen deer; and the flocks of a Lapp Crœsus amount sometimes to two thousand head. As soon as a young lady is born—after having been duly rolled in the snow—she is dowered by her father with a certain number of deer, which are immediately branded with her initials, and thenceforth kept apart as her especial property. In proportion as they increase and multiply does her chance improve of making a good match. Lapp courtships are conducted pretty much in the same fashion as in other parts of the world. The aspirant, as soon as he discovers that he has lost his heart, goes off in search of a friend and a bottle of brandy. The friend enters the tent, and opens simultaneously—the brandy—and his business; while the lover remains outside, engaged in hewing wood, or some other menial employment. If, after the brandy and the proposal have been duly discussed, the eloquence of his friend prevails, he is himself called into the conclave, and the young people are allowed to rub noses. The bride then accepts from her suitor a present of a reindeer's tongue, and the espousals are considered concluded. The marriage does not take place for two or three years afterwards; and during the interval the intended is obliged to labour in the service of his father-in-law, as diligently as Jacob served Laban for the sake of his long-loved Rachel.

I cannot better conclude this summary of what I have been able to learn about the honest Lapps, than by sending you the tourist's stock specimen of a Lapp love-ditty. The author is supposed to be hastening in his sledge towards the home of his adored one :—

"Hasten, Kulnasatz! my little reindeer! long is the way, and boundless are the marshes. Swift are we, and light of foot, and soon we shall have come to whither we are speeding. There shall I behold my fair one pacing. Kulnasatz, my reindeer, look forth! look around! Dost thou not see her somewhere—*bathing?*"

As soon as we had thoroughly looked over the Lapp lady and her companions, a process to which they submitted with the greatest complacency, we proceeded to inspect the other lions of the town; the church, the lazar-house,— principally occupied by Lapps,—the stock fish establishment, and the hotel. But a very few hours were sufficient to exhaust the pleasures of Hammerfest; so having bought an extra suit of jerseys for my people, and laid in a supply of other necessaries, likely to be useful in our cruise to Spitzbergen, we exchanged dinners with the Consul, a transaction by which, I fear, he got the worst of the bargain, and then got under way for this place,—Alten.

The very day we left Hammerfest our hopes of being able to get to Spitzbergen at all—received a tremendous shock. We had just sat down to dinner, and I was helping the Consul to fish, when in comes Wilson, his face, as usual, upside down, and hisses something into the Doctor's ear. Ever since the famous dialogue which had taken place between them on the subject of sea-sickness, Wilson had got to look upon Fitz as in some sort his legitimate prey; and whenever the burden of his own misgivings became greater than he could bear, it was to the Doctor that he unbosomed himself. On this occasion, I guessed, by the look of gloomy triumph in his eyes, that some great calamity had occurred, and it turned out that the following was the agreeable announcement he had been in such haste to make: "Do you know, Sir?"—This was always the preface to tidings unusually doleful. "No— what?" said the Doctor, breathless. "Oh nothing, Sir; only two sloops have just arrived, Sir, from Spitzbergen, Sir—where they couldn't get, Sir;—such a precious lot of ice —two hundred miles from the land—and, oh, Sir— they've come back with all their bows stove in!" Now, immediately on arriving at Hammerfest, my first care had been to inquire how the ice was lying this year to the northward, and I had certainly been told that the season was a very bad one, and that most of the sloops that go every summer to kill sea-horses (*i.e.*, walrus) at Spitzbergen, being unable to reach the land, had returned empty-handed; but as three weeks of better weather had intervened since their discomfiture, I had quite reassured myself with the hope, that in the meantime the advance of the season might have opened for us a passage to the island.

This news of Wilson's quite threw me on my back again. The only consolation was, that probably it was not true; so immediately after dinner we boarded the honest Sea-horseman who was reported to have brought the dismal intelligence. He turned out to be a very cheery intelligent fellow of about five-and-thirty, six feet high, with a dashing "devil-may-care" manner that completely imposed upon me. Charts were got out, and the whole state of the case laid before me in the clearest manner. Nothing could be more unpromising. The sloop had quitted the ice but eight-and-forty hours before making the Norway coast; she had not been able even to reach Bear Island. Two hundred miles of ice lay off the southern and western coast of Spitzbergen—(the eastern side is always blocked up with ice)—and then bent round in a continuous semicircle towards Jan Mayen. That they had not failed for want of exertion—the bows of his ships sufficiently testified. As to *our* getting there it was out of the question. So spake the Sea-horseman. On returning on board the "*Foam*" I gave myself up to the most gloomy reflections. This, then, was to be the result of all my preparations and long-meditated schemes. What likelihood was there of success, after so unfavourable a verdict? *Ipse dixit, equus marinus.* It is true the horse-marines have hitherto been considered a mythic corps, but my friend was too substantial-looking for me to doubt his existence: and unless I was to ride off on the proverbial credulity of the other branch of that amphibious profession, I had no reason to question his veracity. Nevertheless, I felt it would not become a gentleman to turn back at the first blush of discouragement. If it were possible to reach Spitzbergen, I was determined to do so. I reflected that every day that passed was telling in our favour. It was not yet the end of July; even in these latitudes winter does not commence much before September, and in the meantime the tail of the Gulf Stream would still be wearing a channel in the ice towards the pole; so, however unpromising might be the prospect, I determined, at all events, that we should go and see for ourselves how matters really stood.

But I must explain to you why I so counted upon the assistance of the Gulf Stream to help us through.

The entire configuration of the Arctic ice is determined by the action of that mysterious current on its edges. Several theories have been advanced to account for its influence in so remote a region. I give you one which appears to me reasonable. It is supposed, that in obedience to that great law of Nature which seeks to establish equilibrium in the temperature of fluids,—a vast body of gelid water is continually mounting from the Antarctic, to displace and regenerate the over-heated oceans of the torrid zone. Bounding up against the west side of South America, the ascending stream skirts the coasts of Chili and Peru, and is then deflected in a westerly direction across the Pacific Ocean, where it takes the name of the Equatorial Current. Having completely encircled Australia, it enters the Indian Sea, sweeps up round the Cape of Good Hope, and, crossing the Atlantic, twists into the Gulf of Mexico. Here its flagging energies are suddenly accelerated in consequence of the narrow limits within which it finds itself compressed. So marvellous does the velocity of the current now become, so complete its isolation from the deep sea bed it traverses, that by the time it issues again into the Atlantic, its hitherto diffused and loitering waters are suddenly concentrated into what Lieutenant Maury has happily called—"a river in the ocean," swifter and of greater volume than either the Mississippi or the Amazon. Surging forth between the interstices of the Bahamas, that stretch like a weir across its mouth, it cleaves asunder the Atlantic. So distinct is its individuality, that one side of a vessel will be scoured by its warm indigo-coloured water, while the other is floating in the pale, stagnant, weed-encumbered brine of the Mar de Sargasso of the Spaniards. It is not only by colour, by its temperature, by its motion, that this "$ρο\grave{η}$ '$Ωκεανοῖο$" is distinguished; its very surface is arched upwards some way above the ordinary sea-level toward the centre, by the lateral pressure of the elastic liquid banks between which it flows. Impregnated with the warmth of tropic climes, the Gulf Stream—as it has now come to be called,—then pours its genial floods across the North Atlantic, laving the western coasts of Britain, Ireland, and Norway, and investing each shore it strikes upon, with a climate far milder than that enjoyed by other lands situated in the same latitudes. Arrived abreast of the North Cape, the impetus of the current is in a great measure exhausted.

From causes similar (though of less efficacy, in consequence of the smaller area occupied by water) to those which originally gave birth to the ascending energy of the Antarctic waters, a gelid current is also generated in the Arctic Ocean, which, descending in a south-westerly direction, encounters the already faltering Gulf Stream in the space between Spitzbergen and Nova Zembla. A contest for the mastery ensues, which is eventually terminated by a compromise. The warmer stream, no longer quite able to hold its own, splits into two branches, the one squeezing itself round the North Cape, as far as that Varangar Fiord which Russia is supposed so much to covet, while the other is pushed up in a more northerly direction along the west coast of Spitzbergen. But although it has power to split up the Gulf Stream for a certain distance, the Arctic current is ultimately unable to cut across it, and the result is an accumulation of ice to the south of Spitzbergen in the angle formed by the bifurcation, as Mr. Grote would call it, of the warmer current.

It is quite possible, therefore, that the north-west extremity of Spitzbergen may be comparatively clear, while the whole of its southern coasts are enveloped in belts of ice of enormous extent. It was on this contingency that we built our hopes, and determined to prosecute our voyage, in spite of the discouraging report of the Norse skipper.

About eight o'clock in the evening we got under way from Hammerfest; unfortunately the wind almost immediately after fell dead calm, and during the whole night we lay "like a painted ship upon a painted ocean." At six o'clock a little breeze sprang up, and when we came on deck at breakfast time, the schooner was skimming at the rate of five knots an hour over the level lanes of water, which lie between the silver-grey ridges of gneiss and mica slate that hem in the Nordland shore. The distance from Hammerfest to Alten is about forty miles, along a zigzag chain of fiords. It was six o'clock in the evening, and we had already sailed two-and-thirty miles, when it again fell almost calm. Impatient at the unexpected delay, and tempted by the beauty of the evening,—which was indeed most lovely, the moon hanging on one side right opposite to the sun on the other, as in the picture of Joshua's miracle,—Sigurdr, in an evil hour, proposed that we should take a row in the dingy, until the midnight breeze should spring up, and bring the schooner along with it. Away we went, and so occupied did we become with admiring the rocky precipices beneath which we were gliding, that it was not until the white sails of the motionless schooner had dwindled to a speck, that we became aware of the distance we had come.

Our attention had been further diverted by the spectacle of a tribe of fishes, whose habit it appeared to be—instead of swimming like Christian fishes in a horizontal position beneath the water—to walk upon their hind-legs along its surface. Perceiving a little boat floating on the loch not far from the spot where we had observed this phenomenon, we pulled towards it, and ascertained that the Lapp officer in charge was actually intent on stalking the peripatetic *school*—to use a technical expression—whose evolutions had so much astonished us. The great object of the sportsman is to judge by their last appearance what part of the water the fish are likely to select for the scene of their next promenade. Directly he has determined this in his own mind, he rows noiselessly to the spot, and, as soon as they show themselves, hooks them with a landing-net into his boat.

By this time it had become a doubtful point whether it would not be as little trouble to row on to Alten as to return to the schooner, so we determined to go on. Unfortunately we turned down a wrong fiord, and after a long pull, about two o'clock in the morning had the satisfaction of finding ourselves in a *cul-de-sac*. To add to our discomfort, clouds of mosquitoes with the bodies of behemoths and the stings of dragons, had collected from all quarters of the heavens to make a prey of us. In vain we struggled—strove to knock them down with the oars,—plunged our heads under the water,—smacked our faces with frantic violence; on they came in myriads, until I thought our bleaching bones would alone remain to indicate our fate. At last Sigurdr espied a log hut on the shore, where we might at least find some one to put us into the right road again; but on looking in at the open door, we only saw a Lapland gentleman fast asleep. Awaking at our approach he started to his feet, and though nothing could be more gracefully conciliatory than the bow with which I opened the conversation, I regret to say that after staring wildly round for a few minutes, the aboriginal bolted straight away in the most unpolite manner and left us to our fate. There was nothing for it but patiently to turn back, and try some other opening. This time we were more successful, and about three o'clock A.M. had the satisfaction of landing at one of the wharves attached to the copper mines of Kaafiord. We came upon a lovely scene. It was as light and warm as a summer's noon in England; upon a broad plateau, carved by nature out of the side of the grey limestone, stood a bright shining house in the middle of a plot of rich English-looking garden. On one side lay the narrow fiord, on every other rose an amphitheatre of fir-clad mountains. The door of the house was open, so were many of the windows—even those on the ground-floor, and from the road where we stood we could see the books on the library shelves. A swing and some gymnastic appliances on the lawn told us that there were children. Altogether, I thought I had never seen such a charming picture of silent comfort and security. Perhaps the barren prospects we had been accustomed to made the little oasis before us look more cheerful than we might otherwise have thought it.

The question now arose, what was to be done? My principal reason for coming to Alten was to buy some salt provisions and Lapland dresses; but dolls and junk were scarcely a sufficient pretext for knocking up a quiet family at three o'clock in the morning. It is true, I happened to have a letter for Mr. T——, written by a mutual friend, who had expressly told me that—arrive when I might at

Alten,—the more unceremoniously I walked in and took possession of the first unoccupied bed I stumbled on, the better Mr. T—— would be pleased; but British punctilio would not allow me to act on the recommendation, though we were sorely tried. In the meantime the mosquitoes had become more intolerable than ever. At last, half mad with irritation, I set off straight up the side of the nearest mountain, in hopes of attaining a zone too high for them to inhabit; and, poising myself upon its topmost pinnacle, I drew my handkerchief over my head—I was already without coat and waistcoat—and remained the rest of the morning "mopping and mowing" at the world beneath my feet.

About six o'clock, like a phantom in a dream, the little schooner came stealing round the misty headland, and anchored at the foot of the rocks below. Returning immediately on board, we bathed, dressed, and found repose from all our troubles. Not long after, a message from Mr. T——, in answer to a card I had sent up to the house as soon as the household gave signs of being astir—invited us to breakfast; and about half-past nine we presented ourselves at his hospitable door. The reception I met with was exactly what the gentleman who had given me the letter of introduction had led me to expect; and so eager did Mr. T—— seem to make us comfortable, that I did not dare to tell him how we had been prowling about his house the greater part of the previous night, lest he should knock me down on the spot for not having knocked him up. The appearance of the inside of the house quite corresponded with what we had anticipated from the *soigné* air of everything about its exterior. Books, maps, pictures, a number of astronomical instruments, geological specimens, and a magnificent assortment of fishing-rods, betrayed the habits of the practical, well-educated, business-loving English gentleman who inhabited it; and as he showed me the various articles of interest in his study, most heartily did I congratulate myself on the lucky chance which had brought me into contact with so desirable an acquaintance.

All this time we had seen nothing of the lady of the house; and I was just beginning to speculate as to whether that crowning ornament could be wanting to this pleasant home, when the door at the further end of the room suddenly opened, and there glided out into the sunshine— "The White Lady of Avenel." A fairer apparition I have seldom seen,—stately, pale, and fragile as a lily—blond hair, that rippled round a forehead of ivory—a cheek of waxen purity on which the fitful colour went and came— not with the flush of southern blood, or flower-bloom of English beauty,—but rather with a cool radiance, as of "northern streamers" on the snows of her native hills,— eyes of a dusky blue, and lips of that rare tint which lines the conch-shell. Such was the Châtelaine of Kaafiord,—as perfect a type of Norse beauty as ever my Saga lore had conjured up! Frithiof's Ingeborg herself seemed to stand before me. A few minutes afterwards, two little fair-haired maidens, like twin snowdrops, stole into the room; and the sweet home picture was complete.

The rest of the day has been a continued fête. In vain after having transacted my business, I pleaded the turning of the tide, and our anxiety to get away to sea; nothing would serve our kind entertainer but that we should stay to dinner; and his was one of those strong energetic wills it is difficult to resist.

In the afternoon, the Hammerfest steamer called in from the southward, and by her came two fair sisters of our hostess from their father's home in one of the Loffodens which overlook the famous Mälstrom. The stories about the violence of the whirlpool Mr. T—— assures me are ridiculously exaggerated. On ordinary occasions the site of the supposed vortex is perfectly unruffled, and it is only when a strong weather tide is running that any unusual movements in the water can be observed; even then the disturbance does not amount to much more than a rather troublesome race. "Often and often, when she was a girl, had his wife and her sisters sailed over its fabulous crater in an open boat." But in this wild romantic country, with its sparse population, rugged mountains, and gloomy fiords, very ordinary matters become invested with a character of awe and mystery quite foreign to the atmosphere of our own matter-of-fact world; and many of the Norwegians are as prone to superstition as the poor little Lapp pagans who dwell among them.

No later than a few years ago, in the very fiord we had passed on our way to Alten, when an unfortunate boat got cast away during the night on some rocks at a little distance from the shore, the inhabitants, startled by the cries of distress which reached them in the morning twilight, hurried down in a body to the sea-side,—not to afford assistance,—but to open a volley of musketry on the drowning mariners; being fully persuaded that the stranded boat, with its torn sails, was no other than the Kracken or Great Sea-Serpent flapping its dusky wings: and when, at last, one of the crew succeeded in swimming ashore in spite of waves and bullets, —the whole society turned and fled!

And now, again good-bye. We are just going up to dine with Mr. T——; and after dinner, or at least as soon as the tide turns, we get under way—Northward Ho! (as Mr. Kingsley would say) in right good earnest this time!

LETTER XI.

WE SAIL FOR BEAR ISLAND, AND SPITZBERGEN—CHERIE ISLAND—BARENTZ—SIR HUGH WILLOUGHBY—PARRY'S ATTEMPT TO REACH THE NORTH POLE—AGAIN AMONGST THE ICE—ICEBLINK—FIRST SIGHT OF SPITZBERGEN—WILSON—DECAY OF OUR HOPES—CONSTANT STRUGGLE WITH THE ICE—WE REACH THE 80° N. LAT.—A FREER SEA—WE LAND IN SPITZBERGEN—ENGLISH BAY—LADY EDITH'S GLACIER—A MIDNIGHT PHOTOGRAPH—NO REINDEER TO BE SEEN—ET EGO IN ARCTIS—WINTER IN SPITZBERGEN—PTARMIGAN—THE BEAR-SAGA—THE "FOAM" MONUMENT—SOUTHWARDS—SIGHT THE GREENLAND ICE—A GALE—WILSON ON THE MÄLSTROM—BREAKERS AHEAD—ROOST—TAKING A SIGHT—THRONDHJEM.

Throndhjem, Aug. 22nd, 1856.

WE have won our laurels, after all! We have landed in Spitzbergen—almost at its most northern extremity; and the little "*Foam*" has sailed to within 630 miles of the Pole; that is to say, within 100 miles as far north as any ship has ever succeeded in getting.

I think my last letter left us enjoying the pleasant hospitalities of Kaafiord.

The genial quiet of that last evening in Norway was certainly a strange preface to the scenes we have since witnessed. So warm was it, that when dinner was over, we all went out into the garden, and had tea in the open air; the ladies without either bonnets or shawls, merely plucking a little branch of willow to brush away the mosquitoes; and so the evening wore away in alternate intervals of chat and song. At midnight, seawards again began to swirl the tide, and we rose to go,—not without having first paid a visit to the room where the little daughters of the house lay folded in sleep. Then descending to the beach, laden with flowers and kind wishes waved to us by white handkerchiefs held in still whiter hands, we rowed on board; up went the flapping sails, and dipping her ensign in token of adieu—the schooner glided swiftly on between the walls of rock, until an intervening crag shut out from our sight the friendly group that had come forth to bid us "Good speed." In another twenty-four hours we had threaded our way back through the intricate fiords; and leaving Hammerfest three or four miles on the starboard hand, on the evening of the 28th of July, we passed out between the islands of Soroe and Bolsvoe into the open sea.

My intention was to go first to Bear Island, and ascertain for myself in what direction the ice was lying to the southward of Spitzbergen.

Bear—or Cherie Island, is a diamond-shaped island, about ten miles long, composed of secondary rocks—principally sandstone and limestone—lying about 280 miles due north of the North Cape. It was originally discovered by Barentz, the 9th of June, 1596, on the occasion of his last and fatal voyage. Already had he commanded two expeditions sent forth by the United Provinces to discover a north-east passage to that dream-land—Cathay; and each time, after penetrating to the eastward of Nova Zembla, he had been foiled by the impenetrable line of ice. On this occasion he adopted the bolder and more northerly courses which brought him to Bear Island. Thence, plunging into the mists of the frozen sea, he ultimately sighted the western mountains of Spitzbergen. Unable to proceed further in that direction, Barentz retraced his steps, and again passing in sight of Bear Island, proceeded in a south-east direction to Nova Zembla, where his ships got entangled in the ice, and he subsequently perished.

Towards the close of the sixteenth century, in spite of repeated failures, one endeavour after another was made to penetrate to India across these fatal waters.

The first English vessel that sailed on the disastrous quest was the "*Bona Esperanza,*" in the last year of King Edward VI. Her commander was Sir Hugh Willoughby, and we have still extant a copy of the instructions drawn up by Sebastian Cabot—the Grand Pilot of England, for his guidance. Nothing can be more pious than the spirit in which this ancient document is conceived; expressly enjoining that morning and evening prayers should be offered on board every ship attached to the expedition, and that neither dicing, carding, tabling, nor other devilish devices—were to be permitted. Here and there were clauses of a more questionable morality,—recommending that natives of strange lands be "enticed on board, and made drunk with your beer and wine; for then you shall know the secrets of their hearts." The whole concluding with an exhortation to all on board to take especial heed to the devices of " certain creatures, with men's heads, and the tails of fishes, who swim with bows and arrows about the fiords and bays, and live on human flesh."

On the 11th of May the ill-starred expedition got under way from Deptford, and saluting the king, who was then lying sick at Greenwich, put to sea. By the 30th of July the little fleet—three vessels in all—had come up abreast of the Loffoden islands, but a gale coming on, the "*Esperanza*" was separated from the consorts. Ward-huus—a little harbour to the east of the North Cape—had been appointed as the place of rendezvous in case of such an event, but unfortunately, Sir Hugh overshot the mark, and wasted all the precious autumn time in blundering amid the ice to the eastward. At last, winter set in, and they were obliged to run for a port in Lapland. Here, removed from all human aid, they were frozen to death. A year afterwards, the ill-fated ships were discovered by some Russian sailors, and an unfinished journal proved that Sir Hugh and many of his companions were still alive in January, 1554.

The next voyage of discovery in a north-east direction was sent out by Sir Francis Cherie, alderman of London, in 1603. After proceeding as far east as Ward-huus and Kela, the "*Godspeed*" pushed north into the ocean, and on the 16th of August fell in with Bear Island. Unaware of its previous discovery by Barentz, Stephen Bennet—who commanded the expedition—christened the island Cherie Island, in honour of his patron, and to this day the two names are used almost indiscriminately.

In 1607, Henry Hudson was despatched by the Muscovy Company, with orders to sail, if possible, right across the pole. Although perpetually baffled by the ice, Hudson at last succeeded in reaching the north-west extremity of Spitzbergen, but finding his further progress arrested by an impenetrable barrier of fixed ice, he was forced to return. A few years later, Jonas Poole—having been sent in the same direction, instead of prosecuting any discoveries, wisely set himself to killing the sea-horses that frequent the Arctic ice-fields, and in lieu of tidings of new lands—brought back a valuable cargo of walrus tusks. In 1615, Fotherby started with the intention of renewing the attempt to sail across the north pole, but after encountering many dangers he also was forced to return. It was during the course of his homeward voyage that he fell in with the island of Jan Mayen. Soon afterwards, the discovery by Hudson and Davis, of the seas and straits to which they have given their names, diverted the attention of the public from all thoughts of a north-east passage, and the Spitzbergen waters were only frequented by ships engaged in the fisheries. The gradual disappearance of the whale, and the discovery of more profitable fishing stations on the west coast of Greenland, subsequently abolished the sole attraction for human being which this inhospitable region ever possessed, and of late years, I understand, the Spitzbergen seas have remained as lonely and unvisited as they were before the first adventurer invaded their solitude.

Twice only, since the time of Fotherby, has any attempt been made to reach the pole on a north-east course. In 1773, Captain Phipps, afterwards Lord Mulgrave, sailed in the "*Carcass*" towards Spitzbergen, but he never reached a higher latitude than 81°. It was in this expedition that Nelson made his first voyage, and had that famous encounter with the bear. The next and last endeavour was undertaken by Parry, in 1827. Unable to get his ship even as far north as

Phipps had gone, he determined to leave her in a harbour in Spitzbergen, and push across the sea in boats and sledges. The uneven nature of the surface over which they had to travel, caused their progress northward to be very slow, and very laborious. The ice too, beneath their feet, was not itself immovable, and at last they perceived they were making the kind of progress a criminal makes upon the treadmill,—the floes over which they were journeying drifting to the southward faster than they walked north; so that at the end of a long day's march of ten miles, they found themselves four miles further from their destination than at its commencement. Disgusted with so Irish a manœuvre, Parry determined to return, though not until he had almost reached the 83rd parallel, a higher latitude than any to which man is known to have penetrated. Arctic authorities are still of opinion, that Parry's plan for reaching the pole might prove successful, if the expedition were to set out earlier in the season, ere the intervening field of ice is cast adrift by the approach of summer.

Our own run to Bear Island was very rapid. On getting outside the islands, a fair fresh wind sprung up, and we went spinning along for two nights and two days as merrily as possible, under a double-reefed mainsail and staysail, on a due north course. On the third day we began to see some land birds, and a few hours afterwards, the loom of the island itself; but it had already begun to get fearfully cold, and our thermometer, which I consulted every two hours, plainly indicated that we were approaching ice. My only hope was that, at all events, the southern extremity of the island might be disengaged; for I was very anxious to land, in order to examine some coal-beds which are said to exist in the upper strata of the sandstone formation. This expectation was doomed to complete disappointment. Before we had got within six miles of the shore, it became evident that the report of the Hammerfest Sea-horseman was too true.

Between us and the land there extended an impenetrable

barrier of packed ice, running due east and west, as far as the eye could reach.

What was now to be done? If a continuous field of ice lay 150 miles off the southern coast of Spitzbergen, what would be the chance of getting to the land by going further north? Now that we had received ocular proof of the veracity of the Hammerfest skipper in this first particular, was it likely that we should have the luck to find the remainder of his story untrue? According to the track he had jotted down for me on the chart, the ice in front stretched right away west in an unbroken line, to the wall of ice which we had seen running to the north, from the upper end of Jan Mayen. Only a week had elapsed since he had actually ascertained the impracticability of reaching a higher latitude,—what likelihood could there be of a channel having been opened up to the northward during so short an interval? Such was the series of insoluble problems by which I posed myself, as we stood vainly smacking our lips at the island, which lay so tantalizingly beyond our reach.

Still, unpromising as the aspect of things might appear, it would not do to throw a chance away; so I determined to put the schooner round on the other tack, and run westwards along the edge of the ice, until we found ourselves again in the Greenland sea. Bidding, therefore, a last adieu to Mount Misery, as its first discoverers very appropriately christened one of the higher hills in Bear Island, we suffered it to melt back into a fog,—out of which, indeed, no part of the land had ever more than partially emerged,—and with no very sanguine expectations as to the result, sailed west away towards Greenland. During the next four-and-twenty hours we ran along the edge of the ice, in nearly a due westerly direction, without observing the slightest indication of anything approaching to an opening towards the North. It was weary work, scanning that seemingly interminable barrier, and listening to the melancholy roar of waters on its icy shore.

At last, after having come about 140 miles since leaving

Bear Island,—the long, white, wave-lashed line suddenly ran down into a low point, and then trended back with a decided inclination to the North. Here, at all events, was an improvement; instead of our continuing to steer W. by S., or at most W. by N., the schooner would often lay as high up as N.W., and even N.W. by N. Evidently the action of the Gulf Stream was beginning to tell, and our spirits rose in proportion. In a few more hours, however, this cheering prospect was interrupted by a fresh line of ice being reported, not only ahead, but as far as the eye could reach on the port bow; so again the schooner's head was put to the westward, and the old story recommenced. And now the flank of the second barrier was turned, and we were able to edge up a few hours to the northward; but only to be again confronted by another line, more interminable, apparently. than the last. But why should I weary you with the detail of our various manœuvres during the ensuing days? They were too tedious and disheartening at the time, for me to look back upon them with any pleasure. Suffice it to say, that by dint of sailing north whenever the ice would permit us, and sailing west when we could not sail north, we found ourselves on the 2nd of August, in the latitude of the southern extremity of Spitzbergen, though divided from the land by about fifty miles of ice. All this while the weather had been pretty good, foggy and cold enough, but with a fine stiff breeze that rattled us along at a good rate whenever we did get a chance of making any Northing. But lately it had come on to blow very hard, the cold became quite piercing, and what was worse—in every direction round the whole circuit of the horizon, except along its southern segment,—a blaze of iceblink illuminated the sky. A more discouraging spectacle could not have met our eyes. The iceblink is a luminous appearance, reflected on the heavens from the fields of ice that still lie sunk beneath the horizon; it was, therefore on this occasion an unmistakable indication of the encumbered state of the sea in front of us.

IN THE ICE.

I had turned in for a few hours of rest, and release from the monotonous sense of disappointment, and was already lost in a dream of deep bewildering bays of ice, and gulfs whose shifting shores offered to the eye every possible combination of uncomfortable scenery, without possible issue,— when "a voice in my dreaming ear" shouted "*Land!*" and I awoke to its reality. I need not tell you in what double quick time I tumbled up the companion, or with what greediness I feasted my eyes on that longed-for view,—the only sight—as I then thought—we were ever destined to enjoy of the mountains of Spitzbergen !

The whole heaven was overcast with a dark mantle of tempestuous clouds, that stretched down in umbrella-like points towards the horizon, leaving a clear space between their edge and the sea, illuminated by the sinister brilliancy of the iceblink. In an easterly direction, this belt of unclouded atmosphere was etherealized to an indescribable transparency, and up into it there gradually grew—above the dingy line of starboard ice—a forest of thin lilac peaks, so faint, so pale, that had it not been for the gem-like distinctness of their outline, one could have deemed them as unsubstantial as the spires of fairy-land. The beautiful vision proved only too transient ; in one short half hour mist and cloud had blotted it all out, while a fresh barrier of ice compelled us to turn our backs on the very land we were striving to reach.

Although we were certainly upwards of sixty miles distant from the land when the Spitzbergen hills were first observed, the intervening space seemed infinitely less ; but in these high latitudes the eye is constantly liable to be deceived in the estimate it forms of distances. Often, from some change suddenly taking place in the state of the atmosphere, the land you approach will appear even to *recede ;* and on one occasion, an honest skipper—one of the most valiant and enterprising mariners of his day—actually turned back, because, after sailing for several hours with a fair wind towards the land, and finding himself no nearer to it than at first, he concluded that some loadstone rock beneath the sea must have attracted the keel of his ship, and kept her stationary.

The next five days were spent in a continual struggle with the ice. On referring to our log, I see nothing but a repetition of the same monotonous observations.

"July 31st.—Wind W. by S.—Courses sundry to clear ice."

" Ice very thick."

" These twenty-four hours picking our way through ice."

" August 1st.—Wind W.—courses variable—foggy—continually among ice these twenty-four hours."

And in Fitz's diary, the discouraging state of the weather is still more pithily expressed :—

"August 2nd. — Head wind—sailing westward—large hummocks of ice ahead, and on port bow, *i. e.* to the westward —hope we may be able to push through. In evening, ice gets thicker ; we still hold on—fog comes on—ice getting thicker—wind freshens—we can get no farther—ice impassable, no room to tack — struck the ice several times— obliged to sail S. and W.—things look very shady."

Sometimes we were on the point of despairing altogether, then a plausible opening would show itself as if leading towards the land, and we would be tempted to run down it until we found the field become so closely packed, that it was with great difficulty we could get the vessel round,—and only then at the expense of collisions, which made the little craft shiver from stem to stern. Then a fog would come on —so thick, you could almost cut it like a cheese,—and thus render the sailing among the loose ice very critical indeed : then it would fall dead calm, and leave us, hours together, muffled in mist, with no other employment than chess or hopscotch. It was during one of those intervals of quiet that I executed the annexed work of art, which is intended to represent Sigurdr, in the act of meditating a complicated gambit for the Doctor's benefit.

About this period Wilson culminated. Ever since leaving Bear Island he had been keeping a carnival of grief in the pantry, until the cook became almost half-witted by reason of his Jeremiads. Yet I must not give you the impression that the poor fellow was the least wanting in *pluck*—far from it. Surely it requires the highest order of courage to anticipate every species of disaster every moment of the day, and yet to meet the impending fate like a man—as he did. Was it his fault that fate was not equally ready to meet him? *His* share of the business was always done: he was ever prepared for the worst; but the most critical circumstances

SIGURDR.

never disturbed the gravity of his carriage, and the fact of our being destined to go to the bottom before tea-time would not have caused him to lay out the dinner table a whit less symmetrically. Still, I own, the style of his service was slightly depressing. He laid out my clean shirt of a morning as if it had been a shroud; and cleaned my boots as though for a man *on his last legs*. The fact is, he was imaginative and atrabilious,—contemplating life through a medium of the colour of his own complexion.

This was the cheerful kind of report he used invariably to bring me of a morning. Coming to the side of my cot with the air of a man announcing the stroke of doomsday, he used to say, or rather, *toll*—

"Seven o'clock, my Lord!"

"Very well; how's the wind?"

"Dead ahead, my Lord—*dead!*"

"How many points is she off her course?"

"Four points, my Lord—full four points!" (Four points being as much as she could be.)

"Is it pretty clear? eh! Wilson?"

"—Can't see your hand, my Lord!—can't see your hand!"

"Much ice in sight?"

"—Ice all round, my Lord—ice a-all ro-ound!"—and so exit, sighing deeply over my trousers.

Yet it was immediately after one of these unpromising announcements, that for the first time matters began to look a little brighter. The preceding four-and-twenty hours we had remained enveloped in a cold and dismal fog. But on coming on deck, I found the sky had already begun to clear; and although there was ice as far as the eye could see on either side of us, in front a narrow passage showed itself across a patch of loose ice into what seemed a freer sea beyond. The only consideration was—whether we could be certain of finding our way out again, should it turn out that the open water we saw was only a basin without any exit in any other direction. The chance was too tempting to throw away; so the little schooner gallantly pushed her way through the intervening neck of ice where the floes seemed to be least huddled up together, and in half an hour afterwards found herself running up along the edge of the starboard ice, almost in a due northerly direction. And here I must take occasion to say that, during the whole of this rather anxious time, my master—Mr. Wyse—conducted himself in a most admirable manner. Vigilant, cool, and attentive, he handled the vessel most skilfully, and never seemed to lose his presence of mind in any emergency. It is true the silk tartan still coruscated on Sabbaths, but its

brilliant hues were quite a relief to the colourless scenes
which surrounded us, and the dangling chain now only
served to remind me of what firm dependence I could
place upon its wearer.

Soon after, the sun came out, the mist entirely disappeared, and again on the starboard hand shone a vision of the
land ; this time not in the sharp peaks and spires we had first
seen, but in a chain of pale blue egg-shaped islands, floating
in the air a long way above the horizon. This peculiar appearance was the result of extreme refraction, for, later in
the day, we had an opportunity of watching the oval cloudlike forms gradually harden into the same pink tapering
spikes which originally caused the island to be called Spitzbergen : nay, so clear did it become, that even the shadows
on the hills became quite distinct, and we could easily trace
the outlines of the enormous glaciers—sometimes ten or
fifteen miles broad—that fill up every valley along the shore.
Towards evening the line of coast again vanished into the
distance, and our rising hopes received an almost intolerable disappointment by the appearance of a long line of ice
right ahead, running to the westward, apparently, as far as
the eye could reach. To add to our disgust, the wind flew
right round into the North, and increasing to a gale, brought
down upon us—not one of the usual thick arctic mists to
which we were accustomed, but a dark, yellowish brown fog,
that rolled along the surface of the water in twisted columns,
and irregular masses of vapour, as dense as coal smoke.
We had now almost reached the eightieth parallel of north
latitude, and still an impenetrable sheet of ice, extending
fifty or sixty miles westward from the shore, rendered all
hopes of reaching the land out of the question. Our expectation of finding the north-west extremity of the island
disengaged from ice by the action of the currents was—at all
events for this season—evidently doomed to disappointment.
We were already almost in the latitude of Amsterdam Island
—which is actually its north-west point—and the coast
seemed more encumbered than ever. No whaler had ever

succeeded in getting more than about 120 miles further north than we ourselves had already come; and to entangle ourselves any further in the ice—unless it were with the certainty of reaching land—would be sheer folly. The only thing to be done was to turn back. Accordingly, to this course I determined at last to resign myself, if, after standing on for twelve hours longer, nothing should turn up to improve the present aspect of affairs. It was now eleven o'clock; P.M. Fitz and Sigurdr went to bed, while I remained on deck to see what the night might bring forth. It blew great guns, and the cold was perfectly intolerable; billow upon billow of black fog came sweeping down between the sea and sky, as if it were going to swallow up the whole universe; while the midnight sun—now completely blotted out—now faintly struggling through the ragged breaches of the mist—threw down from time to time an unearthly red-brown glare on the waste of roaring waters.

For the whole of that night did we continue beating up along the edge of the ice, in the teeth of a whole gale of wind; at last, about nine o'clock in the morning,—but two short hours before the moment at which it had been agreed we should bear up, and abandon the attempt,—we came up with a long low point of ice, that had stretched further to the Westward than any we had yet doubled; and there, beyond, lay an open sea!—open not only to the Northward and Westward, but also to the Eastward! You can imagine my excitement. "Turn the hands up, Mr. Wyse!" "'Bout ship!" "Down with the helm!" "Helm a-lee!" Up comes the schooner's head to the wind, the sails flapping with the noise of thunder—blocks rattling against the deck, as if they wanted to knock their brains out—ropes dancing about in galvanised coils, like mad serpents—and everything to an inexperienced eye in inextricable confusion; till gradually she pays off on the other tack—the sails stiffen into deal-boards—the staysail sheet is let go—and heeling over on the opposite side, again she darts forward over the

THE MIDNIGHT SUN OFF SPITZBERGEN.

sea like an arrow from the bow. "Stand by to make sail!" "Out all reefs!" I could have carried sail to sink a man-of-war!—and away the little ship went, playing leapfrog over the heavy seas, and staggering under her canvas, as if giddy with the same joyful excitement which made my own heart thump so loudly.

In another hour the sun came out, the fog cleared away, and about noon up again, above the horizon, grow the pale lilac peaks, warming into a rosier tint as we approach. Ice still stretches toward the land on the starboard side ; but we don't care for it now—the schooner's head is pointing E. and by S. At one o'clock we sight Amsterdam Island, about thirty miles on the port bow; then came the "seven ice-hills"—as seven enormous glaciers are called— that roll into the sea between lofty ridges of gneiss and mica slate, a little to the northward of Prince Charles's Foreland. Clearer and more defined grows the outline of the mountains, some coming forward while others recede ; their rosy tints appear less even, fading here and there into pale yellows and greys ; veins of shadow score the steep sides of the hills; the articulations of the rocks become visible ; and now, at last, we glide under the limestone peaks of Mitre Cape, past the marble arches of King's Bay on the one side, and the pinnacle of the Vogel Hook on the other, into the quiet channel that separates the Foreland from the main.

It was at one o'clock in the morning of the 6th of August, 1856, that after having been eleven days at sea, we came to an anchor in the silent haven of English Bay, *Spitzbergen*.

And now, how shall I give you an idea of the wonderful panorama in the midst of which we found ourselves ? I think, perhaps, its most striking feature was the stillness, and deadness, and impassibility of this new world : ice, and rock, and water surrounded us ; not a sound of any kind interrupted the silence ; the sea did not break upon the shore ; no bird or any living thing was visible ; the midnight sun, by this time muffled in a transparent mist, shed an awful, mysterious lustre on glacier and mountain; no atom of vegetation gave token of the earth's vitality : an universal numbness and dumbness seemed to pervade the solitude. I suppose in scarcely any other part of the world is this appearance of deadness so strikingly exhibited. On the stillest summer day in England, there is always perceptible an under-tone of life thrilling through the atmosphere; and though no breeze should stir a single leaf, yet — in default of motion—there is always a sense of growth; but here not so much as a blade of grass was to be seen on the sides of the bald excoriated hills. Primeval rocks and eternal ice constitute the landscape.

The anchorage where we had brought up is the best to be found, with the exception perhaps of Magdalena Bay, along the whole west coast of Spitzbergen; indeed it is almost the only one where you are not liable to have the ice set in upon you at a moment's notice. Ice Sound, Bell Sound, Horn Sound—the other harbours along the west coast—are all liable to be beset by drift-ice during the course of a single night, even though no vestige of it may have been in sight four-and-twenty hours before; and many a good ship has been inextricably imprisoned in the very harbour to which she had fled for refuge. This bay is completely landlocked, being protected on its open side by Prince Charles's Foreland, a long island lying parallel with the mainland. Down towards either horn run two ranges of schistose rocks, about 1,500 feet high, their sides almost precipitous, and the topmost ridge as sharp as a knife, and jagged as a saw ; the intervening space is entirely filled up by an enormous glacier, which,—descending with one continuous incline from the head of a valley on the right, and sweeping like a torrent round the roots of an isolated clump of hills in the centre— rolls at last into the sea. The length of the glacial river from the spot where it apparently first originated, could not have been less than thirty, or thirty-five miles, or its greatest breadth less than nine or ten; but so completely did it fill up the higher end of the valley, that it was as much as you could do to distinguish the further mountains peeping up above its surface. The height of the precipice where it fell into the sea, I should judge to have been about 120 feet.

On the left a still more extraordinary sight presented itself. A kind of baby glacier actually hung suspended half way on the hill side, like a tear in the act of rolling down the furrowed cheek of the mountain.

I have tried to convey to you a notion of the falling impetus impressed on the surface of the Jan Mayen ice rivers; but in this case so unaccountable did it seem that the overhanging mass of ice should not continue to thunder down upon its course, that one's natural impulse was to shrink from crossing the path along which a breath—a sound—might precipitate the suspended avalanche into the valley. Though, perhaps, pretty exact in outline and general effect, the sketch I have made of this wonderful scene, will never convey to you a correct notion of the enormous scale of the distances, and size of its various features.

These glaciers are the principal characteristic of the scenery in Spitzbergen; the bottom of every valley in every part of the island, is occupied and generally completely filled by them, enabling one in some measure to realize the look of England during her glacial period, when Snowdon was still being slowly lifted towards the clouds, and every valley in Wales was brimful of ice. But the glaciers in English Bay are by no means the largest in the island. We ourselves got a view—though a very distant one—of ice rivers which must have been more extensive; and Dr. Scoresby mentions several which actually measured forty or fifty miles in length, and nine or ten in breadth; while the precipice formed by their fall into the sea, was sometimes upwards of 400 or 500 feet high. Nothing is more dangerous than to approach these cliffs of ice. Every now and then huge masses detach themselves from the face of the crystal steep, and topple over into the water; and woe be to the unfortunate ship which might happen to be passing below.

Scoresby himself actually witnessed a mass of ice, the size of a cathedral, thunder down into the sea from a height of 400 feet; frequently during our stay at Spitzbergen we ourselves observed specimens of these ice avalanches; and scarcely an hour passed without the solemn silence of the bay being disturbed by the thunderous boom resulting from similar catastrophes occurring in adjacent valleys.

As soon as we had thoroughly taken in the strange features of the scene around us, we all turned in for a night's rest. I was dog tired, as much with anxiety as want of sleep; for in continuing to push on to the northward in spite of the ice, I naturally could not help feeling that if any accident occurred, the responsibility would rest with me ; and although I do not believe that we were at any time in any real danger, yet from our inexperience in the peculiarities of arctic navigation, I think the coolest judgment would have been liable to occasional misgivings as to what might arise from possible contingencies. Now, however, all was right; the result had justified our anticipations; we had reached the so longed-for goal; and as I stowed myself snugly away in the hollow of my cot, I could not help heartily congratulating myself that—for that night at all events— there was no danger of the ship knocking a hole in her bottom against some hummock which the lookout had been too sleepy to observe ; and that Wilson could not come in the next morning and announce "ice all round, a-all ro-ound!" In a quarter of an hour afterwards, all was still on board the "*Foam;*" and the lonely little ship lay floating on the glassy bosom of the sea, apparently as inanimate as the landscape.

My feelings on awakening next morning were very pleasant ; something like what one used to feel the first morning after one's return from school, on seeing pink curtains glistening round one's head, instead of the dirty-white boards of a turned-up bedstead. When Wilson came in with my hot water, I could not help triumphantly remarking to him, —"Well, Wilson, you see we've got to Spitzbergen, after all!"

But Wilson was not a man to be driven from his convictions by facts; he only smiled grimly, with a look which meant —" Would we were safe back again!" Poor Wilson! he would have gone only half way with Bacon in his famous Apothegm ; he would willingly "commit the Beginnings of all actions to Argus with his hundred eyes, and the Ends"— to Centipede, with his hundred legs. " First to watch, and then to speed "—*away!* would have been his pithy emendation.

Immediately after breakfast we pulled to the shore, carrying in the gig with us the photographic apparatus, tents, guns, ammunition, and the goat. Poor old thing! she had suffered dreadfully from sea-sickness, and I thought a run ashore might do her good. On the left-hand side of the bay, between the foot of the mountain and the sea, there ran a low flat belt of black moss, about half a mile broad; and as this appeared the only point in the neighbourhood likely to offer any attraction to reindeer, it was on this side that I determined to land. My chief reason for having run into English Bay rather than Magdalena Bay was because we had been told at Hammerfest that it was the more likely place of the two for deer; and as we were sadly in want of fresh meat this advantage quite decided us in our choice. As soon, therefore, as we had superintended the erection of the tent, and set Wilson hard at work cleaning the glasses for the photographs, we slung our rifles on our backs, and set off in search of deer. But in vain did I peer through my telescope across the dingy flat in front; not a vestige of a horn was to be seen, although in several places we came upon impressions of their track. At last our confidence in the reports of their great plenty became considerably diminished. Still the walk was very refreshing after our confinement on board; and although the thermometer was below freezing, the cold only made the exercise more pleasant. A little to the northward I observed, lying on the sea-shore, innumerable logs of driftwood. This wood is floated all the way from America by the Gulf Stream, and as I walked from one huge bole to another, I could not help wondering in what

primeval forest each had grown, what chance had originally
cast them on the waters, and piloted them to this desert
shore. Mingled with this fringe of unhewn timber that
lined the beach lay waifs and strays of a more sinister kind ;
pieces of broken spars, an oar, a boat's flagstaff, and a
few shattered fragments of some long-lost vessel's planking.
Here and there, too, we would come upon skulls of walrus,
ribs and shoulder-blades of bears, brought possibly by the
ice in winter. Turning again from the sea, we resumed our
search for deer ; but two or three hours' more very stiff walking produced no better luck. Suddenly a cry from Fitz,
who had wandered a little to the right, brought us helter-
skelter to the spot where was standing. But it was not a
stag he had called us to come and look upon. Half im-
bedded in the black moss at his feet, there lay a grey deal
coffin falling almost to pieces with age ; the lid was gone—
blown off probably by the wind—and within were stretched
the bleaching bones of a human skeleton. A rude cross at
the head of the grave still stood partially upright, and a half
obliterated Dutch inscription preserved a record of the dead
man's name and age.

   . . . . . VANDER SCHELLING . . . .
   COMMAN . . . . JACOB MOOR . . . .
   OB 2 JUNE 1758 ÆT 44.

It was evidently some poor whaler of the last century to
whom his companions had given the only burial possible in
this frost-hardened earth, which even the summer sun has no
force to penetrate beyond a couple of inches, and which will
not afford to man the shallowest grave. A bleak resting-
place for that hundred years' slumber, I thought, as I gazed
on the dead mariner's remains !—

    " I was snowed over with snow,
    And beaten with rains,
    And drenched with the dews ;
    Dead have I long been,"—

— murmured the Vala to Odin in Nifelheim,—and whispers

'ET EGO IN ARCADIA'

of a similar import seemed to rise up from the lidless coffin before us. It was no brother mortal that lay at our feet, softly folded in the embraces of "Mother Earth," but a poor scarecrow, gibbeted for ages on this bare rock, like a dead Prometheus; the vulture, frost, gnawing for ever on his bleaching relics, and yet eternally preserving them!

On another part of the coast we found two other corpses yet more scantily sepulchred, without so much as a cross to mark their resting-place. Even in the palmy days of the whale-fisheries, it was the practice of the Dutch and English sailors to leave the wooden coffins in which they had placed their comrades' remains, exposed upon the shore; and I have been told by an eye-witness, that in Magdalena Bay there are to be seen, even to this day, the bodies of men who died upwards of 250 years ago, in such complete preservation that, when you pour hot water on the icy coating which encases them, you can actually see the unchanged features of the dead, through the transparent incrustation.

As soon as Fitz had gathered a few of the little flowering mosses that grew inside the coffin, we proceeded on our way, leaving poor Jacob Moor—like his great namesake—alone in his glory.

Turning to the right, we scrambled up the spur of one of the mountains on the eastern side of the plain, and thence dived down among the lateral valleys that run up between them. Although by this means we opened up quite a new system of hills, and basins, and gullies, the general scenery did not change its characteristics. All vegetation—if the black moss deserves such a name—ceases when you ascend twenty feet above the level of the sea, and the sides of the mountains become nothing but steep slopes of schist, split and crumbled into an even surface by the frost. Every step we took unfolded a fresh succession of these jagged spikes and break-neck acclivities, in an unending variety of quaint configuration. Mountain climbing has never been a hobby of mine, so I was not tempted to play the part of Excelsior on any of these hill sides; but for those who love such exercise a fairer or a more dangerous opportunity of distinguishing themselves could not be imagined. The supercargo or owner of the very first Dutch ship that ever came to Spitzbergen, broke his neck in attempting to climb a hill in Prince Charles's Foreland. Barentz very nearly lost several of his men under similar circumstances; and when Scoresby succeeded in making the ascent of another hill near Horn Sound, it was owing to his having taken the precaution of marking each upward step in chalk, that he was ever able to get down again. The prospect from the summit, the approach to which was by a ridge so narrow that he sat astride upon its edge, seems amply to have repaid the exertion; and I do not think I can give you a better idea of the general effect of Spitzbergen scenery, than by quoting his striking description of the panorama he beheld:—

"The prospect was most extensive and grand. A fine sheltered bay was seen to the east of us, an arm of the same on the north-east, and the sea, whose glassy surface was unruffled by a breeze, formed an immense expanse on the west; the icebergs rearing their proud crests almost to the tops of mountains between which they were lodged, and defying the power of the solar beams, were scattered in various directions about the sea-coast and in the adjoining bays. Beds of snow and ice filling extensive hollows, and giving an enamelled coat to adjoining valleys, one of which commencing at the foot of the mountain where we stood extended in a continued line towards the north, as far as the eye could reach—mountain rising above mountain, until by distance they dwindled into insignificancy—the whole contrasted by a cloudless canopy of deepest azure, and enlightened by the rays of a blazing sun, and the effect aided by a feeling of danger, seated as we were on the pinnacle of a rock almost surrounded by tremendous precipices,—all united to constitute a picture singularly sublime.

"Our descent we found really a very hazardous, and in some instances a painful undertaking. Every movement was a work of deliberation. Having by much care, and with some anxiety, made good our descent to the top of the secondary hills, we took our way down one of the steepest banks, and slid forward with great facility in a sitting posture. Towards the foot of the hill, an expanse of snow stretched across the line of descent. This being loose and soft, we entered upon it without fear; but on reaching the middle of it, we came to a surface of solid ice, perhaps a hundred yards across, over which we launched with astonishing velocity, but happily escaped without injury. The men whom we left below, viewed this latter movement with astonishment and fear."

So universally does this strange land bristle with peaks and needles of stone, that the views we ourselves obtained —though perhaps from a lower elevation, and certainly without the risk—scarcely yielded either in extent or picturesque grandeur to the scene described by Dr. Scoresby.

Having pretty well overrun the country to the northward, without coming on any more satisfactory signs of deer than their hoof-prints in the moss, we returned on board. The next day—but I need not weary you with a journal of our daily proceedings ; for, however interesting each moment of our stay in Spitzbergen was to ourselves—as much perhaps from a vague expectation of what we might see, as from anything we actually did see—a minute account of every walk we took, and every bone we picked up, or every human skeleton we came upon, would probably only make you wonder why on earth we should have wished to come so far to see so little. Suffice it to say that we explored the neighbourhood in the three directions left open to us by the mountains, that we climbed the two most accessible of the adjacent hills, wandered along the margin of the glaciers, rowed across to the opposite side of the bay, descended a certain distance along the sea-coast, and in fact exhausted all the lions of the vicinity.

During the whole period of our stay in Spitzbergen, we

had enjoyed unclouded sunshine. The nights were even brighter than the days, and afforded Fitz an opportunity of taking some photographic views by the light of a *midnight sun*. The cold was never very intense, though the thermometer remained below freezing; but about four o'clock every evening, the salt-water bay in which the schooner lay was veneered over with a pellicle of ice one-eighth of an inch in thickness, and so elastic, that even when the sea beneath was considerably agitated, its surface remained unbroken, the smooth, round waves taking the appearance of billows of oil. If such is the effect produced by the slightest modification of the sun's power, in the month of August,—you can imagine what must be the result of his total disappearance beneath the horizon. The winter is, in fact, unendurable. Even in the height of summer, the moisture inherent in the atmosphere is often frozen into innumerable particles, so minute as to assume the appearance of an impalpable mist. Occasionally persons have wintered on the island, but unless the greatest precautions have been taken for their preservation, the consequences have been almost invariably fatal. About the same period as when the party of Dutch sailors were left at Jan Mayen, a similar experiment was tried in Spitzbergen. At the former place it was scurvy, rather than cold, which destroyed the poor wretches left there to fight it out with winter; at Spitzbergen, as well as could be gathered from their journal, it appeared that they had perished from the intolerable severity of the climate,—and the contorted attitudes in which their bodies were found lying, too plainly indicated the amount of agony they had suffered. No description can give an adequate idea of the intense rigour of the six months' winter in this part of the world. Stones crack with the noise of thunder; in a crowded hut the breath of its occupants will fall in flakes of snow; wine and spirits turn to ice; the snow burns like caustic; if iron touches the flesh, it brings the skin away with it; the soles of your stockings may be burnt off your feet, before you feel the slightest warmth from the fire; linen taken out of boiling water, instantly stiffens to the consistency of a wooden board; and heated stones will not prevent the sheets of the bed from freezing. If these are the effects of the climate within an air-tight, fire-warmed, crowded hut—what must they be among the dark, storm-lashed mountain-peaks outside?

It was now time to think of going south again; we had spent many more days on the voyage to Spitzbergen than I had expected, and I was continually haunted by the dread of your becoming anxious at not hearing from us. It was a great disappointment to be obliged to return without having got any deer; but your peace of mind was of more consequence to me than a ship-load of horns; and accordingly we decided on not remaining more than another day in our present berth leaving it still an open question whether we should not run up to Magdalena Bay, if the weather proved very inviting, the last thing before quitting for ever the Spitzbergen shores.

We had killed nothing as yet, except a few eider ducks, and one or two ice-birds—the most graceful winged creatures I have ever seen, with immensely long pinions, and plumage of spotless white. Although enormous seals from time to time used to lift their wise, grave faces above the water, with the dignity of sea-gods, none of us had any very great inclination to slay such rational human-looking creatures; and —with the exception of these and a white fish, a species of whale—no other living thing had been visible. On the very morning, however, of the day settled for our departure, Fitz came down from a solitary expedition up a hill with the news of his having seen some ptarmigan. Having taken a rifle with him instead of a gun, he had not been able to shoot more than one, which he had brought back in triumph as proof of the authenticity of his report; but the extreme juvenility of his victim hardly permitted us to identify the species; the hole made by the bullet being about the same size as the bird. Nevertheless, the slightest prospect of obtaining a supply of fresh meat was enough to reconcile us to any amount of exertion; therefore, on the strength of the pinch of feathers which Fitz kept gravely assuring us was the game he had bagged, we seized our guns—I took a rifle in case of a possible bear—and set our faces toward the hill. After a good hour's pull we reached the shoulder which Fitz had indicated as the scene of his exploit, but a patch of snow was the only thing visible. Suddenly I saw Sigurdr, who was remarkably sharp-sighted, run rapidly in the direction of the snow, and bringing his gun up to his shoulder, point it—as well as I could distinguish—at his own toes. When the smoke of the shot had cleared away, I fully expected to see the Icelander prostrate; but he was already reloading with the greatest expedition. Determined to prevent the repetition of so dreadful an attempt at self-destruction, I rushed to the spot. Guess then my relief when the bloody body of a ptarmigan—driven by so point blank a discharge a couple of feet into the snow—was triumphantly dragged forth by instalments from the sepulchre which it had received contemporaneously with its death wound, and thus happily accounted for Sigurdr's extraordinary proceeding. At the same moment I perceived two or three dozen other birds, brothers and sisters of the defunct, calmly strutting about under our very noses. By this time Sigurdr had reloaded, Fitz had also come up, and a regular massacre began. Retiring to a distance—for it was the case of Mahomet and the mountain reversed—the two sportsmen opened fire upon the innocent community, and in a few seconds sixteen corpses strewed the ground.

Scarcely had they finished off the last survivor of this Niobean family, when we were startled by the distant report of a volley of musketry, fired in the direction of the schooner. I could not conceive what had happened. Had a mutiny taken place? Was Mr. Wyse re-enacting, with a less docile ship's company, the pistol scene on board the Glasgow steamer? Again resounded the rattle of the firing. At all events, there was no time to be lost in getting back; so, tying up the birds in three bundles, we flung ourselves down into the gully by which we had ascended, and leaping on from stone to stone, to the infinite danger of our limbs and necks, rolled rather than ran down the hill. On rounding the lower wall of the curve which hitherto had hid what was passing from our eyes, the first I observed was Wilson breasting up the hill, evidently in a state of the greatest agitation. As soon as he thought himself within earshot, he stopped dead short, and, making a speaking-trumpet with his hands, shrieked, rather than shouted, " If you please, my Lord!"—(as I have already said, Wilson never forgot *les convenances*)—" If you please, my Lord, there's a b-e-a-a-a-a-r!" prolonging the last word into a polysyllable of fearful import. Concluding by the enthusiasm he was exhibiting, that the animal in question was at his heels,—hidden from us probably by the inequality of the ground,—I cocked my rifle, and prepared to roll him over the moment he should appear in sight. But what was my disappointment, when, on looking towards the schooner, my eye caught sight of our three boats fastened in a row, and towing behind them a white floating object, which my glass only too surely resolved the next minute into the dead bear!

On descending to the shore, I learned the whole story.

As Mr. Wyse was pacing the deck, his attention was suddenly attracted by a white speck in the water, swimming across from Prince Charles's Foreland,—the long island which lies over against English Bay. When first observed, the creature, whatever it might be, was about a mile and a half off,—the width of the channel between the island and the main being about five miles. Some said it was a bird, others a whale, and the cook suggested a mermaid. When the fact was ascertained that it was a *bonâ fide* bear, a gun was fired as a signal for us to return; but it was evident that unless at once intercepted, Bruin would get ashore. Mr. Wyse, therefore, very properly determined to make sure of him. This was a matter of no difficulty: the poor beast showed very little fight. His first impulse was to swim away from the boat; and even after he had been wounded, he only turned round once or twice upon his pursuers. The honour of having given him his death wound rests between the steward and Mr. Wyse; both contend for it. The evidence is conflicting, as at least half-a-dozen mortal wounds were found in the animal's body; each may be considered to have had a share in his death. Mr. Grant rests his claim principally upon the fact of his having put two bullets in my new rifle—which must have greatly improved the bore of that instrument. On the strength of this precaution, he now wears as an ornament about his person one of the bullets extracted from the gizzard of our prize.

All this time, Wilson was at the tent, busily occupied in taking photographs. As soon as the bear was observed, a signal was made to him from the ship, to warn him of the visitor he might shortly expect on shore. Naturally concluding that the bear would in all probability make for the tent as soon as he reached land, it became a subject of consideration with him what course he should pursue. Weapons he had none, unless the chemicals he was using might be so regarded. Should he try the influence of chloroform on his enemy; or launch the whole photographic apparatus at his grisly head, and take to his heels? Thought is rapid, but the bear's progress seemed equally expeditious; it was necessary to arrive at some speedy conclusion. To fly—was to desert his post and leave the camp in possession of the spoiler; life and honour were equally dear to him. Suddenly a bright idea struck him.

At the time the goat had been disembarked to take her pleasure on *terra firma*, our crow's-nest barrel had been landed with her. At this moment it was standing unoccupied by the side of the tent. By creeping into it, and turning its mouth downward on the ground, Wilson perceived that he should convert it into a tower of strength for himself against the enemy, while its legitimate occupant, becoming at once a victim to the bear's voracity, would probably prevent the monster from investigating too curiously its contents. It was quite a pity that the interposition of the boats prevented h putting this ingenious plan into execution. He had been regularly *done* out of a situation, in which the most poignant agony of mind and dreary anticipations would have been absolutely required of him. He pictured the scene to himself; he lying fermenting in the barrel, like a curious vintage; the bear sniffing querulously round it, perhaps cracking it like a cocoa-nut, or extracting him like a periwinkle! Of these chances he had been deprived by the interference of the crew. Friends are often injudiciously meddling.

Although I felt a little vexation that one of us should not have had the honour of slaying the bear in single combat, which would certainly have been for the benefit of his skin, the unexpected luck of having got one at all, made us quite forget our personal disappointment. As for my people, they were beside themselves with delight. To have killed a polar bear was a great thing, but to eat him would be a greater. If artistically dealt with, his carcase would probably cut up into a supply of fresh meat for many days. One of the hands happened to be a butcher. Whenever I wanted anything a little out of the way to be done on board, I was sure to find that it happened to be the *spécialité* of some one of the ship's company. In the course of a few hours, the late bear was converted into a row of the most tempting morsels of beef, hung about the rigging. Instead of in flags, the ship was dressed in joints. In the meantime it so happened that the fox, having stolen a piece of offal, was in a few minutes afterwards seized with convulsions. I had already given orders that the bear's liver should be thrown overboard, as being, if not poisonous, at all events very unwholesome. The seizure of the fox, coupled with this injunction, brought about a complete revolution in the men's minds, with regard to the delicacies they had been so daintily preparing for themselves. Silently, one by one, the pieces were untied and thrown into the sea: I do not think a mouthful of bear was eaten on board the "*Foam.*" I never heard whether it was in consequence of any prognostics of Wilson's that this act of self-denial was put into practice. I observed, however, that for some days after the slaughter and dismemberment of the bear, my ship's company presented an unaccountably sleek appearance. As for the steward, his head and whiskers seemed carved out of black marble: a varnished boot would not have looked half so bright: I could have seen to shave myself in his black hair. I conclude, therefore, that the ingenious cook must, at all events, have succeeded in manufacturing a supply of genuine bear's grease, of which they had largely availed themselves.

The bagging of the bear had so gloriously crowned our visit to Spitzbergen, that our disappointment about the deer was no longer thought of; it was therefore with light hearts, and most complete satisfaction, that we prepared for departure.

Maid Marian had already carved on a flat stone an inscription, in Roman letters, recording the visit of the "*Foam*" to English Bay; and a cairn having been erected to receive it, the tablet was solemnly lifted to its resting-place. Underneath I placed a tin box, containing a memorandum similar to that left at Jan Mayen, as well as a printed dinner invitation from Lady ———, which I happened to have on board. Having planted a boat's flag beside the rude monument, and brought on board with us a load of driftwood, to serve hereafter as Christmas yule-logs, we bade an eternal adieu to the silent hills around us; and weighing anchor, stood out to sea. For some hours a lack of wind still left us hanging about the shore, in the midst of a grave society of seals; but soon after, a gentle breeze sprang up in the south, and about three o'clock on Friday, the 11th of August, we again found ourselves spanking along before a six-knot breeze, over the pale green sea.

In considering the course on which I should take the vessel home, it appeared to me that in all probability we should have been much less pestered by the ice on our way to Spitzbergen, if, instead of hugging the easterly ice, we had kept more away to the westward; I determined therefore—as soon as we got clear of the land—to stand right over to the Greenland shore, on a due west course, and not to attempt to make any southing, until we should have struck the Greenland ice. The length of our tether in that direction being ascertained, we could then judge of the width of the channel down which we were to beat, for it was still blowing pretty fresh from the southward.

Up to the evening of the day on which we quitted English Bay, the weather had been most beautiful; calm, sunshiny, dry, and pleasant. Within a few hours of our getting under weigh, a great change had taken place, and by midnight it had become as foggy and disagreeable as ever. The sea was pretty clear. During the few days we had been on shore, the northerly current had brushed away the great angular field of ice which had lain off the shore, in a north-west direction; so that instead of being obliged to run up very nearly to the 80th parallel, in order to round it, we were enabled to sail to the westward at once. During the course of the night, we came upon one or two wandering patches of drift ice, but so loosely packed that we had no difficulty in pushing through them. About four o'clock in the morning, a long line of close ice was reported right a-head, stretching south as far as the eye could reach. We had come about eighty miles since leaving Spitzbergen. The usual boundary of the Greenland ice in summer runs, according to Scoresby, along the second parallel of west longitude. This we had already crossed; so that it was to be presumed the barricade we saw before us was a frontier of the fixed ice. In accordance, therefore, with my predetermined plan, we now began working to the southward, and the result fully justified my expectations.

The sea became comparatively clear, as far as could be seen from the deck of the vessel; although small vagrant patches of ice that we came up with occasionally—as well as the temperature of the air and the sea—continued to indicate the proximity of larger bodies on either side of us.

It was a curious sensation with which we had gradually learnt to contemplate this inseparable companion: it had become a part of our daily existence, an element, a thing without which the general aspect of the universe would be irregular and incomplete. It was the first thing we thought of in the morning, the last thing we spoke of at night. It glittered and grinned maliciously at us in the sunshine; it winked mysteriously through the stifling fog; it stretched itself like a prostrate giant, with huge, portentous shoulders and shadowy limbs, right across our course; or danced gleefully in broken groups in the little schooner's wake. There was no getting rid of it, or forgetting it; and if at night we sometimes returned in dreams to the green summer world—to the fervent harvest fields of England, and heard "the murmurs of innumerous bees," or the song of larks on thymy uplands—thump! bump! splash! gra-a-ate!—came the sudden reminder of our friend on the starboard bow; and then sometimes a scurry on deck, and a general "scrimmage" of the whole society, in endeavours to prevent more serious collisions. Moreover, I could not say, with your old French friend, that "Familiar'ty breeds despise." The more we saw of it, the less we liked it; its cold presence sent a chilly sense of discouragement to the heart, and I had daily to struggle with an ardent desire to throw a boot at Wilson's head, every time his sepulchral voice announced the "Ice *all round!*"

It was not until the 14th of August, five days after quitting Spitzbergen, that we lost sight of it altogether. From that moment the temperature of the sea steadily rose, and we felt that we were sailing back again into the pleasant summer.

A sad event which occurred soon after, in some measure marred our enjoyment of the change. Ever since she had left Hammerfest, it had become too evident that a sea-going life did not agree with the goat. Even the run on shore at Spitzbergen had not sufficed to repair her shattered constitution, and the bad weather we had had ever since completed its ruin. It was certain that the butcher was the only doctor who could now cure her. In spite, therefore, of the distress it occasioned Maid Marian, I was compelled to issue orders for her execution. Sigurdr was the only person who regarded the *tragical* event with indifference, nay, almost with delight. Ever since we had commenced sailing in a southerly direction, we had been obliged to beat; but during the last four-and-twenty hours the wind kept dodging us every time we tacked, as a nervous pedestrian sets to you sometimes on a narrow *trottoir*. This spell of ill-luck the Icelander heathenishly thought would only be removed by a sacrifice to Rhin, the goddess of the sea, in which light he trusted she would look upon the goat's body when it came to be thrown overboard.

Whether the change which followed upon the consignment of her remains to the deep really resulted from such an influence, I am not prepared to say. The weather immediately thereafter certainly *did* change. First the wind dropped altogether; but though the calm lasted several hours, the sea strangely enough appeared to become all the rougher, tossing and tumbling restlessly *up and down*—(not over and over as in a gale)—like a sick man on a fever bed; the impulse to the waves seeming to proceed from all four quarters of the world at once. Then, like jurymen with a verdict of death upon their lips, the heavy, ominous clouds slowly passed into the north-west.

A dead stillness followed—a breathless pause—until, at some mysterious signal, the solemn voice of the storm hurtled over the deep. Luckily we were quite ready for it; the gale came from the right quarter, and the fiercer it blew the better. For the next three days and three nights it was a scurry over the sea such as I never had before; nine or ten knots an hour was the very least we ever went, and 240 miles was the average distance we made every four-and-twenty hours.

Anything grander and more exciting than the sight of the sea under these circumstances you cannot imagine. The vessel herself remains very steady; when you are below you scarcely know you are not in port. But on raising your head above the companion the first sight which meets your eye is an upright wall of black water, towering, you hardly know how many feet, into the air over the stern. Like a lion walking on its hind legs, it comes straight at you, roaring and shaking its white mane with fury—it overtakes the vessel—the upright shiny face curves inwards—the white mane seems to hang above your very head; but ere it topples over, the nimble little ship has already slipped from underneath. You hear the disappointed jaws of the sea-monster snap angrily together,—the schooner disdainfully kicks up her heel—and raging and bubbling up on either side the quarter, the unpausing wave sweeps on, and you see its round back far ahead, gradually swelling upwards, as it gathers strength and volume for a new effort.

We had now got considerably to the southward of North Cape. We had already seen several ships, and you would hardly imagine with what childish delight my people hailed these symptoms of having again reached more "Christian latitudes," as they called them.

I had always intended, ever since my conversation with Mr. T. about the Mälstrom, to have called in at Loffoden Islands on our way south, and ascertain for myself the real truth about this famous vortex. To have blotted such a bugbear out of the map of Europe, if its existence really was a myth, would at all events have rendered our cruise not altogether fruitless. But, since leaving Spitzbergen, we had never once seen the sun, and to attempt to make so dangerous a coast in a gale of wind and a thick mist, with no more certain knowledge of the ship's position than our dead reckoning afforded, was out of the question; so about one o'clock in the morning, the weather giving no signs of improvement, the course I had shaped in the direction of the island was altered, and we stood away again to the southward. This manœuvre was not unobserved by Wilson, but he mistook its meaning. Having, I suppose, overheard us talking at dinner about the Mälstrom, he now concluded the supreme hour had arrived. He did not exactly comprehend the terms we used, but had gathered that the spot was one fraught with danger. Concluding from the change made in the vessel's course that we were proceeding towards the dreadful locality, he gave himself up to despair, and lay tossing in his hammock in sleepless anxiety. At last the load of his forebodings was greater than he could bear; he gets up, steals into the Doctor's cabin, wakes him up, and standing over him—as the messenger of ill tidings cnce stood over Priam—whispers, " *Sir !*" " What is it? " says Fitz, thinking, perhaps, some one was ill. " Do you know where we are going?" "Why, to Throndhjem," answered Fitz. "We *were* going to Throndhjem," rejoins Wilson, " but we ain't now—the vessel's course was altered two hours ago. Oh, Sir! we are going to Whirlpool—to *Whirl-rl-pooo-l!* Sir!" in a quaver of consternation,—and so glides back to bed like a phantom, leaving the Doctor utterly unable to divine the occasion of his visit.

The whole of the next day the gale continued. We had now sailed back into night; it became therefore a question how far it would be advisable to carry on during the ensuing hours of darkness, considering how uncertain we were as to our real position. As I think I have already described to you, the west coast of Norway is very dangerous; a con tinuous sheet of sunken rocks lies out along its entire edge for eight or ten miles to sea. There are no lighthouses to warn the mariner off; and if we were wrong in our reckon- ing, as we might very well be, it was possible we might stumble on the land sooner than we expected. I knew the proper course would be to lie to quietly until we could take an observation; but time was so valuable, and I was so fearful you would be getting anxious. The night was pretty clear. High mountains, such as we were expecting to make, would be seen, even at night, several miles off. Ac- cording to our log we were still 150 miles off the land, and, however inaccurate our calculation might be, the error could not be of such magnitude as that amounted to. To throw away so fair a wind seemed such a pity, especially as it might be days before the sun appeared; we had already been at sea about a fortnight without a sight of him, and his appearance at all during the summer is not an act *de rigueur* in this part of the world; we might spend yet another fortnight in lying to, and then after all have to poke our way blindfold to the coast; at all events it would be soon enough to lie to the next night. Such were the considerations, which—after an anxious consultation with Mr. Wyse in the cabin, and much fingering of the charts,—determined me to carry on during the night.

Nevertheless, I confess I was very uneasy. Though I went to bed and fell asleep—for at sea nothing prevents that process—my slumbers were constantly agitated by the most vivid dreams that I ever remember to have had. Dreams of an arrival in England, and your coming down to meet us, and all the pleasure I had in recounting our adventures to you; then suddenly your face seemed to fade away beneath a veil of angry grey surge that broke over low, sharp-pointed rocks; and the next moment there resounded over the ship that cry which has been the preface to so many a disaster—the ring of which, none who have ever heard it are likely to forget—" Breakers ahead!"

In a moment I was on deck, dressed—for it is always best to dress,—and there, sure enough, right ahead, about a mile and a half off, through the mist, which had come on very thick, I could distinguish the upward shooting fluff of seas shattering against rocks. No land was to be seen, but the line of breakers every instant became more evident; at the pace we were going, in seven or eight minutes we should be upon them. Now, thought I to myself, we shall see whether a stout heart beats beneath the silk tartan! The result covered that brilliant garment with glory and salt water. To tack was impossible, we could only wear,—and to wear in such a sea was no very pleasant operation. But the little ship seemed to know what she was about, as well as any of us: up went the helm, round came the schooner into the trough of the sea,—high over her quarter toppled an enormous sea, built up of I know not how many tons of water, and hung over the deck;—by some unaccoun'-

able wriggle, an instant ere it thundered down she had twisted her stern on one side, and the waves passed underneath. In another minute her head was to the sea, the mainsail was eased over, and all danger was past.

What was now to be done? That the land we had seen was the coast of Norway I could not believe. Wrong as our dead reckoning evidently was, it could not be so wrong as that. Yet only one other supposition was possible, viz., that we had not come so far south as we imagined, and that we had stumbled upon Roost—a little rocky island that lies about twenty miles to the southward of the Loffoden Islands. Whether this conjecture was correct or not, did not much matter; to go straight away to sea, and lie to until we could get an observation, was the only thing to be done. Away then we went, struggling against a tremendous sea for a good nine hours, until we judged ourselves to be seventy or eighty miles from where we had sighted the breakers,— when we lay to, not in the best of tempers. The next morning, not only was it blowing as hard as ever, but all chance of getting a sight that day seemed also out of the question. I could have eaten my head with impatience. However, as it is best never to throw a chance away, about half-past eleven o'clock, though the sky resembled an even sheet of lead, I got my sextant ready, and told Mr. Wyse to do the same.

Now, out of tenderness for your feminine ignorance I must state, that in order to take an observation, it is necessary to get a sight of the sun at a particular moment of the day: this moment is noon. When, therefore, twelve o'clock came, and one could not so much as guess in what quarter of the heavens he might be lying *perdu*, you may suppose I almost despaired. Ten minutes passed. It was evident we were doomed to remain, kicking our heels for another four-and-twenty hours where we were. No!—yes!—no! By Phœbus! there he is! A faint spongy spot of brightness gleamed through the grey roof overhead. The indistinct outline grew a little clearer; one-half of him, though still behind a cloud, hardened into a sharp edge. Up went the sextant. "52.43!" (or whatever it was) I shouted to Mr. Wyse. "52.41, my Lord!" cried he, in return; there was only the discrepancy of a mile between us. We had got the altitude; the sun might go to bed for good and all now, we did not care,—we knew our position to an inch. There had been an error of something like forty miles in our dead reckoning, in consequence—as I afterwards found—of a current that sets to the northward, along the west coast of Norway, with a velocity varying from one to three miles an hour. The island upon which we had so nearly run *was* Roost. We were still nearly 200 miles from our port. "Turn the hands up! Make sail!" and away we went again in the same course as before, at the rate of ten knots an hour.

"The girls at home have got hold of the tow-rope, I think, my Lord," said Mr. Wyse, as we bounded along over the thundering seas.

By three o'clock next day we were up with Vigten; and now a very nasty piece of navigation began. In order to make the northern entrance of the Throndhjem Fiord, you have first to find your way into what is called the Froh Havet,—a kind of oblong basin about sixteen miles long, formed by a ledge of low rocks running parallel with the mainland, at a distance of ten miles to seaward. Though the space between this outer boundary and the coast is so wide, in consequence of the network of sunken rocks which stuffs it up, the passage by which a vessel can enter is very narrow, and the only landmark to enable you to find the channel is the head one of the string of outer islets. As this rock is about the size of a dining-table, perfectly flat, and rising only a few feet above the level of the sea, to attempt to make it is like looking for a needle in a bottle of hay. It was already beginning to grow very late and dark by the time we had come up with the spot where it ought to have been, but not a vestige of such a thing had turned up. Should we not sight it in a quarter of an hour, we must go

"THE GIRLS AT HOME HAVE GOT HOLD OF THE TOW-ROPE."

to sea again, and lie to for the night,—a very unpleasant alternative for any one so impatient as I was to reach a port. Just as I was going to give the order, Fitz—who was certainly the Lynceus of the ship's company—espied its black back just peeping up above the tumbling water on our starboard bow. We had hit it off to a yard!

In another half-hour we were stealing down in quiet water towards the entrance of the fiord. All this time not a rag of a pilot had appeared; and it was without any such functionary that the schooner swept up next morning between the wooded, grain-laden slopes of the beautiful loch, to Throndhjem—the capital of the ancient sea-kings of Norway.

LETTER XII.

THRONDHJEM—HARALD HAARFAGER—KING HACON'S LAST BATTLE—
OLAF TRYGGVESSON—THE "LONG SERPENT"—ST. OLAVE—THORMOD
THE SCALD — THE JARL OF LADÉ—THE CATHEDRAL—HARALD
HARDRADA—THE BATTLE OF STANFORD BRIDGE—A NORSE BALL
—ODIN—AND HIS PALADINS.

Off Munkholm, Aug. 27, 1856.

THRONDHJEM (pronounced Tronyem) looked very pretty and picturesque, with its red-roofed wooden houses sparkling in the sunshine, its many windows filled with flowers, its bright fiord covered with vessels gaily dressed in flags, in honour of the Crown Prince's first visit to the ancient capital of the Norwegian realm. Tall, pretentious warehouses crowded down to the water's edge, like bullies at a public show elbowing to the foremost rank; orderly streets stretched in quiet rows at right angles with each other, and pretty villas with green cinctures sloped away towards the hills. In the midst rose the king's palace, the largest wooden edifice in Europe; while the old grey cathedral—stately and grand, in spite of the slow destruction of the elements, the mutilations of man's hands, or his yet more degrading rough-cast and stucco reparations—still towered above the perishable wooden buildings at his feet, with the solemn pride which befits the shrine of a royal saint.

I cannot tell you with what eagerness I drank in all the features of this lovely scene; at least, such features as Time can hardly alter—the glancing river, from whence the city's ancient name of Nidaros, or "mouth of the Nid," is derived,—the rocky island of Munkholm, the bluff of Ladé,—the land-locked fiord and its pleasant hills, beyond whose grey stony ridges I knew must lie the fatal battle-field of Sticklestad. Every spot to me was full of interest,—but an interest noways connected with the neat green villas, the rectangular streets, and the obtrusive warehouses. These signs of a modern humdrum prosperity seemed to melt away before my eyes as I gazed from the schooner's deck, and the accessories of an elder time came to furnish the landscape;—the clumsy merchantmen lazily swaying with the tide, darkened into armed galleys with their rows of glittering shields,—the snug, bourgeois-looking town shrank into the quaint proportions of the huddled ancient Nidaros,—and the old marauding days, with their shadowy line of grand old pirate kings, rose up with welcome vividness before my mind.

What picture shall I try to conjure from the past, to live in your fancy, as it does in mine?

Let the setting be these very hills,—flooded by this same cold, steely sunshine. In the midst stands a stalwart form, in quaint but regal attire. Hot blood deepens the colour of his sun-bronzed cheek; an iron purpose gleams in his earnest eyes, like the flash of a drawn sword; a circlet of gold binds the massive brow, and from beneath it stream to below his waist thick masses of hair, of that dusky red which glows like the heart of a furnace in the sunlight, but deepens earth-brown in the shadow. By his side stands a fair woman; her demure and heavy-lidded eyes are seldom lifted from the earth, which yet they seem to scorn; but the king's eyes rest on her, and many looks are turned towards him. A multitude is present, moved by one great event, swayed by a thousand passions;—some with garrulous throats full of base adulation and an unworthy joy;—some pale, self-scorning, with averted looks, and hands that twitch instinctively at their idle daggers, then drop hopeless, harmless at their sides.

The king is Harald Haarfager, "of the fair hair;" the woman is proud and beautiful Gyda, whose former scorn for him, in the days when he was nothing but the petty chief of a few barren mountains, provoked that strange wild vow of his, "That he would never clip or comb his locks till he could woo her as sole king of Norway."

Among the crowd are those who have bartered, for ease,

and wealth, and empty titles born of the king's breath—their ancient Udal rights, their Bonder privileges; others have sunk their proud hearts to bear the yoke of the stronger hand, yet gaze with yearning looks on the misty horizon that opens between the hills. A dark speck mars that shadowy line. Thought follows across the space. It is a ship. Its sides are long, and black, and low; but high in front rises the prow, fashioned into the semblance of a gigantic golden dragon, against whose gleaming breast the divided waters angrily flash and gurgle. Along the top sides of the deck are hung a row of shining shields, in alternate breadths of red and white, like the variegated scales of a sea-monster, whilst its gilded tail curls aft over the head of the steersman. From either flank projects a bank of some thirty oars, that look, as they smite the ocean with even beat, like the legs on which the reptile crawls over its surface. One stately mast of pine serves to carry a square sail made of cloth, brilliant with stripes of red, white, and blue.

And who are they who navigate this strange, barbaric vessel?—why leave they the sheltering fiords of their beloved Norway? They are the noblest hearts of that noble land—freemen, who value freedom,—who have abandoned all rather than call Harald master, and now seek a new home even among the desolate crags of Iceland, rather than submit to the tyranny of a usurper.

"Nord—oder Süd! wenn nur die Seelen glühen!"

Another picture, and a sadder story; but the scene is now a wide dun moor, on the slope of a seaward hill; the autumn evening is closing in, but a shadow darker than that of evening broods over the desolate plain,—the shadow of *Death*. Groups of armed men, with stern sorrow in their looks, are standing round a rude couch, hastily formed of fir branches. An old man lies there—dying. His ear is dulled even to the shout of victory; the mists of an endless night are gathering in his eyes; but there is passion yet in the quivering lip, and triumph on the high-resolved brow; and the gesture of his hand has kingly power still. Let me tell his saga, like the bards of that old time.

KING HACON'S LAST BATTLE.

I.

All was over: day was ending
As the foeman turned and fled.
Gloomy red
Glowed the angry sun descending;
While round Hacon's dying bed,
Tears and songs of triumph blending,
Told how fast the conqueror bled.

II.

"Raise me," said the King. We raised him—
Not to ease his desperate pain;
That were vain!
"Strong our foe was—but we faced him:
Show me that red field again."
Then, with reverent hands, we placed him
High above the bloody plain.

III.

Silent gazed he; mute we waited,
Kneeling round—a faithful few,
Staunch and true,—
Whilst above, with thunder freighted,
Wild the boisterous north wind blew,
And the carrion-bird, unsated,
On slant wing around us flew.

IV.

Sudden, on our startled hearing,
Came the low-breathed, stern command—
"Lo! ye stand?
Linger not, the night is nearing;
Bear me downwards to the strand,
Where my ships are idly steering
Off and on, in sight of land."

V.

Every whispered word obeying,
Swift we bore him down the steep,
O'er the deep,
Up the tall ship's side, low swaying
To the storm-wind's powerful sweep,
And—his dead companions laying
Round him,—we had time to weep.

VI.

But the King said—" Peace ! bring hither
Spoil and weapons—battle-strown,
Make no moan ;
Leave me and my dead together,
Light my torch, and then—begone."
But we murmured, each to other,
" Can we leave him thus alone ? "

VII.

Angrily the King replieth ;
Flash the awful eyes again,
With disdain—
" Call him not *alone* who lieth
Low amidst such noble slain ;
Call him not alone who dieth
Side by side with gallant men."

VIII.

Slowly, sadly, we departed :
Reached again that desolate shore,
Nevermore
Trod by him, the brave true-hearted—
Dying in that dark ship's core !
Sadder keel from land ne'er parted,
Nobler freight none ever bore !

IX.

There we lingered, seaward gazing,
Watching o'er that living tomb,
Through the gloom—
Gloom ! which awful light is chasing—
Blood-red flames the surge illume !
Lo ! King Hacon's ship is blazing ;
'Tis the hero's self-sought doom.

X.
Right before the wild wind driving,
Madly plunging—stung by fire—
No help nigh her—
Lo! the ship has ceased her striving!
Mount the red flames higher—higher!
Till—on ocean's verge arriving,
Sudden sinks the Viking's pyre—
Hacon's gone!

Let me call one more heroic phantom from Norway's romantic past.

A kingly presence, stately and tall; his shield held high above his head—a broken sword in his right hand. Olaf Tryggvesson! Founder of Nidaros;—that cold Northern Sea has rolled for many centuries above your noble head, and yet not chilled the battle heat upon your brow, nor staunched the blood that trickles down your iron glove, from hidden, untold wounds, which the tender hand of Thyri shall never heal!

To such ardent souls it is indeed given "to live for ever" (the for ever of this world); for is it not "Life" to keep a hold on *our* affections, when their own passions are at rest,—to influence our actions (however indirectly)—when action is at an end for them? Who shall say how much of modern heroism may owe its laurels to that first throb of fiery sympathy which young hearts feel at the relation of deeds such as Olaf Tryggvesson's?

The forms of those old Greeks and Romans whom we are taught to reverence, may project taller shadows on the world's stage; but though the scene be narrow here, and light be wanting, the interest is not less intense, nor are the passions less awful that inspired these ruder dramas.

There is an individuality in the Icelandic historian's description of King Olaf that wins one's interest—at first as in an acquaintance—and rivets it at last as in a personal friend. The old Chronicle lingers with such loving minuteness over his attaching qualities, his social, generous nature, his gaiety and "frolicsomeness;" even his finical taste in dress, and his evident proneness to fall too hastily in love, have a value in the portrait, as contrasting with the gloomy colours in which the story sinks at last. The warm, impulsive spirit speaks in every action of his life, from the hour when—a young child, in exile—he strikes his axe into the skull of his foster-father's murderer, to the last grand scene near Svälderöe. You trace it in his absorbing grief for the death of Geyra, the wife of his youth; the saga says, " he had no pleasure in Vinland after it," and then naïvely observes, " he *therefore* provided himself with war-ships, and went a-plundering," one of his first achievements being to go and pull down London Bridge. This peculiar kind of "distraction" (as the French call it) seems to have had the desired effect, as is evident in the romantic incident of his second marriage, when the Irish Princess Gyda chooses him—apparently an obscure stranger—to be her husband, out of a hundred wealthy and well-born aspirants to her hand. But neither Gyda's love, nor the rude splendours of her father's court, can make Olaf forgetful of his claims upon the throne of Norway—the inheritance of his father; and when that object of his just ambition is attained, and he is proclaimed King by general election of the Bonders, as his ancestor Harald Haarfager had been, his character deepens in earnestness as the sphere of his duties is enlarged. All the energies of his ardent nature are put forth in the endeavour to convert his subjects to the true Faith. As he himself expresses it, " he would bring it to this,—that all Norway should be Christian or *die!*" In the same spirit he meets his heretic and rebellious subjects at the Thing of Ladé, and boldly replies, when they require him to sacrifice to the false gods, " If I turn with you to offer sacrifice, then shall it be the greatest sacrifice that can be made; I will not offer slaves, nor malefactors to your gods,—I will sacrifice *men;*—and they shall be the noblest men among you!" It was soon after this that he despatched the exemplary Thangbrand to Iceland.

With a front not less determined does he face his country's

foes. The king of Sweden, and Svend "of the forked beard," king of Denmark, have combined against him. With them is joined the Norse jarl, Eric, the son of Hacon. Olaf Tryggvesson is sailing homewards with a fleet of seventy ships,—himself commanding the famous "*Long Serpent*," the largest ship built in Norway. His enemies are lying in wait for him behind the islands.

Nothing can be more dramatic than the description of the sailing of this gallant fleet—(piloted by the treacherous Earl Sigwald)—within sight of the ambushed Danes and Swedes, who watch from their hiding-place the beautiful procession of hostile vessels, mistaking each in turn for the "*Long Serpent*," and as often undeceived by a new and yet more stately apparition. She appears at length, her dragon prow glittering in the sunshine, all canvas spread, her sides bristling with armed men; "and when they saw her, none spoke,—all knew it to be indeed the '*Serpent*,'—and they went to their ships to arm for the fight." As soon as Olaf and his forces had been enticed into the narrow passage, the united fleets of the three allies pour out of the Sound; his people beg Olaf to hold on his way and not risk battle with such a superior force; but the King replied, high on the quarter-deck where he stood, " Strike the sails ! I never fled from battle : let God dispose of my life, but flight I will never take !" He then orders the war-horns to sound, for all his ships to close up to each other. " Then," says Ulf the Red, captain of the forecastle, "if the '*Long Serpent*' is to lie so much a-head of the other vessels, we shall have hot work of it here on the forecastle."

The King replies, "I did not think I had a forecastle man *afraid*, as well as *red*." [1]

Says Ulf, "Defend thou the quarter-deck, as I shall the forecastle."

The King had a bow in his hands; he laid an arrow on the string, and made as if he aimed at Ulf.

[1] There is a play on these two words in the Icelandic, "Raudan oc Ragan."

Ulf said, "Shoot another way, King, where it is more needful,—my work is thy gain."

Then the King asks, "Who is the chief of the force right opposite to us?" He is answered, "Svend of Denmark, with his army."

Olaf replies, "We are not afraid of these soft Danes! Who are the troops on the right?"

They answer, "Olaf of Sweden, and his forces."

"Better it were," replies the King, "for these Swedes to be sitting at home, killing their sacrifices, than venturing under the weapons of the '*Long Serpent.*' But who owns the large ships on the larboard side of the Danes?"

"That is Jarl Eric, son of Hacon," say they.

The King says, "*He* has reason for meeting us; we may expect hard blows from these men; they are Norsemen like ourselves."

The fierce conflict raged for many hours. It went hard with the "soft Danes," and idolatrous Swedes, as Olaf had foreseen: after a short struggle they turn and fly. But Jarl Eric in his large ship the "*Iron Beard*" is more than a match for Olaf's lighter vessels. One by one their decks are deluged with blood, their brave defenders swept into the sea; one by one they are cut adrift and sent loose with the tide. And now at last the "*Iron Beard*" lies side by side with the "*Long Serpent*," and it is indeed "hot work" both on forecastle and quarter-deck.

"Einar Tambarskelvar, one of the sharpest of bowmen, stood by the mast, and shot with his bow." His arrow hits the tiller-end, just over the Earl's head, and buries itself up to the shaft in the wood. "Who shot that bolt?" says the Jarl. Another flies between his hand and side, and enters the stuffing of the chief's stool. Then said the Jarl to a man named Fin, "Shoot that tall archer by the mast!" Fin shoots; the arrow hits the middle of Einar's bow as he is in the act of drawing it, and the bow is split in two.

"What is that," cried King Olaf, "that broke with such a noise?"

DEATH OF OLAF.

"*Norway*, King, from thy hands!" cried Einar.

"No! not so much as that," says the King; "take my bow, and shoot,"—flinging the bow to him.

Einar took the bow, and drew it over the head of the arrow. "Too weak, too weak," said he, "for the bow of a mighty King!" and throwing the bow aside, "he took sword and buckler, and fought valiantly."

But Olaf's hour is come. Many slain lie around him: many that have fallen by his hand, more that have fallen at his side. The thinned ranks on board the "*Iron Beard*" are constantly replenished by fresh combatants from other vessels, even by the Swedes and soft Danes, now "strong, upon the stronger side,"—while Olaf, cut off from succour, stands almost alone upon the "*Serpent's*" deck, made slippery by his people's blood. The Jarl had laid out boats to intercept all who might escape from the ship; but escape is not in the King's thoughts. He casts one look around him, glances at his sword—broken like Einar's bow—draws a deep breath, and, holding his shield above his head, springs overboard. A shout—a rush! who shall first grasp that noble prisoner? Back, slaves! the shield that has brought him scathless through a hundred fights, shall yet shelter him from dishonour.

Countless hands are stretched to snatch him back to worthless life, but the shield alone floats on the swirl of the wave;—King Olaf has sunk beneath it.

Perhaps you have already had enough of my Saga lore; but with that grey cathedral full in sight, I cannot but dedicate a few lines to another Olaf, king and warrior like the last, but to whom after times' have accorded a yet higher title.

Saint Olaf's—Saint Olave, as we call him—early history savours little of the odour of sanctity, but has rather that "ancient and fish-like smell" which characterised the doings of the Vikings, his ancestors. But those were days when honour rather than disgrace attached to the ideas of booty and plunder, especially in an enemy's country; it was a "spoiling of the Egyptians" sanctioned by custom, and even permitted by the Church, which did not disdain occasionally to share in the profits of a successful cruise, when presented in the decent form of silver candlesticks and other ecclesiastical gauds. As to the ancient historian, he mentions these matters as a thing of course. "Here the King landed, burnt, and ravaged;" "there the Jarl gained much booty;" "this summer, they took a cruise in the Baltic, to gather property," etc., much as a modern biographer would speak of a gentleman's successful railroad speculations, his taking shares in a coal mine, or coming into a "nice little thing in the Long Annuities." Nevertheless, there is something significant of his future vocation, in a speech which Olaf makes to his assembled friends and relations, imparting to them his design of endeavouring to regain possession of the throne: "I and my men have nothing for our support save what we captured in war, *for which we have hazarded both life and soul;* for many an innocent man have we deprived of his property, and some of their lives, and foreigners are now sitting in the possessions of my fathers." One sees here a faint glimmer of the Saint's nimbus, over the helmet of the Viking, a dawning perception of the "rights of property," which, no doubt, must have startled his hearers into the most ardent conservative zeal for the good old marauding customs.

But though years elapsed, and fortunes changed, before this dim light of the early Church became that scorching and devouring flame which, later, spread terror and confusion among the haunts of the still lingering ancient gods, an earnest sense of duty seems to have been ever present with him. If it cannot be denied that he shared the errors of other proselytizing monarchs, and put down Paganism with a stern and bloody hand, no merely personal injury ever weighed with him. How grand is his reply to those who advise him to ravage with fire and sword the rebellious district of Throndhjem, as he had formerly punished numbers of his subjects who had rejected Christianity:—"We had then *God's* honour to defend; but this treason against their sovereign is a much less grievous crime; it is more in my power to spare those who have dealt ill with me, than those whom God hated." The same hard measure which he meted to others he applied to his own actions: witness that curiously characteristic scene, when, sitting in his high seat, at table, lost in thought, he begins unconsciously to cut splinters from a piece of fir-wood which he held in his hand. The table servant, seeing what the King was about, says to him, (mark the respectful periphrasis!) "*It is Monday, Sire, to-morrow.*" The King looks at him, and it came into his mind what he was doing on a Sunday. He sweeps up the shavings he had made, sets fire to them, and lets them burn on his naked hand; "showing thereby that he would hold fast by ·God's law, and not trespass without punishment."

But whatever human weaknesses may have mingled with the pure ore of this noble character, whatever barbarities may have stained his career, they are forgotten in the pathetic close of his martial story.

His subjects,—alienated by the sternness with which he administers his own severely religious laws, or corrupted by the bribes of Canute, king of Denmark and England, are fallen from their allegiance. The brave, single-hearted monarch is marching against the rebellious Bonders, at the head of a handful of foreign troops, and such as remained faithful among his own people. On the eve of that last battle, on which he stakes throne and life, he intrusts a large sum of money to a Bonder, to be laid out "on churches, priests, and alms-men, as gifts for thê souls of such as may fall in battle *against himself*,"—strong in the conviction of the righteousness of his cause, and the assured salvation of such as upheld it.

He makes a glorious end. Forsaken by many whom he had loved and served,—yet forgiving and excusing them; rejecting the aid of all who denied that holy Faith which had become the absorbing interest of his life,—but surrounded by a faithful few, who share his fate ; "in the lost battle, borne down by the flying"—he falls, transpierced by many wounds, and the last words on his fervent lips are prayer to God.[1]

Surely there was a gallant saint and soldier. Yet he was not the only one who bore himself nobly on that day. Here is another episode of that same fatal fight.

A certain Thormod is one of the Scalds (or Poets) in King Olaf's army. The night before the battle he sings a spirited song at the King's request, who gives him a gold ring from his finger in token of his approval. Thormod thanks him for the gift, and says, " It is my prayer, Sire, that we shall never part, either in life or death." When the King receives his death-wound Thormod is near him,—but, wounded himself, and so weak and weary that in a desperate onslaught by the King's men,—nicknamed *" Dag's storm,"* —*he only stood by his comrade in the ranks, although he could do nothing.*

The noise of the battle has ceased ; the King is lying dead where he fell. The very man who had dealt him his death-wound has laid the body straight out on the ground, and spread a cloak over it. "And when he wiped the blood from the face it was very beautiful, and there was red in the cheeks, as if he only slept."

Thormod, who had received a second wound as he stood in the ranks—(an arrow in his side, which he breaks off at the shaft),—wanders away towards a large barn, where other wounded men have taken refuge. Entering with his drawn sword in his hand, he meets one of the Bonders coming out, who says, "It is very bad there, with howling and screaming ; and a great shame it is, that brisk young fellows cannot bear their wounds. The King's men may have done bravely to-day, but truly they bear their wounds ill."

Thormod asks what his name is, and if he was in the battle. Kimbe was his name, and he had been " with the

[1] The exact date of the battle of Sticklestad is known : an eclipse of the sun occurred while it was going on.

Bonders, which was the best side." "And hast thou been in the battle too?" asks he of Thormod.

Thormod replies, " I was with them that had the best."

"Art thou wounded?" says Kimbe.

"Not much to signify," says Thormod.

Kimbe sees the gold ring, and says, " Thou art a King's man : give me thy gold ring, and I will hide thee."

Thormod replies, "Take the ring if thou canst get it; *I have lost that which is more worth.*"

Kimbe stretches out his hand to seize the ring ; but Thormod, swinging his sword, cuts off his hand; "and it is related, that Kimbe behaved no better under his wound than those he had just been blaming."

Thormod then enters the house where the wounded men are lying, and seats himself in silence by the door.

As the people go in and out, one of them casts a look at Thormod, and says, " Why art thou so dead pale? Art thou wounded?" He answers carelessly, with a half-jesting rhyme ; then rises and stands awhile by the fire. A woman, who is attending on those who are hurt, bids him "go out, and bring in firewood from the door." He returns with the wood, and the girl then looking him in the face, says, " Dreadfully pale is this man ;" and asks to see his wounds. She examines his wound in his side, and feels that the iron of the arrow is still there ; she then takes a pair of tongs and tries to pull it out, "but it sat too fast, and as the wound was swelled, little of it stood out to lay hold of." Thormod bids her " cut deep enough to reach the iron, and then to give him the tongs, and let him pull." She did as he bade. He takes the ring from his hand, and gives it to the girl, saying, " It is a good man's gift ! King Olaf gave it to me this morning." Then Thormod took the tongs and pulled the iron out. The arrow-head was barbed, and on it there hung some morsels of flesh. When he saw that he said, " *The King has fed us well !* I am fat, even at the heart-roots!" And so saying, he leant back, and died.[1]

[1] When a man was wounded in the abdomen, it was the habit of the

Stout, faithful heart! if they gave you no place in your master's stately tomb, there is room for you by his side in heaven!

I have at last received—I need not say how joyfully—two letters from you; one addressed to Hammerfest. I had begun to think that some Norwegian warlock had bewitched the post-bags, in the approved old ballad fashion, to prevent their rendering up my dues; for when the packet of letters addressed to the "*Foam*" was brought on board, immediately after our arrival, I alone got nothing. From Sigurdr and the Doctor to the cabin-boy, every face was beaming over "news from home!" while I was left to walk the deck, with my hands in my pockets, pretending not to care. But the spell is broken now, and I retract my evil thoughts of the warlock and you.

Yesterday, we made an excursion as far as Ladé, saw a waterfall, which is one of the lions of this neighbourhood (but a very mitigated lion, which "roars you as soft as any sucking dove"), and returned in the evening to attend a ball given to celebrate the visit of the Crown Prince.

At Ladé, I confess I could think of nothing but "the great Jarl" Hacon, the counsellor, and maker of kings, king himself in all but the name, for he ruled over the western sea-board of Norway, while Olaf Tryggvesson was yet a wanderer and exile. He is certainly one of the most picturesque figures of these Norwegian dramas; what with his rude wit, his personal bravery, and that hereditary beauty of his race for which he was conspicuous above the rest. His very errors, great as they were, have a dash and prestige about them, which in that rude time must have dazzled men's eyes, and especially *women's*, as his story proves. It was his sudden passion for the beautiful Gudrun Lyrgia (the "Sun of Lunde," as she was called), which precipitated the avenging fate which years of heart-burnings and discontent among his subjects had been preparing. Gudrun's husband incites the Bonders to throw

Norse leeches to give him an onion to eat; by this means they learnt whether the weapon had perforated the viscera.

off the yoke of the licentious despot,—Olaf Tryggvesson is proclaimed king,—and the "great Jarl of Ladé" is now a fugitive in the land he so lately ruled, accompanied by a single thrall, named Karker.

In this extremity, Jarl Hacon applies for aid to Thora of Rimmol, a lady whom he had once dearly loved; she is faithful in adversity to the friend of happier days, and conceals the Jarl and his companion in a hole dug for this purpose, in the swine-stye, and covered over with wood and litter; as the only spot likely to elude the hot search of his enemies. Olaf and the Bonders seek for him in Thora's house, but in vain; and finally, Olaf, standing on the very stone against which the swine-stye is built, promises wealth and honours to him who shall bring him the Jarl of Ladé's head. The scene which follows is related by the Icelandic historian with Dante's tragic power.

There was a little daylight in their hiding-place, and the Jarl and Karker both hear the words of Olaf.

"Why art thou so pale?" says the Jarl, "and now again as black as earth? Thou dost not mean to betray me?"

"By no means," said Karker.

"We were born on the same night," said the Jarl, "and the time will not be long between our deaths."

When night came, the Jarl kept himself awake,—but Karker slept;—a troubled sleep. The Jarl awoke him, and asked of what he was dreaming. He answered, "I was at Ladé, and Olaf was laying a gold ring about my neck."

The Jarl said, "It will be a *red* ring about thy neck, if he catches thee: from me thou shalt enjoy all that is good,—therefore, betray me not!"

Then they both kept themselves awake; "*the one, as it were, watching upon the other.*" But towards day, the Jarl dropped asleep, and in his unquiet slumber he drew his heels under him, and raised his neck as if going to rise, "and shrieked fearfully." On this, Karker, "dreadfully alarmed," drew a knife from his belt, stuck it into the Jarl's throat, and cut off his head. Late in the day he came to Ladé, brought the Jarl's head to Olaf, and told his story.

It is a comfort to know that "*the red ring*" was laid round the traitor's neck: Olaf caused him to be beheaded.

What a picture that is, in the swine-stye, those two haggard faces, travel-stained and worn with want of rest, watching each other with hot, sleepless eyes through the half darkness, and how true to nature is the nightmare of the miserable Jarl!

It was on my return from Ladé, that I found your letters; and that I might enjoy them without interruption, I carried them off to the churchyard—(such a beautiful place!)—to read in peace and quiet. The churchyard was *not* "populous with young men, striving to be alone," as Tom Hood describes it to have been in a certain sentimental parish; so I enjoyed the seclusion I anticipated.

I was much struck by the loving care and ornament bestowed on the graves; some were literally loaded with flowers, and even those which bore the date of a long past sorrow had each its own blooming crown, or fresh nosegay. These good Throndhjemers must have much of what the French call *la religion des souvenirs*, a religion in which we English (as a nation) are singularly deficient. I suppose no people in Europe are so little addicted to the keeping of sentimental anniversaries as we are; I make an exception with regard to our living friends' birthdays, which we are ever tenderly ready to cultivate, when called on; turtle, venison, and champagne, being pleasant investments for the affections. But time and business do not admit of a faithful adherence to more sombre reminiscences; a busy gentleman "on 'Change" cannot conveniently shut himself up, on his "lost Araminta's natal-day," nor will a railroad committee allow of his running down by the 10.25 A.M., to shed a tear over that neat tablet in the new Willow-cum-Hatband Cemetery. He is necessarily content to regret his Araminta in the gross, and to omit the petty details of a too pedantic sorrow.

The fact is, we are an eminently practical people, and are

easily taught to accept "the irrevocable," if not without regret, at least with a philosophy which repudiates all superfluous methods of showing it. *Decent* is the usual and appropriate term applied to our churchyard solemnities, and we are not only "content to dwell in decencies for ever," but to die, and be buried in them.

The cathedral loses a little of its poetical physiognomy on a near approach. Modern restoration has done something to spoil the outside, and modern refinement a good deal to degrade the interior with pews and partitions; but it is a very fine building, and worthy of its metropolitan dignity. I am told that the very church built by Magnus the Good, —son of Saint Olave—over his father's remains, and finished by his uncle Harald Hardrada, is, or rather was, included in the walls of the cathedral; and though successive catastrophes by fire have perhaps left but little of the original building standing, I like to think that some of these huge stones were lifted to their place under the eyes of Harald the Stern. It was on the eve of his last fatal expedition against our own Harold of England that the shrine of St. Olave was opened by the king, who, having clipped the hair and nails of the dead saint (most probably as relics, efficacious for the protection of himself and followers), then locked the shrine, and threw the keys into the Nid. Its secrets from that day were respected until the profane hands of Lutheran Danes carried it bodily away, with all the gold and silver chalices, and jewelled pyxes, which, by kingly gifts and piratical offerings, had accumulated for centuries in its treasury.

He must have been a fine, resolute fellow, that Harald the Stern, although, in spite of much church-building and a certain amount of Pagan-persecuting, his character did not in any way emulate that of his saintly brother. The early part of his history reads like a fairy tale, and is a favourite subject for Scald songs; more especially his romantic adventures in the East,—

"Well worthy of the golden prime
Of good Haroun Alraschid;"

where Saracens flee like chaff upon the wind before him, and impregnable Sicilian castles fall into his power by impossible feats of arms, or incredible stratagems. A Greek empress, "the mature Zoe," as Gibbon calls her, falls in love with him, and her husband, Constantine Monomachus, puts him in prison; but Saint Olaf still protects his *mauvais sujet* of a brother, and inspires "a lady of distinction" with the successful idea of helping Harald out of his inaccessible tower by the prosaic expedient of a ladder of ropes. A boom, however, across the harbour's mouth still prevents the escape of his vessel. The Sea-king is not to be so easily baffled. Moving all his ballast, arms, and men, into the afterpart of the ship, until her stem slants up out of the sea, he rows straight at the iron chain. The ship leaps almost half-way over. The weight being then immediately transferred to the fore-part, she slips down into the water on the other side,—having topped the fence like an Irish hunter. A second galley breaks her back in the attempt. After some questionable acts of vengeance on the Greek court, Harald and his bold Væringers go fighting and plundering their way through the Bosphorus and Black Sea back to Novogorod, where the first part of the romance terminates, as it should, by his marriage with the object of his secret attachment, Elisof, the daughter of the Russian king.

Hardrada's story darkens towards the end, as most of the tales of that stirring time are apt to do. His death on English ground is so striking, that you must have patience with one other short Saga; it will give you the battle of Stanford Bridge from the Norse point of view.

The expedition against Harold of England commences ill; dreams and omens affright the fleet; one man dreams he sees a raven sitting on the stern of each vessel; another sees the fair English coast;

"But glancing shields
Hide the green fields;"

and other fearful phenomena mar the beautiful vision. Harald himself dreams that he is back again at Nidaros, and that his brother Olaf meets him with a prophecy of ruin and death. The bold Norsemen are not to be daunted by these auguries, and their first successes on the English coast seem to justify their persistence. But on a certain beautiful Monday in September (A.D. 1066, according to the Saxon Chronicle), part of his army being encamped at Stanford Bridge, "Hardrada, *having taken breakfast*, ordered the trumpets to sound for going on shore;" but he left half his force behind, to guard the ships: and his men, anticipating no resistance from the castle, which had already surrendered, "went on shore (the weather being hot), with only their helmets, shields, and spears, and girt with swords; some had bows and arrows,—and all were very merry." On nearing the castle, they see "a cloud of dust as from horses' feet, and under it shining shields and bright armour." English Harold's army is before them. Hardrada sends back to his ship for succour, and sets up his banner, "Land Ravager," undismayed by the inequality of his force, and their comparatively unarmed condition. The men on each side are drawn up in battle array, and the two kings in presence; each gazes eagerly to discover his noble foe among the multitude. Harald Hardrada's black horse stumbles and falls; "the King got up in haste, and said, 'A fall is lucky for a traveller.'"

The English King said to the Northmen who were with him, "Do you know the stout man who fell from his horse, with the blue kirtle, and beautiful helmet?"

"That is the Norwegian King," said they.

English Harold replied, "A great man, and of stately appearance is he; but I think his luck has left him."

And now twenty gallant English knights ride out of their ranks to parley with the Northmen. One advances beyond the rest and asks if Earl Toste, the brother of English Harold (who has banded with his enemy against him), is with the army.

The Earl himself proudly answers, "It is not to be denied that you will find him here."

The Saxon says, "Thy brother, Harold, sends his salutation, and offers thee the third part of his kingdom, if thou wilt be reconciled and submit to him."

The Earl replies, at the suggestion of the Norse King, "What will my brother the King give to Harald Hardrada for his trouble?"

"He will give him," says the Knight, "*seven feet of English ground, or as much more as he may be taller than other men.*"

"Then," says the Earl, "let the English King, my brother, make ready for battle, for it never shall be said that Earl Toste broke faith with his friends when they came with him to fight west here in England."

When the knights rode off, King Harald Hardrada asked the Earl, "Who was the man who spoke so well?"

The Earl replied, "That knight was Harold of England."

The stern Norwegian King regrets that his enemy had escaped from his hands, owing to his ignorance of this fact; but even in his first burst of disappointment, the noble Norse nature speaks in generous admiration of his foe, saying to the people about him, "That was but a little man, yet he sat firmly in his stirrups."

The fierce, but unequal combat is soon at an end, and when tardy succour arrives from the ships, Harald Hardrada is lying on his face, with the deadly arrow in his throat, never to see Nidaros again. Seven feet of English earth, and no more, has the strong arm and fiery spirit conquered.

But enough of these gallant fellows; I must carry you off to a much pleasanter scene of action. After a very agreeable dinner with Mr. K——, who has been most kind to us, we adjourned to the ball. The room was large and well lighted—plenty of pretty faces adorned it;—the floor was smooth, and the scrape of the fiddles had a festive accent so extremely inspiriting, that I besought Mr. K—— to present me to one of the fair personages whose tiny feet were already tapping the floor with impatience at their own inactivity.

I was led up in due form to a very pretty lady, and heard my own name, followed by a singular sound purporting to be that of my charming partner, Madame Hghelghghagllaghem. For the pronunciation of this polysyllabic cognomen, I can only give you a few plain instructions; commence it with a slight cough, continue with a gurgling in the throat, and finish with the first convulsive movement of a sneeze, imparting to the whole operation a delicate nasal twang. If the result is not something approaching to the sound required, you must relinquish all hope of achieving it, as I did. Luckily, my business was to dance, and not to apostrophize the lady; and accordingly, when the waltz struck up, I hastened to claim, in the dumbest show, the honour of her hand. Although my dancing qualifications have rather rusted during the last two or three years, I remembered that the time was not so very far distant when even the fair Mad^{elle.} E—— had graciously pronounced me to be a very tolerable waltzer, "for an Englishman," and I led my partner to the circle already formed with the "*air capable*" which the object of such praise is entitled to assume. There was a certain languid rhythm in the air they were playing which rather offended my ears, but I suspected nothing until, observing the few couples who had already descended into the arena, I became aware that they were twirling about with all the antiquated grace of "*la valse à trois temps.*" Of course my partner would be no exception to the general rule! nobody had ever danced anything else at Throndhjem from the days of Odin downwards; and I had never so much as attempted it. What was to be done? I could not explain the state of the case to Madame Hghelghghagllaghem; she could not understand English, nor I speak Norse. My brain reeled with anxiety to find some solution of the difficulty, or some excuse for rushing from her presence. What if I were taken with a sudden bleeding at the nose, or had an apoplectic fit on the spot? Either case would necessitate my being carried decently out, and consigned to oblivion, which would have been a comfort under the circumstances. There was nothing for it but the courage of despair; so, casting reflection to the winds, and my arm round her waist, I suddenly whisked her off her legs, and dashed madly down the room, "*à deux temps.*" At the first perception that something unusual was going on, she gave such an eldritch scream, that the whole society suddenly came to a standstill. I thought it best to assume an aspect of innocent composure and conscious rectitude which had its effect, for though the lady began with a certain degree of hysterical animation to describe her wrongs she finished with a hearty laugh, in which the compan: cordially joined, and I delicately chimed in. For the re: of the dance she seemed to resign herself to her fate, and floated through space, under my guidance, with all the *abandon* of Francesca di Rimini, in Scheffer's famous picture.

The Crown Prince is a tall, fine-looking person; he was very gracious, and asked many questions about my voyage.

At night there was a general illumination, to which the "*Foam*" contributed some blue lights.

We got under way early this morning, and without a pilot—as we had entered—made our way out to sea again. I left Throndhjem with regret, not for its own sake, for in spite of balls and illuminations I should think the pleasures of a stay there would not be deliriously exciting; but this whole district is so intimately associated in my mind with all the brilliant episodes of ancient Norwegian History, that I feel as if I were taking leave of all those noble Haralds, and Olafs, and Hacons, among whom I have been living in such pleasant intimacy for some time past.

While we are dropping down the coast, I may as well employ the time in giving you a rapid sketch of the commencement of this fine Norse people, though the story "*remonte jusqu'à la nuit des temps,*" and has something of the vague magnificence of your own M'Donnell genealogy, ending a long list of great potentates, with "somebody, who was the son of somebody else, who was the son of Scotha, who was the daughter of Pharaoh!"

In bygone ages, beyond the Scythian plains and the fens of the Tanaïs, in that land of the morning, to which neither Grecian letters nor Roman arms had ever penetrated, there was a great city called Asgaard. Of its founder, of its history, we know nothing; but looming through the mists of antiquity we can discern an heroic figure, whose superior attainments won for him the lordship of his own generation, and divine honours from those that succeeded. Whether moved by an irresistible impulse, or impelled by more powerful neighbours, it is impossible to say; but certain it is that at some period, not perhaps very long before the Christian era, under the guidance of this personage, a sun-nurtured people moved across the face of Europe, in a north-westerly direction, and after leaving settlements along the southern shores of the Baltic, finally established themselves in the forests and valleys of what has come to be called the Scandinavian Peninsula. That children of the South should have sought out so inclement a habitation may excite surprise; but it must always be remembered that they were, probably, a comparatively scanty congregation, and that the unoccupied valleys of Norway and Sweden, teeming with fish and game, and rich in iron, were a preferable region to lands only to be colonised after they had been conquered.

Thus, under the leadership of Odin and his twelve Paladins,—to whom a grateful posterity afterwards conceded thrones in the halls of their chief's Valhalla,—the new emigrants spread themselves along the margin of the out-ocean, and round about the gloomy fiords, and up and down the deep valleys that fall away at right angles from the backbone, or *keel*, as the seafaring population soon learnt to call the flat, snow-capped ridge that runs down the centre of Norway.

Amid the rude but not ungenial influences of its bracing climate, was gradually fostered that gallant race which was destined to give an imperial dynasty to Russia, a nobility to England, and conquerors to every sea-board in Europe.

Upon the occupation of their new home, the ascendency of that mysterious hero, under whose auspices the settlement was conducted, appears to have remained more firmly established than ever, not only over the mass of the people, but also over the twelve subordinate chiefs who accompanied him; there never seems to have been the slightest attempt to question his authority, and, though afterwards themselves elevated into an order of celestial beings, every tradition which has descended is careful to maintain his human and divine supremacy. Through the obscurity, the exaggeration, and the ridiculous fables, with which his real existence has been overloaded, we can still see that this man evidently possessed a genius as superior to his contemporaries, as has ever given to any child of man the ascendency over his generation. In the simple language of the old chronicler, we are told, "that his countenance was so beautiful that, when sitting among his friends, the spirits of all were exhilarated by it; that when he spoke, all were persuaded; that when he went forth to meet his enemies, none could withstand him." Though subsequently made a god by the superstitious people he had benefited, his death seems to have been noble and religious. He summoned his friends around his pillow, intimated a belief in the immortality of his soul, and his hope that hereafter they should meet again in Paradise. "Then," we are told, "began the belief in Odin, and their calling upon him."

On the settlement of the country, the land was divided and subdivided into lots—some as small as fifty acres—and each proprietor held his share—as their descendants do to this day—by udal right; that is, not as a fief of the Crown, or of any superior lord, but in absolute, inalienable possession, by the same udal right as the kings wore their crowns, to be transmitted, under the same title, to their descendants unto all generations.

These landed proprietors were called the Bonders, and formed the chief strength of the realm. It was they, their friends and servants, or thralls, who constituted the army.

Without their consent the king could do nothing. On stated occasions they met together, in solemn assembly, or Thing, (*i.e.* Parliament,) as it was called, for the transaction of public business, the administration of justice, the allotment of the scatt, or taxes.

Without a solemn induction at the Ore or Great Thing, even the most legitimately-descended sovereign could not mount the throne, and to that august assembly an appeal might ever lie against his authority.

To these Things, and to the Norse invasion that implanted them, and not to the Wittenagemotts of the Latinised Saxons, must be referred the existence of those Parliaments which are the boast of Englishmen.

Noiselessly and gradually did a belief in liberty, and an unconquerable love of independence, grow up among that simple people. No feudal despots oppressed the unprotected, for all were noble and udal born; no standing armies enabled the Crown to set popular opinion at defiance, for the swords of the Bonders sufficed to guard the realm; no military barons usurped an illegitimate authority, for the nature of the soil forbade the erection of feudal fortresses. Over the rest of Europe despotism rose up rank under the tutelage of a corrupt religion; while, year after year, amid the savage scenery of its Scandinavian nursery, that great race was maturing whose genial heartiness was destined to invigorate the sickly civilization of the Saxon with inexhaustible energy, and preserve to the world, even in the nineteenth century, one glorious example of a free European people.

LETTER XIII.

COPENHAGEN—BERGEN—THE BLACK DEATH—SIGURDR—
HOMEWARDS.

Copenhagen, Sept. 12th, 1856.

OUR adventures since the date of my last letter have not been of an exciting character. We had fine weather and prosperous winds down the coast, and stayed a day at Christiansund, and another at Bergen. But though the novelty of the cruise had ceased since our arrival in lower latitudes, there was always a certain raciness and oddity in the incidents of our coasting voyage; such as—waking in the morning, and finding the schooner brought up under the lee of a wooden house, or—riding out a foul wind with your hawser rove through an iron ring in the sheer side of a mountain,—which took from the comparative flatness of daily life on board.

Perhaps the queerest incident was a visit paid us at Christiansund. As I was walking the deck I saw a boat coming off, with a gentleman on board; she was soon alongside the schooner, and as I was gazing down on this individual, and wondering what he wanted, I saw him suddenly lift his feet lightly over the gunwale and plunge them into the water, boots and all. After cooling his heels in this way for a minute or so, he laid hold of the side ropes and gracefully swung himself on deck. Upon this, Sigurdr, who always acted interpreter on such occasions, advanced towards him, and a colloquy followed, which terminated rather abruptly in Sigurdr walking aft, and the web-footed stranger ducking down into his boat again. It was not till some hours later that the indignant Sigurdr explained the meaning of the visit. Although not a naval character, this gentleman certainly came into the category of men "who do business in great waters," his *business* being to negotiate a loan; in short, to ask me to lend him 100*l*. There must have been something very innocent and confiding in "the cut of our jib" to encourage his boarding us on such an errand; or perhaps it was the old marauding, toll-taking spirit coming out strong in him: the politer influences of the nineteenth century toning down the ancient Viking into a sort of a cross between Paul Jones and Jeremy Diddler. The seas which his ancestors once swept with their galleys, he now sweeps with his telescope, and with as keen an eye to the *main* chance as any of his predecessors displayed. The feet-washing ceremony was evidently a propitiatory homage to the purity of my quarter-deck.

Bergen, with its pale-faced houses grouped on the brink of the fiord, like invalids at a German Spa, though picturesque in its way, with a cathedral of its own, and plenty of churches, looked rather tame and spiritless after the warmer colouring of Throndhjem; moreover it wanted novelty to me, as I called in there two years ago on my return from the Baltic. It was on that occasion that I became possessed of my ever-to-be-lamented infant Walrus.

No one, personally unacquainted with that "most delicate monster," can have any idea of his attaching qualities. I own that his figure was not strictly symmetrical, that he had a roll in his gait, suggestive of heavy seas, that he would not have looked well in your boudoir; but he never seemed out of place on my quarter-deck, and every man on board loved him as a brother. With what a languid grace he would wallow and roll in the water, when we chucked him overboard; and paddle and splash, and make himself thoroughly cool and comfortable, and then come and "beg to be taken up," like a fat baby, and allow the rope to be slipped round his extensive waist, and come up—sleek and dripping—among us again with a contented grunt, as much as to say, "Well, after all, there's no place like *home!*" How he would compose himself to placid slumber in every possible inconvenient place, with his head on the binnacle (especially when careful steering was a matter of moment), or across the companion entrance, or the cabin skylight, or on the shaggy back of "Sailor," the Newfoundland, who positively abhorred him. But how touching it was to see him waddle up and down the deck after Mr. Wyse, whom he evidently regarded in a maternal point of view—begging for milk with the most expressive snorts and grunts, and embarrassing my good-natured master by demonstrative appeals to his fostering offices!

I shall never forget Mr. Wyse's countenance that day in Ullapool Bay, when he tried to command his feelings sufficiently to acquaint me with the creature's death, which he announced in this graphic sentence, "Ah, my Lord!—the poor thing!—*toes up at last!*"

Bergen is not as neat and orderly in its architectural arrangements as Drontheim; a great part of the city is a confused network of narrow streets and alleys, much resembling, I should think, its early inconveniences, in the days of Olaf Kyrre. This close and stifling system of street building must have ensured fatal odds against the chances of life in some of those world-devastating plagues that characterised past ages. Bergen was, in fact, nearly depopulated by that terrible pestilence which, in 1349, ravaged the North of Europe, and whose memory is still preserved under the name of "The Black Death."

I have been tempted to enclose you a sort of ballad, which was composed while looking on the very scene of this disastrous event; its only merit consists in its local inspiration, and in its conveying a true relation of the manner in which the plague entered the doomed city.

THE BLACK DEATH OF BERGEN.

I.

> WHAT can ail the Bergen Burghers
> That they leave their stoups of wine?
> Flinging up the hill like jagers,
> At the hour they're wont to dine!

See, the shifting groups are fringing
  Rock and ridge with gay attire,
Bright as Northern streamers tinging
  Peak and crag with fitful fire !

II.

Towards the cliff their steps are bending,
  Westward turns their eager gaze,
Whence a stately ship ascending,
  Slowly cleaves the golden haze.
Landward floats the apparition—
  " Is it, *can* it be the same ? "
Frantic cries of recognition
  Shout a long-lost vessel's name !

III.

Years ago had she departed—
  Castled poop and gilded stern ;
Weeping women, broken-hearted,
  Long had waited her return.
When the midnight sun wheeled downwards,
  But to kiss the ocean's verge—
When the noonday sun, a moment
  Peeped above the Wintry surge,

IV.

Childless mothers, orphaned daughters,
  From the seaward-facing crag,
Vainly searched the vacant waters
  For that unreturning flag !
But, suspense and tears are ended,
  Lo ! it floats upon the breeze !
Ne'er from eager hearts ascended
  Thankful prayers as warm as these.

V.

See the good ship proudly rounding
  That last point that blocks the view ;
" Strange ! no answering cheer resounding
  From the long home-parted crew ! "
Past the harbour's stony gateway,
  Onwards borne by sucking tides,
Tho' the light wind faileth—straightway
  Into port she safely glides.

VI.

Swift, as by good angels carried,
　Right and left the news has spread.
Wives long widowed—yet scarce married—
　Brides that never hoped to wed,
From a hundred pathways meeting
　Crowd along the narrow quay,
Maddened by the hope of meeting
　Those long counted cast away.

VII.

Soon a crowd of small boats flutter
　O'er the intervening space,
Bearing hearts too full to utter
　Thoughts that flush the eager face!
See young Eric foremost gaining—
　(For a father's love athirst!)
Every nerve and muscle straining,
　But to touch the dear hand *first*.

VIII.

In the ship's green shadow rocking
　Lies his little boat at last :
Wherefore is the warm heart knocking
　At his side, so loud and fast?
" What strange aspect is she wearing,
　Vessel once so taut and trim ?
Shout !—*my* heart has lost its daring ;
　Comrades, search !—*my* eyes are dim."

IX.

Sad the search, and fearful finding !
　On the deck lay parched and dry
Men—who in some burning, blinding
　Clime—had laid them down to die !
Hands—prayer-clenched—that would not sever,
　Eyes that stared against the sun,
Sights that haunt the soul for ever,
　Poisoning life—till life is done !

X.

Strength from fear doth Eric gather,
　Wide the cabin door he threw—
Lo ! the face of his dead father,
　Stern and still, confronts his view !

Stately as in life he bore him,
  Seated—motionless and grand ;
On the blotted page before him
  Lingers still the livid hand !

XI.

What sad entry was he making,
  When the death-stroke fell at last ?
" Is it then God's will, in taking
  All, that I am left the last ?
I have closed the cabin doorway,
  That I may not see them die :—
Would our bones might rest in Norway,—
  'Neath our own cool Northern sky ! "

XII.

Then the ghastly log-book told them
  How—in some accursed clime,
Where the breathless land-swell rolled them,
  For an endless age of time—
Sudden broke the plague among them,
  'Neath that sullen Tropic sun ;
As if fiery scorpions stung them—
  Died they raving, one by one !

XIII.

—Told the vain and painful striving,
  By shot-weighted shrouds to hide
(Last fond care), from those surviving,
  What good comrade last had died ;
Yet the ghastly things kept showing,
  Waist deep in the unquiet grave—
To each other gravely bowing
  On the slow swing of the wave !

XIV.

Eric's boat is near the landing—
  From that dark ship bring they aught ?
In the stern sheets *one* is standing,
  Though their eyes perceive him not ;
But a curdling horror creepeth
  Thro' their veins, with icy darts,
And each hurried oar-stroke keepeth
  Time with their o'er-labouring hearts !

XV.

Heavy seems their boat returning,
    Weighted with a world of care!
Oh, ye blind ones—none discerning
    What the spectral freight ye bear.
Glad they hear the sea-beach grating
    Harsh beneath the small boat's stem—
Forth they leap, for no man waiting—
    But *the Black Death lands with them.*

XVI.

Viewless—soundless—stalks the spectre
    Thro' the city chill and pale,
Which like bride, this morn, had decked her
    For the advent of that sail.
Oft by Bergen women, mourning,
    Shall the dismal tale be told,
Of that lost ship home returning,
    With "THE BLACK DEATH" in her hold!

I would gladly dwell on the pleasures of my second visit to Christiansund, which has a charm of its own, independent of its interest as the spot from whence we really "start for home." But though strange lands, and unknown or indifferent people, are legitimate subjects for travellers' tales, our *friends* and their pleasant homes are *not;* so I shall keep all I have to say of gratitude to our excellent and hospitable Consul, Mr. Mörch, and of admiration for his charming wife, until I can tell you *vivâ voce* how much I wish that you also knew them.

And now, though fairly off from Norway, and on our homeward way, it was a tedious business—what with fogs, calms, and headwinds—working towards Copenhagen. We rounded the Scaw in a thick mist, saw the remains of four ships that had run aground upon it, and were nearly run into ourselves by a clumsy merchantman, whom we had the relief of being able to abuse in our native vernacular, and the most racy sea-slang.

Those five last days were certainly the only tedious period of the whole cruise. I suppose there is something magnetic

in the soil of one's own country, which may account for that
impatient desire to see it again, which always grows, as the
distance from it diminishes; if so, London clay,—and its
superstratum of foul, greasy, gas-discoloured mud—began
about this time to exercise a tender influence upon me,
which has been increasing every hour since: it is just possible that the thoughts of seeing you again may have some
share in the matter.

Somebody (I think Fuller) says somewhere, that "every
one with whom you converse, and every place wherein you
tarry awhile, giveth somewhat to you, and taketh somewhat
away, either for evil or for good;" a startling consideration
for circumnavigators, and such like restless spirits; but a
comfortable thought, in some respects, for voyagers to Polar
regions, as (except seals and bears) few things could suffer
evil from us there; though for our own parts, there were
solemn and wholesome influences enough "to be taken
away" from those icy solitudes, if one were but ready and
willing to "stow" them.

To-morrow I leave Copenhagen, and my good Sigurdr,
whose companionship has been a constant source of enjoyment, both to Fitz and myself, during the whole voyage; I
trust that I leave with him a friendly remembrance of our too
short connexion, and pleasant thoughts of the strange places
and things we have seen together; as I take away with me
a most affectionate memory of his frank and kindly nature,
his ready sympathy, and his imperturbable good humour.
From the day on which I shipped him—an entire stranger
—until this eve of our separation—as friends, through scenes
of occasional discomfort, and circumstances which might
sometimes have tried both temper and spirits—shut up as
we were for four months in the necessarily close communion of life on board a vessel of eighty tons,—there has
never been the shadow of a cloud between us; henceforth,
the words "an Icelander" can convey no cold or ungenial
associations to my ears, and however much my imagination
has hitherto delighted in the past history of that singular

island, its Present will always claim a deeper and warmer interest from me, for Sigurdr's sake.

To-morrow Fitz and I start for Hamburg, and very soon after—at least as soon as railroad and steamer can bring me—I look for the joy of seeing your face again.

By the time this reaches Portsmouth, the "*Foam*" will have perfomed a voyage of six thousand miles.

I have had a most happy time of it, but I fear my amusement will have cost you many a weary hour of anxiety and suspense.

THE END.

Watson and Hazell, Printers, London and Aylesbury.

www.ingramcontent.com/pod-product-compliance
Lightning Source LLC
Chambersburg PA
CBHW031957230426
43672CB00010B/2185